Macoy's Worshipful Master's Assistant
By Robert Macoy

ISBN: 978-1-63923-239-0

Printed: June 2022

Cover Art By: Amit Paul

Published and Distributed By:
Lushena Books
607 Country Club Drive, Unit E
Bensenville, IL 60106
www.lushenabooksinc.com/books

ISBN: 978-1-63923-239-0

*"I want each of you to learn
and be a better Worshipful Master than I have been"*

Macoy's Worshipful Master's Assistant

A Manual For All Lodge Officers

ROBERT MACOY

ROBERT MACOY

October 4, 1815   January 9, 1895

FOUR months after ROBERT MACOY was born in Armagh, Ulster County, Ireland, his Scotch-Irish parents brought him to the United States. He received a liberal education, and early in life was apprenticed to a printer. It was in the printing-publishing business he was to spend his life and earn his living.

It was to Freemasonry, and its appendant organizations, he gave his life. From the day he was made a Master Mason in Lebanon Lodge No. 13, New York City, February 13, 1848, he worked for the Craft. In 1849 he was elected Worshipful Master, certainly an unusual occurrence. In this office he served for two years. In 1850 he was elected Grand Secretary of the St. John's Grand Lodge of New York.

In his capacity as Grand Secretary he worked to bring about the union of the two New York Grand Lodges. When this was successful he was given the rank of Past Grand Secretary. He was elected a Grand Warden and in 1856 he became Deputy Grand Master. For 44 years he served as Grand Recorder of the Grand Commandery.

Macoy became a Royal Arch Mason in Orient Chapter No. 1 (now No. 138) New York City. At the time of his death he was a member of DeWitt Clinton Chapter No. 142, Brooklyn, and Americus Lodge No. 535, New York City.

He is perhaps remembered most for his work for the Order of the Eastern Star. He was the founder and organizer of the "Chapter" system and became the first Grand Secretary of the Grand Chapter of New York. At the 5th Annual Session of that Grand Chapter Bro. Rob Morris conferred the title of "Supreme Grand Patron of the World" on Macoy. Harold V.B. Voorhis in his *The Eastern Star* (Macoy, 1976) covers his activities extensively. What Rob Morris had to say about Macoy speaks volumes for the type of person he was:

> "In 1868, when I sailed for the Holy Land, I resigned to Brother Robert Macoy the title and prerogatives of Grand Patron, which I assumed as the author of the system, he consenting to undergo the heavy cares incumbent upon the office...I would not have divested myself of this prerogative, but that I knew my successor to be a man of pure life, of singular zeal in Masonry, and one who had exhibted, for several years, a warm love for this particular system. I need not say that Brother Macoy has

fully justified my choice. His assiduity in extending the Eastern Star has been a marvel to us all."

All Freemasonry can be thankful he decided to form a Masonic publishing house in 1849. From that date to this he and his successors have furnished the Masonic world with the best in Masonic literature.

The *Adoptive Rite Ritual* for the Order of the Eastern Star (from which all Eastern Star rituals used today have been taken), the *Amaranth Ritual*, and *Worshipful Master's Assistant* have remained in print since they were first published.

Robert Macoy died on January 9, 1895 and his passing was noted by the Grand Chapters throughout the entire world. He was buried in Greenwood Cemetery in Brooklyn, New York.

PREFACE

It has been forcibly said by an English writer, "that nothing dissipates the ardor of an aspiring brother; nothing destroys his love and zeal for Masonry, like the incapacity of his Worshipful Master." In correspondence with this idea, the Lodge Master is told at his installation, "that the honor, reputation and usefulness of his Lodge will materially depend upon the skill and assiduity with which he (the Master) manages its concerns, while the happiness of its member will be generally promoted in proportion to the zeal and abillity with which he propagates the genuine principles of the institution." The history of ten thousand Lodges in this country amply substantiates and bears out these assertions.

I have long considered the ideal of a practical work directed solely to the interests of the Worshipful Master; something that, while it informs him of the *duties* and *responsibilities* of his office, will at the same time cheer and encourage him with the assurance of his *reward*. This ideal has more and more grown upon me as I have advanced in the understanding of the wants and ways of American Lodges; and now that my life is tending toward its sunset, I would fain leave as a fitting legacy a PRACTICAL CYCLOPEDIA of counsel and instruction to Worshipful Masters, bearing in mind how much of the success and prosperity of the Lodge, and of the Masonic Order itself, depend upon them.

The topics which seem to me of the greatest practical importance at the present time are those given in the synopsis of the subjects.

A logical system of PARLIAMENTARY USAGE will doubtless be welcomed by Worshipful Masters everywhere, for they are often embarrassed in debates by the intricacies of questions sprung upon them unexpectedly, sometimes mischievously, by contestants. In the sense in which the Lodge is a deliberative assembly, the system here given will be found, I am confident, a valuable compend of Parliamentary Law and Usage.

The MASONIC DISCIPLINE, a popular treatise on the Principles and Practice of Masonic Law, embellished with numerous opinions and decisions, carefully selected from the best authorities, is herein presented. This part of the work will prove of great value to the Master, thus affording information which would otherwise cost much time and labor to procure.

A practical guide to INTERMENT OF DEAD, and particularly to LODGES OF SORROW, has long been asked for by Worshipful Masters. How meagre and barren the various monitors are, under this head, I need not say. The ceremonial, of all others most solemn, most impressive, demanding most knowledge, dignity and skill—the ceremonial performed publicly and under the critical eye of rival societies and observers often unfriendly, is usually performed with less impressiveness than any other part of Masonic ritualism. To leave nothing wanting under this head, I have first given a chapter to the simple forms of WEBB and his followers, and a second to the more ornate and popular methods preferred in many jurisdictions.

All my counsels to Worshipful Masters will be found brotherly, affectionate, and strictly within the limits of personal experience. Having frequently been intrusted with positions of responsibility, I have surveyed the entire field of Masonic duty and prerogative, and endeavored to describe it here in a manner pleasant and effective.

I have placed myself in the attitude of a "Father in Masonry," conversing familiarly with a brother just elected Master, young, inexpreienced, but anxious to make a brilliant record in his official career.

Courteously,
ROBERT MACOY

COMMENTARY

ROBERT MACOY deserves the appreciation and commendation of the Masonic World. In 1849 he formed a Masonic publishing company (still in existence) when such a company was desperately needed.

When his *Worshipful Master's Assistant* was published in 1885 few Grand Lodges had the ceremonies he described. It was from this book, in many instances, they evolved. They found his "Encyclopedia of Useful Knowledge" invaluable. He actually paved the way for much of the esoteric cermonies in use today.

What Macoy had to say in 1885 is, for the most part, just as vital today. For this reason much of the original book has been left intact. But because all Grand Lodges have forms and ceremonies for "The Public Exercise of Freemasonry," Macoy's version has been reduced.

Where applicable, notations endeavor to clarify changes generally made during the ninety-four years since the book was first published.

Many requests have been made for sample By-laws to be included. To satisfy this need I have included in Chapter 12 a sample used by many Grand Lodges. There have been even more requests for a suggested list of Committees and their duties. While I prefer to call these "Teams" I fully realize the word "Committee" will be with us until the end of time. But if we can use these as Teams, the wording won't hurt. I'll have more to say about this in Chapter 13 where Committees and their duties will be covered.

It has been a privilege to be "associated" with the great Robert Macoy. He has taught me much. Hopefully, his vast knowledge will prove a benefit to you, your Lodge, and your Grand Lodge.

On one important point I must disagree with Brother Macoy. He makes the mistake far too many leaders still make. An officer should not wait until he has reached the Oriental Chair in the East to learn his duties. This learning should start no later than the day he is elected, or appointed, to the line. Learning is a long and continuous process. It can't be covered in a day, a year, or even a lifetime. This book, and others, should be presented to the young officer as a first step toward making his Lodge the best in the jurisdiction. This and other books should be used for group study.

On another important point we must all agree with Robert Macoy. The law is what your Grand Lodge says it is. The ceremonies adopted by your Grand Lodge are the ones that must be followed. What is written here, and everywhere, can only be used for historical purposes if there is a conflict with the laws, rules, and regulations of your Grand Lodge.

I hope you will enjoy, as I have, the wisdom and vast knowledge of Robert Macoy.

Highland Springs, Virginia
February 22, 1980

CONTENTS

Contents continued

CHAPTER 1

THE WORSHIPFUL MASTER

To become Master of his Lodge is the legitimate object of every young brother who takes an interest in our society. The very questionable policy of our present regulations seems to be, to open to each, in succession, the way to the Mastership—almost, if not altogether, as a matter of course. Now, my younger brethren may rest assured, that although in deference to a usage which it is perhaps too late to abolish, we may place a careless or ignorant Mason in the Chair, invest him with the badge of authority, and address him with the external forms of respect, we cannot command for him the deference and consideration which will be sure to follow the enlightened and expert. He will be like that figure-head of a ship—placed foremost, and gaudily decorated; but, after all, it is a mere effigy, not contributing in the least to the management of the vessel. In small, as in great things, *knowledge* is power—*intellectual superiority* is real preeminence.— T. Fitz-Henry Townsend.

In the whole series of offices recognized in Freemasonry there is no other so important to Masonic unity as that of the Worshipful Master. Upon his skill, integrity and prudence depend, in great part, the usefulness and welfare of the Lodge.

To become Master of a Lodge, "worthy and well qualified," should be the legitimate object of ambition to every brother interested in the prosperity of the society. That he should be "of good report, true and trusty," and be held in high esteem by the brethren; that he should be exemplary in conduct, easy in address, courteous in manners, but steady and firm in principle. All this is essential to the office.

The powers of the Master in his own Lodge are great; far greater and more varied than the governor of any other organization. From his decisions there can be no appeal to the Lodge; he is amenable for his conduct only to the Grand Master, or the Grand Lodge. He should possess a thorough knowledge of the Ritual, Ancient Charges, Landmarks, and Parliamentary Rules of the Craft. He is supposed to have served a full term as a Warden (except in the case of a newly-constituted Lodge, when there is no Warden or Past Master to serve). His record demands a legal election, a compliance with the covenants of the installation service, and induction into the oriental chair.

Before entering fully into the details of the subject now before us, it is important that we should at once recognize the fact that wherever the views we lay down are in any manner opposed to those established by the Grand Lodge, or the *dictum* of the Grand Master, the *latter must rule*. In such cases the reader will simply take the opinions herein expressed as not authoritative, but only those of one of some experience, and only valuable as showing how authorities may differ upon leading Masonic questions.

In Chase's *Digest of Masonic Law* it is shown that almost every question of Masonic jurisprudence lay in the arena of debate and unsettled. During these twenty years, however, the labors of men experienced and learned in such matters have placed the subject of Masonic usage upon a better footing; and there is reason to hope that in time all important questions will thus be disposed of. We shall rejoice, if the views expressed with clearness and simplicity, in the present volume, will aid in bringing about so desirable a result.

The position of Worshipful Master is eminently important and honorable. In all public ceremonials he takes the lead, either in his own character or as the representative of the Grand Master, when that officer is absent. The Lodge is called *his* Lodge... The checks upon his misuse of high powers are sufficient... His term of office is limited to a single year, and his re-election is dependent solely upon the good record he shall make. An appeal to the Grand Master, properly sustained, deprives him of office. He cannot draw money from the treasury save by vote of the Lodge. He has no power to inflict penalties. He cannot confer degrees save by the clear voice of his members...The crowning feature in the high dignity of this officer lies in the fact, that he represents in duties, prerogatives and responsibilities, Solomon, King of Israel.—Morris' *Dictionary of Freemasonry*.

PREROGATIVES OF THE WORSHIPFUL MASTER

The prerogatives of the W.M. are so numerous, so varied, and so interwoven with one another, it is difficult to lay them out as so many threads from a tangled skein, and discuss them separately. For convenience we divide them into fourteen sections:

I. It is the prerogative of the W.M. to congregate (that is, call together) his Lodge at his discretion.

This function is performed by notifying the members through the public press, or by written or printed notices through the Secretary, or by oral notifications through the Tyler. Whether notices are publications in the press, or upon written or printed sheets from the Secretary, they are to be subscribed, "By Order of the W.M. A.B., Secretary." If the notifications are upon written or printed sheets, they should be signed by the Secretary, and impressed with the seal of the Lodge, which is in the keeping of the Secretary. If the notifications are sent by the Tyler, his own oral notifications are deemed official. It is not the prerogative of the Master to "Summon" the members; that is a power reserved to the Lodge itself.

The particular subjects for which the W.M. is likely to call his Lodge in the interval between the regular communications, are funerals; invitations from neighboring Lodges; emergencies produced by conflagrations, inundations, defalcations, etc.; proposed visits from Grand Officers; lectures and addresses proposed for the benefit of the members; conferring degrees upon candidates duly elected by the Lodge, etc., etc. In every instance the particular business for which the Lodge is called must be named in the notification. The charter of the Lodge being in the keeping of the W.M, it is plainly impossible for the Lodge to be congregated against his consent. Should this, however, be attempted, should the charter be furtively procured, and the Lodge opened by any officer *against the orders or wishes* of the W.M., the work would be clandestine, the parties leading in the affair would be liable to discipline, and the Lodge itself placed in an unfortunate attitude before the community and the Grand Lodge.

The distinction between a "Notification" and a "Summons" is so great that it is strange how many writers overlook it. The former issues from the W.M., or the Lodge, and is practically a strong *Invitation*. It is in the option of the brother receiving it to attend the meeting or not, at his convenience. If he absents himself there is no penalty, for no discipline follows. But a "Summons" comes directly under the province of his obligation, and for its neglect he may be disciplined, and may be punished. To *disobey a Summons* is a most heinous form of Masonic stubbornness.

II. It is the prerogative of the W.M. to preside at all communications of his Lodge, whether regular or called, when present.

The W.M. may (and sometimes will) temporarily resign the East to an experienced Past Master, but he is all the time *responsible to the Grand Lodge* for the proceedings, as much as though he held the gavel in person. And he may resume the East at any moment in his own discretion.

But in the case of his absence, or in his absenting himself after the opening of the Lodge, he must surrender charter, gavel and prerogative to the Senior Warden, or close the Lodge.

One W.M. in the very outset of his official career, drew off and committed to memory the following as his rules of action:

1. I will perform all my official duties as between myself and my conscience, being guided therein by my Installation vows.

2. I will rule my Lodge without fear, favor or reward, save the approbation of my conscience and the favor of God.

3. I will endeavor to win my brethren to attend all the

meetings of the Lodge by the allurements of abundant Masonic instruction for their wages.

4. I will at all times, and by all means, seek out the ancient work and lectures of Masonry, and be satisfied with nothing less.

5. I will see that the distressed worthy brother shall never go disappointed from the door of the Lodge, if in my power to aid him.

6. I will strive in knowledge, charity, truth, courtesy and love, to be a model to my brethren.

7. The evil-doer under my jurisdiction shall have no rest until he reforms; but if he will not reform, he shall be cut off.

8. My fellow-officers shall be urged to acquire and perform their respective duties accurately and thoroughly, according to their Installation vows.

9. My Lodge shall have honor and respect among its fellows.

Need we say that such a W.M. was a success? Re-elected year after year, honored and respected throughout the neighboring Lodges as "the Model Master," sought for in Grand Lodge, for the highest officer, the man who began with such a code of private resolutions, left a name brilliant upon the scroll of time, and passed to his reward the blessings of all who knew him.

III. It is the prerogative of the W.M. to fill all vacancies that may occur in the roster of his Lodge.

There is no such thing as *advancement* recognized in this. If the Senior Warden is absent the Junior Warden does not *ex officio* fill the West; but the W.M. appoints a Senior Warden *pro tempore*. So of every other officer.

IV. It is the prerogative of the W.M. to regulate the admission of visitors.

A glance at the 15th and last of the Installation Charges of this volume, will show this to be as much a *duty as a prerogative*. "You agree that no visitors should be received into your Lodge without due examination, and producing proper vouchers of their having been initiated in a regular Lodge."

If any Mason, not a member of your Lodge, proposes to visit it, and you discover that his presence is objectionable to *any* member, you will use your kindly influence to reconcile the two brethren, or, failing in that, will forbid the visit. This is both prerogative and duty. It is a poor incentive to peace and harmony to admit a living cause of offence. According to the English rituals, the following elegant and impressive charge upon this subject is delivered to the newly admitted candidate when he receives his white apron:

> You are never to put on that apron if there is any brother in the Lodge which you are about to visit, with whom you are at variance, or against whom you entertain any animosity. In such a case it is expected you will invite him to withdraw in order amicably to settle your differences; which, if happily effected, you may clothe yourselves, enter the Lodge, and work with that love and harmony which should at all times characterize Freemasons. But if, unfortunately, your differences are of such a nature as not to be so easily adjusted, it were better that one or both of you should retire than that the harmony of the Lodge should be disturbed by your presence.

In regard to vouching for visitors in general, you will do well to require every brother who tenders an avouchal to rise, and say, "I vouch for A.B. as a Mason, having sat with him in a Lodge of Master Masons."

In visiting a Lodge—not your own—you should notify the Committee of Examination, or if avouched for, the brother who introduces you, that *you are a Past Master.* This is an intimation to the W.M. not to be slighted. In introducing you to the Lodge he will invite you to the *dais* as a Past Master, and, if such is the custom in his jurisdiction, lead in saluting you with the private Grand Honors of Masonry. We have little respect for men who do not respect themselves. If a brother, who has been elevated to Masonic rank, has so little regard for the proprieties that he will not report *his title,* he is unworthy to bear a title.

No stranger, however expert, can pass through the ordeal of "strict trial, due examination and lawful information," so as to enter the Lodge in a less period than half an hour. [Today a five minute examination, after viewing a visitor's current dues cards, should prove a man is a Master Mason.] Thousands with their poverty of information could never pass it at all.

What we have said concerning the stern, unyielding methods of avouchal, and examination of visitors, must not be construed as an intimation that *such persons are ever unwelcome.* Far from it. While, indeed, in the trials of offences, there may be occasions when it is best to confine the attendance *to the membership alone,* yet at all regular and called communications of any ordinary character, visitors are made welcome in the broadest sense of the term. Even before the Lodge is opened, special attention is paid them. A kind word to one far from home ("a stranger in a strange land") is as "the shadow of a great rock in a weary land," a favor never to be forgotten. With his address in the Visitors' Book, assure him that as soon as the Lodge is opened he shall have proper attention from a Committee of Examination. Give him a copy of the by-laws. Exhibit to him the Lodge-room, pointing out with pride its orderly and correct arrangement, its cleanliness, the extent of its library and furnishings, the elegent and instructive symbolisms on the walls, the appropriate jewels, the commanding pillars, the wheat-sheaf—all that attracts the eye and informs the mind.

In foreign countries, especially Continental countries, the examination of visitors consists in little more than the exhibition of the diploma (certificate), borne by the visitor. The sight of this, and the autograph of the visiting brother, will, as a rule, satisfy the committee, and secure to the visitor the desired welcome. [Today this diploma or certificate is obtained from the office of the Grand Secretary. It bears his signature and the seal of the Grand Lodge. A Mason traveling overseas should always carry one if he plans on visiting foreign Lodges.]

V. It is the prerogative of the W.M. to control and terminate discussions.

In Chapter 8, "Parliamentary Law," and elsewhere, this prerogative is accurately defined. It is a Landmark essential to the position which you occupy, the only method by which you can sustain yourself in your responsibility to the Grand Lodge, and, happily for your position, one that will rarely bring you in contact with the brethren. The Installation vow, which forbids a haughty and arbitrary exercise of the Master's prerogative, will *preserve you,* while the sense of obedience, inculcated in every degree of Masonry, will bend the minds of the brethren to support you in a judicious exercise of power. There is little or no danger of rebellion, even in extremest cases. Some of the more wilful members, the older ones perhaps, may withdraw their countenance from you for a time, and cease to attend Lodge. They may whisper of a change of officers at the next election. But, if you exercise the *fifth prerogative* in a mild, firm, straightforward and determined manner, you will be rejoiced ere your term expires, in the restoration of confidence. The surest method of *electioneering* for re-election to office as W.M. is to fill worthily the office of W.M. *while you occupy it.*

VI. It is the prerogative of the W.M. to determine all questions of order

and the Order of Business without appeal, save to the Grand Master or the Grand Lodge.

What is said on this subject in the last paragraph, is applicable here. The instructions in Chapter 8, upon Parliamentary Law are more full and explicit. It cannot be controverted that this whole subject, "Order of Business," however it may be introduced into the by-laws of the Lodge, is within the prerogatives of the W.M. And while he may refer himself to the by-laws for the usual forms, and defer to the customs and choice of the brethren in this matter, yet in any case of emergency he may and ought to deviate from them, reversing the order of subjects, omitting some, in his discretion, ever bearing in mind that "the good of Masonry in his Lodge" is in his keeping, and that he alone is responsible to the Grand Lodge for the good order, peace and harmony of his members.

We introduce here, for convenience, the most practical Order of Business within our knowledge, and recommend it to the reader's use, as one that serves every purpose sought for in such a syllabus:

1. Opening the Lodge.
2. Calling Roll of Officers.
3. Reading Minutes of last regular and special Communications.
4. Sickness and Distress.
5. Presenting and referring petitions for Affiliation and Degress.
6. Reports on petitions referred at previous regular Communication.
7. Balloting on petitions.
8. Reports of Committees, regular or special.
   Annual Election of Officers.
9. Unfinished Business.
10. New Business.
11. Work—Conferring Degrees.
12. Reading Minutes of present Communication.
13. Closing.

To secure a thorough clearance of the business on the trestleboard of the communications, the Secretary should place upon the table of the W.M., before the opening of the Lodge, an *Agenda Paper* that is a memorandum of the unfinished items of business, taken from the minutes of the Lodge. These unfinished items may and often do, run back through several communications of the Lodge.

VII. It is the prerogative of the W.M. to appoint all Committees. [However, see suggestions in Chapter 13, "Committees and Their Duties."]

VIII. It is the prerogative of the W.M. to be the custodian of the charter (warrant).

This is seen in the Installation service, Part II., Chapter II. The Lodge cannot be opened or business lawfully performed in the absence of this document, from which we draw the conclusion that it is in the possession of the W.M. during his term of office. The impropriety of framing it and leaving it suspended upon the walls of the Lodge will appear obvious from these considerations. [Framing the charter and leaving it in the Lodge room is an accepted practice today.]

IX. It is the prerogative of the W.M. to order the issuance of notifications requiring the attendance of members. (See our commentary upon section one, for a sufficient reference to this.)

X. It is the prerogative of the W.M. to give the casting vote in case of a tie, in addition to his own vote.

The W.M. may vote upon ordinary questions or not as he chooses, but it is not usual for him to do so. Upon questions requiring the ballot he should *always vote.*

In ordinary questions, if there is a tie, he should settle the question by his vote. This prerogative does not extend to the ballot box.

XI. It is the prerogative of the W.M. to sign all drafts upon the Treasurer, for the payment of Lodge disbursements, by consent of the Lodge.

The Treasurer may not lawfully pay out the funds without such order. In most jurisdictions today money from the general fund of the Lodge can be expended "by order of the W.M." *or* by vote of the Lodge.

In some cases this is limited to exclusively Masonic purposes; in others there are no stipulations. Few, if any, Grand Lodges limit the Master's disgression in matters of charity or relief.

XII. It is the prerogative of the W.M. to represent the Lodge in Grand Lodge, in conjunction with the two Wardens.

The ancient title of the Grand Lodge (*Assemblie*) suggests that social enjoyment, unrestrained communication, leveling of varied ranks, harmony of diverse interests threw an air of pleasure around the meetings. If there were no other advantages in these Grand Lodge Assemblies than "the making Masons better acquainted with each other," all the trouble, time and expense associated with them would be justified. Friendships are established there, lasting as life. Hearts are bound together there that would otherwise move in remote circles. Innovations are frowned down, errors adjusted, appeals adjudicated, Masonic light disseminated, peace and harmony established through the utmost bounds of the jurisdiction by the influence of Grand Lodge Assemblies.

You will find in Grand Lodge, if it is your first visit, that a few old members claim the largest share of honors on the score of faithful service. Now Grand Lodge business is so clearly defined by its own Constitution as to lie within the ability of ordinary minds. Each member, therefore, should claim his share in what is passing, for each member shares the responsibility. The oldest and most influential veteran must have no more time or attention than the new-comer. Any system of cliques, if such a thing prevails, should be discountenanced, and the various positions on committees as well as the Grand Lodge offices should be so distributed that modest merit shall enjoy its full share.

XIII. It is the prerogative of the W.M. to appoint the Senior Deacon and such other officers as may be prescribed in the by-laws of the Lodge. See the third prerogative, which strengthens this.

In foreign countries it is the prerogative of the W.M. to appoint *all the officers of the Lodge*, save, perhaps, the Treasurer and Tyler; but in this country the privilege is commonly restricted to the appointment of the Senior Deacon, Chaplain, Organist, and other supernumerary officers.

The Senior Deacon is the proxy, the assistant, the executive of the W.M.; as the W.M. is the embodiment of the Lodge itself. He is the active, forward personage in its *drill* and *drama*. How important then that the W.M. should make a cautious selection. In the opening and closing of the Lodge, much of the beauty and effectiveness of the ceremony depends upon the Senior Deacon; if he knows his duty thoroughly and performs it quietly and expeditiously, its effectiveness will be marked and impressive. In conducting the candidate in either degree (that proceeding so vital to the future character of the neophyte), the Senior Deacon stands alone in impressing the *white paper* of the youthful mind; the work fails or succeeds according as he succeeds or fails in his part. To endeavor to make a Mason without his co-operation is to undertake Hamlet without a

Hamlet. In the reception and introduction of the visitor how prominent is his part! With suavity to polish he will rejoice the stranger's heart with all the graces of the time-honored institution, whose honor at that moment rests in his keeping. In the lecture to the newly-admitted candidate, the Senior Deacon is his sponsor, pointing out to him, successively and unerringly, the proper emblems, and rendering the whole subject practical and instructive. [What an excellent concept! In most jurisdictions, though, the W.M. has little choice in selecting his Senior Deacon. This officer, as well as the others, progresses up the line.]

XIV. It is the prerogative of the W.M. to install his successor.

In Chapter 4, instructions under the head of INSTALLATION are sufficiently precise as to forms and ceremonies. But in none of the Monitors can we discover any form of address, any kind breathings of counsel and encouragement suitable to this occasion. There is no other place in the history of a Lodge where such an address is so appropriate, and we venture to devote a little space to it.

Supposing the Installation vows taken, the stereotyped instructions given, and the Installing Officer (having placed the gavel and its power, in the hand of his successor) stepped aside and "homaged" with the rest, he may with great propriety deliver to the new W.M. in hearing of the audience, Masonic and secular, the following:

The Master of the Lodge must be a moral and a good man. —He is an exemplar to his flock. *Like master like man* is an adage older than Aesop, wiser than Plato. If, in your daily walk and conversation, you fail to practice *out of the Lodge* what you teach *in it,* your labor is vain. Your seat is but a shadowy throne. Your Lodge is as a body without a head. How absurd to suppose that an immoral man can teach *morality,* a profane man *reverence to God,* an intemperate man *temperance,* a licentious man *purity of life.* The influence of an immoral Master is destructive to its growth, to its honorable standing, and to those social enjoyments permitted at hours of refreshment. No Lodge will be better than its Master; the spring will not rise higher than its fountain; the public will measure the honor and respectability of this Lodge, Worshipful Brother, by you!

The Master of a Lodge must be a law-abiding man. —In all mobs, riots and public lawlessness of every form, in all violations of statute and common law by which the current history of our country is disgraced, you should be found *in the lead* in the preservation of public order. Never let it be charged upon you that you are engaged in the infraction of law, but conform yourself and teach others to conform to the public peace. How else can you say that Masonry interferes not with the duty a man owes to his country?

The Master of the Lodge must be no conspirator or secret enemy of government.—Midnight plots, schemes of self-aggrandizement at the expense of the country; these are abhorrent to the conscience of the man who remembers that he is engaged, as you are, in the covenants of the Mastership. Prove then, Worshipful Brother, before a vigilant inspection, that the secrecy of Freemasonry is not the secrecy of the assassin, its profits are not those of piracy, its wages not the thirty pieces of Judas Iscariot.

The Master of the Lodge must be of good report before the community.—In the nervous language of old, "he must work diligently, live creditably, and act honorably by all men." This implies that he will recommend it by his life to the hearts of observers; he will disseminate that charity to the needy which is so acceptable to the Most High. But if he is idle or extravagant, that body of which he is the head will fall into merited contempt.

The Master of the Lodge must be temperate and meek.—"As the sons of Rechab were temperate, as the leader of Israel was meek," thus wrote the Masonic historian a century ago, and none more worthly has sat in Solomon's seat. Your gavel, Worshipful Brother, having knocked off the rough corners of your own mind and conscience, has brought you the golden rewards of well-doing, and therefore your brethren will honor you.

The Master of the Lodge must be cautious, courteous, and faithful, and must practice self-government.—In behavior *cautious*, lest the vigilant eye mark the weak spot, the flawy place, and disgrace you before your constituents; *courteous*, for have they not *chosen you*, Worshipful Brother, and promised to *obey you*, and thus earned all that you can give them of courtesy and gentleness? *Faithful*, for are you not pledged before God to be faithful? Are you not bound, secretly and publicly, by every tie that can bind an honest heart? All the precepts of the Sinaitic law are so many injunctions to you to *govern yourself*, to apply the working tools to *yourself*, and so to secure *for yourself* a title honorable and lasting; "The Master in Israel."

The Master of the Lodge must posess an ardent love for genuine Masonry.—To this end, Worshipful Brother, you will learn to abhor impostors and discountenance innovation. Qualified by experience and study to separate the pure gold from the base, you will exhibit a genuine admiration for the pure and abhorrence for the base in Masonry. It does not look well, Worshipful Brother, to see men who hold the Lodge-gavel

seeking with prurient curiosity the stagnant pools of imitative associations. Rather let your heart, soul, mind, be engrossed in this one work to
which you pledged your best endeavors—*the work of Masonry.*

The Master of the Lodge must respect his Masonic superiors.—How can
you expect to be obeyed, Worshipful Brother, if you have not yourself
learned obedience? Of the three sources of authority upon which your
right to exact obedience is based, two are *from above*—the DEITY,
through *His Word*, the GRAND LODGE, through its *Charter.* Thus, while
you command once, you obey twice.

The Master of the Lodge must be a zealous Mason.—It is your part,
Worshipful Brother, to propagate the knowledge of Masonry. You are as
the messenger of this evangel. You should be exact in logic, close in
debate, read up in Masonic literature, familiar with mankind, that you
may lead in the war against opposition and overcome it. The Masonic
East is no place for cold-blooded indifference.

*The Master of the Lodge must be versed in the Landmarks of
Masonry.*—As the Scripture hath it, you must often "walk about
Jerusalem and mark the bulwarks thereof." You must know your ground
well—how far the pillars are from the centre. If a Landmark be removed
by accident or design, you must raise the warning voice before it is too
late.

The Master of the Lodge must be a lover of old-time things.—To you,
Worshipful Brother, as the Master of the Lodge, "progressiveness in
Masonry" can have no meaning. The religion of departed saints was "to
learn the will of God," *to perform it* followed in due course; the true
Masonry is *to know* its behests and *to do* them. The better you know them
the more earnest you will be to do them.

The Master of Lodge must be zealous of its honor.—Its chastity must be
kept without reproach. You will receive visitors and applicants with
zealous scrutiny, and not permit any to enjoy the honors and rewards of
the time-honored institution until you are positive of their ability and
worthiness.

*The Master of the Lodge must communicate statedly with Grand
Lodge.*—You are the one of all, Worshipful Brother, who constitutes the
chain of connection between this Lodge and the mother Grand Lodge to
which it is subordinate.

*The Master of the Lodge must recognize no clandestine
rivals.*—Inspired with a sense of the importance of Masonic purity, you
will have no heart or hand for organizations without tribe, kindred, or
genealogical honors.

The Master of the Lodge must maintain the regularity of the Masonic system as essential to the very life and usefulness of Masonry itself.—Let these precepts, Worshipful Brother, be as lamps to your feet. "A place for everything; everything in its place." "Nothing in Freemasonry without a rational explanation."

DUTIES OF THE WORSHIPFUL MASTER

1.It is the duty of the W.M. to attend regularly the communications of his Lodge.

One has only to consider the relation which the W.M. bears to the organization over which he is installed, to concur in the propriety of this first requisition. As few things weaken and demoralize the Lodge as much as the Master's frequent absence, so there are few things that more thoroughly justify the Lodge in appealing to the Grand Master to have him removed from office, and his place given to the Senior Warden.

The rule adopted by an eminent Mason, long a W.M., and for three years Grand Master, was "never to be absent without a positive necessity, from the *regular monthly communications.* If there is a necessity for absence, let it be at called communications, when no business can regularly come up save that which is mentioned in the notifications."

Going into further details, we add that the W.M. should make his appearance at the Lodge-room at least a quarter of an hour (half is better) prior to the opening moment, to see that matters are in readiness. Tylers need looking after as much as other people. The W.M. must be ready to make *pro tem.* appointments to offices whose incumbents are absent. This ought not to be left to the last minute. The appointee should know of his appointment in season to refresh his memory and prepare himself for duty. If visitors are in attendance, the W.M. is ready to meet them with the genial "word of welcome," so acceptable to the stranger, and, if convenient, they may be put in care of the Committee of Examination *even before the Lodge is opened.*

2. It is the duty of the W.M. to open his Lodge at the time specified in the by-laws, and close it at a suitable hour.

In the 7th of the 15 Installation Charges the W.M. declares that "he will be faithful to his Lodge." Precisely at the time specified in the by-laws, he should congregate his Lodge "by one knock." No clock is more punctually to sound forth the hour with its hammer than a well-disposed W.M. with his gavel. If, after he has done this, there is not present a sufficient number for opening, it is optional with him to wait a while for the dilatory members, or to dismiss those who are in attendance, and all go home together. The latter method was adopted on a certain occasion, by a sharp-set young W.M. just installed, whose Lodge in preceding years had become inexcusably tardy. At the first communication he congregated his Lodge at the time specified in the by-laws, and then, there being but a handful present, dismissed them, pocketed the charter, and went home. Then he brought the members together in a *Called Communication* the succeeding week, explained the matter to them, pointed out the evils of tardiness, and so worked upon their better nature that he had but little difficulty under that head for the balance of his term. The true theory is, that the Lodge establishes the moment of opening *in its by-laws,* and the W.M., at his installation, solemnly covenants to *see the by-laws carefully and punctually executed.* If the members of the Lodge disapprove of the time established there, the same being too early or too late, they have authority to change it at pleasure. But, while the rule stands, let the W.M. see it rigidly enforced, as far as his power extends.

Two hours well employed is ample time for a Lodge meeting, quite as long as the tired, the feeble, the sick, the active business man cares to stay. It is as long as the ordinary mind has power to imbibe instruction, and after that the rest is weariness. It is as long as one's family patiently assents to the absence of its head. If degrees are to be conferred, let there be called communications of the Lodge, although these should not be too frequent. It is a good rule, established long ago by an aged and venerable brother, now at rest, "when you venture home, if the family scowl and complain at your absence, take it that you have exceeded the by-laws!"

The ability of the W.M. is shown more in his style of opening and closing the Lodge than in any other part of official duty. This has been styled the *experimentum crucis* of his efficiency. As the test of a good Lodge is a *good Master,* so the test of a good W.M. is his capacity for opening and closing his Lodge wisely, accurately, instructively. In this part of Masonry he is the be-all and the do-all of the Order.

3. It is the duty of the W.M. to preserve order in the Lodge.

The Mason must be dull indeed who cannot see that this matter is the sole province of the W.M. That he may be properly strengthened for it, the officers of his Lodge are all commanded and installed by *himself.* The Wardens are commended to assist him in his trust. The Secretary is informed that "he is to observe the will and pleasure of the W.M." The Deacons learn that their charge is to attend upon him. Finally, the brethren of his Lodge, one and all, are commended *to obey him* according to the Old Charges and Regulations "with all humility, reverence, love and alacrity." His very name MASTER suggests the authority with which he is invested to keep order, and his implement, the GAVEL, placed in his hand by the Past Master who placed him in the Oriental Chair of King Solomon, is an emblem of power indisputable, recognized the Masonic world over by every beholder, and every hearer.

The fifth prerogative is "to control and determine discussions," and the sixth "to determine all questions of order and the Order of Business without appeal, save to the Grand Master or the Grand Lodge." This clears up the question of authority beyond controversy. If the W.M. cannot, by proper use of his gavel and other appliances within his prerogatives, preserve that order and decorum essential to true Masonry—if reproof and rebuke, counsel and appeal, reference to written authority, the aid of aged reverend Past Masters—if all these fail in the hands of the W.M., he ought, as a last resort, to pocket his charter and declare the Lodge summarily closed. By this he justifies his position before the Grand Lodge, and secures that sympathy at headquarters which alone can compensate him for the mortification he has been compelled to endure at the hands of wicked and contentious brethren.

Lest the reader, especially the un-Masonic reader, should draw the conclusion from the above paragraph, that the W.M. stands in continual danger from the disobedient of his Lodge, we add that in fifteen thousand Lodges now enrolled upon the Catalogue of the forty-nine American Grand Lodges, such incidents are of the rarest. Old Masons are living who never witnessed and never heard of such an occurrence as we have foreshadowed.

4. It is the duty of the W.M. to regulate the admission of visitors.

So many references appear in the present volume to the admission of visitors that it is well to read the language of the Installation forms given in Chapter 4, "You (the W.M.) agree that no visitor shall be received into your Lodge without due examination and producing proper voucher of his having been initiated into a regular Lodge." These "proper vouchers" are variously construed in different jurisdictions.

In foreign countries "due examination" is as much neglected as the "proper voucher" is by most of the American Lodges. We are not prepared to affirm that no visitor shall be admitted without the exhibition of his diploma, but will frankly express our approval of the foreign practice, which is "to furnish each newly-made Mason with a diploma (certificate), and require him to exhibit it whenever he applies to visit a Lodge where he is not otherwise vouched for." The *test* in the exhibition of the diploma is the autograph of its possessor found over *Ne varietur*, in the margin. [A current dues card, with the bearer's signature, is the accepted means of recognition in America.]

Readers familiar with the ordinary methods of avouchal in crowded meetings, need not be informed that there is much room for improvement in these particulars. To secure such an assemblage from impostors, suspended Masons, etc., demands a far more perfect system than is in vogue. The Deacon passing rapidly along the columns three or four files deep, and trusting to a quick glance of the eye or a hasty "I vouch for that brother" for identification, and obliged to limit his work to ten minutes or less, comes very far short of that "strict trial, due examination or lawful information" which shall make the visitors as lawfully entitled to be present at the communication as he (the Deacon) is himself. The matter, however, is commented upon in another chapter.

5. It is the duty of the W.M. to preserve the charter (warrant) of the Lodge inviolate, and transmit it to his successor.

No Masonic Lodge can function without a legitimate charter from the Grand Lodge in its jurisdiction. It must be present at all times when the Lodge is open. A visitor has the right to examine it before he is examined to make certain he is not about to visit a clandestine, or unrecognized, Lodge.

6. It is the duty of the W.M. to perform the ritualistic work of the Lodge (the drill and drama), and instruct the brethren therein.

The Masonic drama presents a beauty and sublimity calculated to arouse a desire of excellence in every intelligent mind. Nothing outside *Inspired Lids* is so grand, solemn, sublime as the dramatic lessons which make up the theory of a Freemason's life from his announcement at the N.E. corner of the Lodge to the instant when the clods of the valley, mingled with the evergreen sprigs of the grave, fall upon his coffin. To each ceremony there is a complete sequence that explains the preceding and hints at the subsequent passage. In each symbol is a practical thought that gavels the harmony together, and each points to higher attainments in the present life and a trembling trust for a place in the world to come. Each suggests, in some degree, kindness to our fellow men as a means of pleasing God, and of pleasing Him as the highest source of human happiness. Is not the place of hierophant of such mysteries a desireable one? Does it not arouse the mind of the W.M. to display these mysteries worthily? Can the man who is covenanted and installed under most sacred sanctions allow his indolence to justify his ignorance?

There is a difference, too great to be overlooked, between the instruction which appears to be absolutely extemporaneous—seems to come from the heart upon the impulse of the moment, that method of instruction in which the W.M. *looks into the eye of the candidate,* and communicates to him the code of morality, science, and religion that make up Freemasonry—a difference we say between that and another method, alas, too popular! wherein the W.M., holding a book in one hand and a smoky lamp in the other, *reads from the Monitor,* through moist and cloudy glasses, the same disquisitions. Who has not seen it?

In dispensing light and knowledge, therefore, the W.M. should early commit to memory everything of that sort, and communicate by the first method named above. One great credit is due to the Masons of Pennsylvania above all other American jurisdictions, that a Monitor is not allowed to be carried into the Lodge room. The officers may acquire their exoteric parts from the book in the ante-room but, like the actor going upon the stage, they must leave it with the prompter and trust to memory in delivering their respective parts.

Each American Grand Lodge has settled the *particular system of work* required by its own jurisdiction, and this involves the necessity, on the part of the W.M., of learning it accurately and communicating it literally. Nothing less than this comes up to the level of his convenants. The establishment of Schools of Instruction, the appointment of Grand Lecturers, the communication of the proper forms and lectures in the Grand Lodge, etc., facilitate the acquirement of the standard system, although it must be admitted that the continued changes of "work" by Grand Lodge make this task a more laborious one than it ought to be.

7. It is the duty of the W.M. to cause an investigation into all un-Masonic conduct committed by persons affiliated with his Lodge; also of non-affiliates and members of other Lodges resident within his jurisdiction.

In the large majority of American Lodges the Junior Warden acts as the party to *present and prosecute* before the Lodge [or trial commission] all misconduct that comes under the head of "Unmasonic Conduct." But in this part of his official duty, he is but the proxy of the W.M., who counsels him from point to point in the proceedings, assuring himself that all things are conducted according to rules of order prepared for such occasions, and that no serious misconduct that has come to light within his jurisdiction shall pass unnoticed. In this category it will be seen that non-affiliated Masons (that is *demitted* Masons) are affected equally with the members of the Lodge, and the same of Masons affiliated in other Lodges but resident within the jurisdiction of the Lodge. Too often such Masons have been permitted to escape the just penalty of their profanity, intemperance, and general lawlessness by the plea of non-affiliation.

8. It is the duty of the W.M. to visit the sick and preside at the funeral rites of deceased Masons.

If it is the duty of the private Mason "to visit the sick and afflicted" affiliated with him in Masonic bonds, how much greater the duty of an installed officer? how much greater the duty of the Installed Master? In the majority of American Lodges there is a standing *Committee on Charity* to which, in general, applications for relief are referred; and this Committee has power to grant relief to a limited extent during the recess of the Lodge. But this scarcely applies to the point involved in the EIGHTH DUTY, VIZ: *obligation to visit the sick.* Few writers have sufficiently dwelt on this. Yet in many instances it ranks in importance above the others. There are but *few Masons* in proportion to the whole, who are poor and need relief; but *many Masons* suffer from long confinement on the sick-bed, and *all Masons* in their turn must die. In the weary hours of sickness, in the painful confinement extending often through weeks and months, the refreshing voice of a beloved brother or a beloved and respected MASTER falls upon the wearied mind as the early dew upon the parched grass. "It is like the dew of Hermon, like the dew that descends upon the mountains of Zion," and twice blessed is the man who has it in his power so easily, so cheaply to impart such pleasure. In some Lodges there are brethren deputed by order of the Master to wait in their turn, upon a sick brother. This will often prove the most systematic method, because it secures the afflicted one from neglect which might follow upon purely voluntary callers.

As to the second clause of the EIGHTH DUTY, "to preside at the funeral rites of deceased Masons," this is too well understood to need argument.

It is well to explain here, that the system of public funerals, so common in American Masonry, is not in use abroad. Nor can we discover from Masonic history, the time when funerals were first admitted as regulations of the Order. Therefore, the expressions "from time immemorial," etc., heard at the western limit of the open grave are scarcely sustained by the facts. But in this Republic, so general is the custom, so dear to the heart of the true Mason is the burial-privilege; so conducive is the practice of Masonic interments, when rightly conducted, that the W.M. knowing that death's shafts fall indiscriminately and without warning, will not

permit a month to pass after his installation before qualifying himself for
the solemn duty, "the Masonic Burial of the Masonic Dead."

A BROTHER'S LAST REQUEST
BY ROBERT MORRIS, LL.D.

[A dying Mason sent a message to another to come and
pronounce the eulogy over his remains.]

How tender must the love of Masons be,
When in a dying moment they can think
Of one another! Few are human ties
That are not severed at the approach of *death;*
Death quenches common friendships, blunts the edge
Of mere acquaintance, rends the cable-tow
Of social ties, and scatters them like chaff;
But on *the love of Masons,* golden chain,
Stronger than iron, *death can lay no hand!*
Powerless, conquered, stingless, hateful death.

Brother, when struggling thus in the last fight
(That fight I, too, must struggle in, and soon)—
Did you remember me? did the bright hours
We've spent together 'midst the Sons of Light
Come o'er your spirit like a happy dream?
Did you recall the Masons' songs we've sung?
Or what in sweet companionship was told
Of gentle Ruth and loving Martha pure,
While from the Sisters round came answering tears?

Those scenes delightful I can ne'er forget:
Would I had seen *you* in the conquering hour,
That I, too, might prepare for victory:
If the blest spirits of the just return
To this cold world, if Mason-love hath power
To call our visitor from brighter scenes,
May I have grace with God to see again
When I shall die, *those whom I love below,*
To tell me how to win the victory,
And what the joys awaiting in the skies!

**9. It is the duty of the W.M. to use his utmost endeavors to preserve peace
and harmony in his Lodge; and by his own deportment both within and
without the Lodge, to be a good example to his brethren.**

The Masonic student will find nowhere a finer comment upon this
passage than the well-known Charge at the Installation of the Worshipful
Master. With slight changes, we read: "Impress upon the members of

your Lodge the dignity and high importance of Masonry. Admonish them never to disgrace it. Charge them to practice *out of the Lodge* those duties which they have been taught *in it*. By amiable, discreet, and virtuous conduct, convince mankind of the goodness of the institution, so that, when anyone is said to be a Freemason, the world may know that he is one to whom the brotherhood may pour forth its sorrows; to whom distress may prefer its suit; whose hand is guided by justice, and his heart expanded by benevolence."

SUGGESTED REMARKS BY THE MASTER

On Acceptance of Office:

My Brethren, one often hears protests from newly elected officers as to their inability to fill the posts to which they have been chosen. I am not going to take that attitude for it would not be complimentary to you, who have elected me, to imply that you have chosen an incompetent person to fill the office of Master of this Lodge. If a mistake has been made, it will be discovered soon enough.

I thank you most heartily for the confidence you have placed in me, and I will endeavor, to the best of my ability, to merit that confidence by discharging my duties zealously and impartially. If errors are made, they will be errors of the mind and not of the heart. I am taking it for granted that you will stand by me throughout my term of office, and I expect to have the benefit of your counsel and advice.

Again, my sincere thanks for the honor you have paid me and my promise that I shall do all in my power to do what the responsibilities and duties of the office require.

Words of Welcome to Delegations from Visiting Lodges:

My Brethren, it is indeed an honor to extend a welcome to you on behalf of _____ Lodge. I do that now with the deepest sincerity. I am not going to burden you with a long and stilted address. We have with us tonight brethren with real ability as orators, some of whom we will hear from, and I feel that any effort by me in this direction and at this time would be superfluous.

The visit of your Lodge and other brethren is the continuance of a happy custom started many years ago; in fact, the custom of visiting brethren elsewhere has come down through the centuries from the days of the Operative Masons when the signs, grips and words were tests of great importance. Masons were strangers to each other until they were proved as brethren by the same tests we use today; happily, we did not have to apply these tests tonight because through long and intimate association in the daily walks of life and by frequent visits back and forth, we know each other for what we are.

I hope your stay with us tonight will be a most happy and pleasant one. Again, I say you are welcome, most welcome, and we are proud to be your hosts upon this occasion. There is only one thought I wish to add, and that is—come again, and often.

Master's Acceptance of his Past Master's Jewel or Apron:

Members of _____ Lodge, the year just closing has been to me a most rewarding one, and in many ways, the happiest of my life. It has brought me into close relationship with each and everyone of you and has given to me a keen appreciation of your worth, your loyalty, as well as the spirit of Masonry that shines in your hearts and lives. We are all human beings with our frailties and weaknesses. We shall never attain perfection, but we are all striving toward the same goal, doing our best with God's help to be true men, true Masons, true citizens and true sons of the one Eternal Father.

It has been a great privilege to serve you, and I can only say that for this beautiful token of your esteem and remembrance, I am grateful indeed. The fact that I am now to be a Past Master will make no difference as far as I am concerned in the interest I shall always have for our Lodge, and I trust that we may all be able to work on and on together just the same for God, for country and for this wonderful Brotherhood. I assure you that I will wear this jewel (or apron) with pride.

CHAPTER 2

THE OTHER OFFICERS
THE WARDENS AND THEIR DUTIES

The Wardens, in theory, are "two officers in a state of preparation for the Mastership." As it cannot be known when the W.M. will be absent, the language directed to the Senior Warden in the Installation Service is particularly applicable. "Your regular attendance at our stated meetings is essentially necessary. In the absence of the Master you are to govern this Lodge; in his presence you are to assist him in the government of it." The Senior Warden is elected annually, and chosen "not for seniority, but for his merit." His specific powers and duties are thus summed up:

1. To succeed to and exercise all the powers of the W.M. in the event of that officer's absence.
2. To represent the Lodge in conjunction with the W.M. and the J.W. at all the Grand Communications of the Grand Lodge, when such rule prevails.
3. To act on the standing Committee of Charity.
4. To appoint the Junior Deacon (this rule is not universal).
5. To take charge of the Craft during the hours of labor.

He is to pay the Craft their wages, if any be due, that is, to make up in his own person any deficiency created by the Master's absence, and particularly to study the peace and harmony of the Lodge. To this end he is conjoined with the W.M. in communicating the catechetical instructions of the ritual. His station is in the west, upon a dais reached by two steps; his jewel is a Level, an emblem of equality and harmony, which should ever exist among Masons. Before him, upon a pedestal is, and he carries in procession, a column of the Doric order, the emblem of strength. He represents HIRAM, King of Tyre, who is also the representative of the column Strength, because he gave aid and strength to King Solomon while erecting the temple at Jerusalem.

The Junior Warden, like his immediate superior, is annually elected, "not by seniority, but by merit." He must be a Master Mason, and a member of the Lodge. His specific powers and duties are thus summed up:

1. To succeed to and exercise all powers of the W.M. in the absence of the two officers above him.

2. To represent the Lodge in conjunction with the W.M. and S.W., at all the Grand Communications of the Grand Lodge, where this rule prevails.
3. To act on the standing Committee of Charity.
4. To take charge of the Craft during the hours of refreshment.

In the absence of the Senior Warden his position is not changed, unless the W.M. desires to make him Senior Warden, *pro tem.* He is eligible to be elected to the office of W.M., after one year's service.

By the older forms the Junior Warden was required to examine visitors and receive candidates. These duties are better entrusted, the first to a special Committee of Examination, the latter to the Senior Deacon. His regular and punctual attendance upon the communications of the Lodge is strongly enjoined. One well-devised theory of the Junior Warden's part is "that he is the counsellor and admonisher of his brethren, and he is to see that the penalties of Masonry are inflicted upon the incorrigible. In many jurisdictions he is the official prosecutor of the Lodge. In the festivals of the society he has the governance, so that the preservation of harmony and order may be secured. His station is in the south; his jewel is a Plumb, emblematical of the rectitude of conduct which should distinguish the brethren when, during the hours of refreshment, they are beyond the precincts of the Lodge. He has placed before him, and carries in processions, a column of the Corinthian order, an emblem of beauty, and a gavel, as an emblem of authority. The crowning feature in the dignity of the Junior Warden is the fact that he represents in duties, prerogatives and responsibilities, HIRAM ABIF, the widow's son.

THE SECRETARY AND HIS DUTIES

It has been well and forciby said that "it is not so much what a Lodge *does*, that makes up its history, as what the Secretary *records.*" A negligent and ignorant Secretary so falsifies and suppresses, as to *devitalize* that which makes up the memory of a Lodge Life, *its Records.* A working member of the Order, undertakng to prepare the history of his Grand Lodge, mourned over this almost to tears. He failed to trace out many of the most important facts in the Lodge records. The dry memorandums of "members present" and "work done" placed in his hands were no more a *History of the Lodge* than a skeleton is the body of a man. He could not find in them the most essential matters of dates. There was no account of corner-stone celebrations, of the visits of Grand officials, of the dates of fires, deaths and other casualties. The minutes were often loose sheets, kept with pencil, partly missing, not paged, not identifiable by signature, soiled with oil and drippings from the roof, or, if copied into the Lodge-books, but little better. In various instances, he found himself unable to trace back the biography of a given member (notably HENRY CLAY), so as to give the dates of initiation, passing, raising and demitting, all of which facts were lost, owing to the negligence of Secretaries, seen in the imperfection of their records.

The propriety of introducing a chapter in this volume upon Secretary rests upon this, that, while in American Lodges the Secretary is elected by the Lodge, and not an appointee of the W.M., yet, in point of fact, he is as *directly under the Master's orders* as though he were. His response shows this. In answer to the query, "What are your duties there, brother Secretary?" he replies "To observe the Worshipful Master's will and pleasure, to record the proceedings of the Lodge, to receive all moneys and pay them into the hands of the Treasurer." ["And to record ALL transactions proper to be written."] Practically the first clause embraces the entire round of the Secretary's duties, viz.: "To observe the Worshipful Master's will and pleasure," for he is not at liberty to read, file or record any document unless it has the approbation of the W.M.

To secure a good Secretary then, or to shape a good one out of imperfect materials, is a matter of prime necessity to the W.M., who is striving to make an Augustan age of his official year.

In the "Memorandum book" of a Grand Lecturer whose experience extends over several States, and over thirty-two years of time, we find the following accounts of eighteen Secretaries in as many Lodges. Appended to each is a pen sketch of the man, very life-like and artistic.

Number One.—A liberal and good Secretary, regularly donates his annual salary ($12) to the charity fund of the Lodge.

Number Two.—Talks too much. Is up in his place upon every question that is moved. Otherwise a worthy officer.

Number Three.—Exceedingly illiterate. Especially a bad reader. To hear him read his minutes aloud is painful to me and mortifying to the W.M. Calls archives, *archeeves*, etc.

Number Four—Has invented a response of his own in place of the one given him at his Installation. Said invention lacks in correctness, grammar and good judgment. Fault of W.M.

Number Five—A fine intellect, but wretched penman. When he passes out of office his records will scarcely be legible.

Number Six—Makes his corner too noisy. Has a crowd of whisperers around him, even in serious parts of the work. Fault of W.M.

Number Seven—Retains his seat and continues his work during prayer. Irreverent. Fault of W.M.

Number Eight—Hard of hearing. Guesses at what is going on, keeps records accordingly. Earnest, conscientious, intelligent, but deaf.

Number Nine—Smokes tobacco during Lodge hours till the south-east fumes and stinks. W.M. firmly rebukes and exhorts. Rev. Chaplain threatens to bring charges. Fault of W.M.

Number Ten—Does not "pay over" the collected funds to the Treasurer as fast as gathered. Fault of W.M.

Number Eleven—Keeps his books at home. Rarely has them at the Lodge when wanted. Fault of W.M.

Number Twelve—Has a voice like a bugle horn. When reading his minutes is heard in the street. Scandal has followed. Fault of W.M.

Number Thirteen—Voice too feeble. Does not reach beyond the altar. Fault of W.M.

Number Fourteen—Fails to rise at the three knocks. Continues his work even while opening proceedings are had. Fault of W.M.

Number Fifteen—Insists upon disbursing the Lodge funds in place of the Treasurer. Fault of W.M.

Number Sixteen—Is incomparably the brightest Mason in the Lodge. So far superior to W.M. as to be employed in the most active parts of drill and drama. Fault of W.M.

Number Seventeen—Splendid penman. As Masonic historio-grapher has no superior. His books are models of internal accuracy and external beauty. Credit of W.M.

Number Eighteen—A life-long official and grows better as he grows older. Has served the Lodge more than forty years. Fine painted por-trait of him over his head. No Ezra ever worthier of honor and respect.

To this list as many more varieties of Secretaries might be added from the memoranda, illustrating every grade of merit and demerit, from the *worst* (the defaulters of Lodge moneys, the terror of Grand Secretaries, the falsifiers of Masonic history), to *the best*. The responsibility for these negligent and unworthy officials rests solely and absolutely upon the W.M. [Yet, because he is an elected officer, he can be removed only by the Lodge, and then only if charges are preferred against him and he is found guilty. He can resign, and probably would if enough pressure was put upon him by the W.M. and other officers.]

The following sketch of duties of the Secretary, given in thirteen parts, is copied from the Model By-laws used in hundreds of American Lodges:

1. To observe the Worshipful Master's will and pleasure.
2. To record the proceedings of the Lodge.
3. To receive all moneys.
4. To pay them (the moneys) into the hands of the Treasurer.
5. To attend upon trials and meetings for taking evidence.
6. To furnish copies of all evidence taken on trials where an appeal to the Grand Lodge is demanded.
7. To furnish diplomas, demits, certificates, etc., duly signed and sealed, by order of the Lodge.

8. To prepare the annual reports for the Grand Lodge and certificates for the representatives.
9. To notify the Grand Secretary promptly of all expulsions from the Lodge.
10. To keep a book of Masonic biography for recording all important facts relative to Masonic history of each member of the Lodge.
11. To keep a visitors' book.
12. To prepare a balance sheet of all the accounts of the members, and a roll of all who are entitled to vote; likewise an official statement of his own acount with the Lodge, and deliver them to the W.M. at the close of the term.
13. To preserve the seal of the Lodge with care, and deliver it to his successor at the close of his offical term.

It is becoming a laudable practice to open, continue and perfect a *Book of Masonic Biography.* Nothing is more creditable to the Lodge than this. In the Commanderies of Knights Templar the Biographical Volume is the pride of the fraters. A convenient form should contain a place:

1. For time and place of birth.
2. Date of petition.
3. Dates of Initiation, Passing and Raising.
4. Date of death.
5. Miscellaneous, to embrace room for Demit, for the infliction of discipline (Suspension or Expulsion), for installation to various offices, etc., etc.

It is not too much to call a Secretary the "Historiographer of the Lodge," who will preform such a noble charge properly. It is in this volume that the affecting "request for Masonic Burial" of each brother should be entered. In some of the New York City Lodges the "Book of Masonic Biography" is so splendidly got up, so intelligently kept, so carefully preserved as to be considered the greatest treasure of the Lodge.

One of the best Secretaries we have ever known, gives a history of his official labors, full of matters worthy of perusal by all who are placed in the South-east. He entered upon his duties knowing that a most disagreeable task was before him, and he secured from the Lodge and the W.M. their consent and a full understanding that he have ample authority to bring order out of confusion. The accounts were years behind; few of the members being less than twelve months in arrears. Debts large and small were due by the Lodge, and its credit was exhausted. Everyone who would trust them had been victimized by the outgoing Secretary (expelled for defalcation and general rascality), from the owner of the hall who threatened to distrain for rent, to the washerwoman who threatened to lay violent hands upon the Lodge aprons! The Grand Lodge dues were much behind; in brief, the Lodge was generally believed to be bankrupt.

Our newly-elected brother, having some leisure and much pride in Masonry, took hold of the joint task of resuscitation and reformation. First, he gave some days and nights to copying the Lodge records from loose sheets, backs of envelopes and waste paper into a new and attractive volume. Though various *lacunae* were left, yet, upon the whole, the continuity of the Lodge history was fairly perserved. Next he attacked the account books and made a ledger, a thing never before attempted by the occupant of the South-east. In conjunction with the treasurer, a balance sheet was prepared and submitted to the W.M. for correction. Great was the uproar that followed upon the consideration of this portentous paper by the members, and several Called Communications were devoted to comparing accounts, planning inordinate charges, and "making buckle and tongue to meet." Old receipts were hunted up, evidences of payment produced, and in the end, an honest exhibit of money matters was made and entered upon the Lodge records.

This, however, was but the first step; to *collect* the long out standing accounts was far more laborious. He drew them off in form and began a course of drumming. He received the smallest amounts and credited them. In three cases he took notes, and by joint consent paid them into the hands of creditors, who deemed the notes of individuals better than the promises of the Lodge. Every dollar, as fast as collected, was paid (through the hands of the Treasurer, of course) to the Lodge creditors, beginning with those whose claims were most pressing, beginning in fact with the washerwoman and the Tyler. Before the end of the first year of his official term (which was afterwards extended to the *twenty-third*, the year of his death), he had paid every cent owed by the Lodge, and before the second had collected all that was collectable, and spread oblivion over the rest. In his report at the end of the second year he gave it as his deliberate opinion that "there would be little injustice in charging the Secretary with the losses sustained by failure of members to pay Lodge dues, for this evil results, in almost every instance, from the neglect of the Secretary to collect the dues in *the small* instead of waiting until they become *too large* for *collection.*"

The Lodge should provide the Secretary with a desk enriched with pigeon-holes and drawers; an ample supply of stationery for himself and his fellow members, for reports, etc.; a sufficiency of lamps; strong, well-bound minute books, records, and ledgers; the seal and press of the

Lodge; a full assortment of blanks for accounts, receipts of the Treasurer, demits, diplomas, and other official papers; and, if the funds of the Lodge justify the expenditure, an iron safe of convenient size. In the large city Lodges this latter object is a regular part of the furniture. As the Secretary is *ex officio* Librarian of the Lodge, proper cabinets or shelving should be furnished him for the reception and preservation of the books. Every Lodge must of necessity have *some volumes* worth preserving, if only the printed proceedings of the Grand Lodge; but there are others, such as monitors, music books, etc., necessary to the instruction and use of members. It has become the custom of old and prosperous Lodges to collect libraries comprehensive enough to embrace many works upon Freemasonry, its ethics, history, poetry, etc., which have been published during the last forty years. Some New York Lodges (notably *Kane Lodge*) have accumulated collections of books that give them a place among the standard libraries of the city. In 1857 a series of volumes on Masonry was published containing more than *fifty* distinct works under the name of *The Universal Masonic Library,* of which several thousand sets are in the hands of as many American and Canadian Lodges. In all these instances the Secretary is considered the Librarian of his Lodge. In brief, all the written papers of the Lodge, every document save the charter, every volume, including the Bible, are within the keeping of the Secretary.

[While the above remarks by Macoy may hold true in many cases, yet, in more modern times, the W.M. more often gives the Tyler the responsibility of seeing that the Bible is properly stored with the Lodge's paraphernalia when Lodge is closed.

Also, the W.M. often appoints a Library Chairman who works with his committee for the acquisition of Masonic literature for the benefit of the members.]

The form of the account book kept by the Lodge Secretary is simple and easy of comprehension. Every member has two pages appropriated to him in the ledger. One of *credits* (on the left hand), one of *debits* (on the right hand.) [Bookkeeping practices today call for the reverse—debits left, credits right.] In the latter appear the various items of dues charged against him, with the other assessments specified in the by-laws, or levied by special order of the Lodge. These should be footed up quarterly. Upon the right hand page appear his various payments and any allowances made him by the Lodge. These, too, should be footed up quarterly, and the balance struck and carried to proper pages. Upon the death, demission, or expulsion of a member, the balance is carried to "Profit and Loss," and the account closed. When a member petitions for a demit he pays to the end of the current quarter, and with that his financial transactions with the Lodge are ended.

A contributor to the present volume furnishes us with the account of an old and venerable Secretary rising three score years and ten, so decrepit in his lower limbs as to be carried to his place in the arms of the brethren, sitting at a capacious table supplied with drawers and recesses, on his left the library, behind him the iron safe, above him a gallery of Masonic worthies old and recent, in various styles of art, and surrounded, each of them, with a running circlet of acacia and black ribbon. Clear in intelligence, ardent in Masonic zeal, stored with Masonic memories of nearly half a century, this venerable father in Masonry is a model Secretary in all the "parts and points" that make up our commentary in the present chapter.

From our personal acquaintances we select another example that will further enforce the counsels and instructions we are giving here. He was for thirteen years Secretary of his Lodge, and a Mason more amiable and unassuming we have never met. Rarely was his voice heard in debate, never in the caucusing (gentle and friendly always) which precedes the annual election in his Lodge. His influence was the greater in the membership because exclusively limited to the affairs of the South-east and the personal duties which every Mason owes to his brethren. As the Masonic Historiographer of his Lodge he was active and efficient. Whenever a new member was enrolled, whether by initiation or affiliation, he sought from him the dates of his birth and parentage, and began a *biographical sketch* which enlarged with the incidents of his life, his social and political career, etc., was made to occupy the first lines of the page devoted to his name.

In his Masonic advances new facts were developed, and sketches given until death cut short the thread. There, then, were the materials for an obituary, not the stereotyped and hackneyed skeleton made to embody all manner of Masonic biographies, but an intelligent, instructive, and truthful story of the dead. Thus, when one of the leading members was accidentally killed, and the reporters sought for details of his honored and useful life, this Secretary had but to refer to his *Golden Book of Biographies*. Thence he sketched in one hour such a body of facts as filled the column, and told the world in eulogistic terms the labors, the social elevation, and the merits of the lamented dead. After his own death, it was found that the record of each member was thus "posted" to the very close of the preceding year!

In those cases, happily infrequent, in which the Secretary is compelled to absent himself from an approaching communication, he should deliver the keys of his several depositories to the W.M., accompanied by a synopsis of the business due at the coming meeting. All papers are supposed to be labeled, pigeon-holed and distributed so as to be available to the *pro-*

tem. appointee; nor is this thought derogatory to a sensible mind when locking his desk at the close of a meeting, "It is possible I may not live to return here. Is there anything neglected that will embarrass my successor?"

In acting as collector of Lodge dues the Secretary should insist upon the payer taking from him a receipt, and preserving it. This is designed as security for both parties. Brethren have been suspended in that unfortunate state of Masonic death, *who owed the Lodge nothing,* but had failed to receive credit on the books and had mislaid (or never taken) receipts. Money should not pass from hand to hand without an interchange of receipts; this will enable the Secretary to avoid the financial confusion that has ruined many an honest man. And if this custom is recommended as between the Secretary and private member, how important as between the Secretary and Treasurer!

It cannot be denied that circumstances may occur to compel the Secretary to take home the Lodge books, or a portion of them. But the necessity is emphatically an unfortunate one, and ought not often to occur. In no case must it be done without the consent of the W.M., and he will discourage the practice as far as possible. Many a Lodge has lost its most valuable records by permitting the Secretary to carry them away from the hall.

There is no warning that we feel impelled to make more solemn and impressive than that directed against the practice of *retaining the funds in the Secretary's hands.* He is solemnly admonished at his installation against it; at every Lodge communication he declares with his own lips against the practice. He is bound to pay them promptly (*at every meeting*) into the hands of the Treasurer, and if the W.M. discovers that he is not doing so, he must bring his great powers of compulsion to bear. The Secretary has no right to pay out a cent of the Lodge funds, or to liquidate a debt due by the Lodge without a special order to that effect. He must not retain a cent of the money, even to the amount of his own monthly or annual stipend. If he presumes thus to infringe upon the duties of the Treasurer and the prerogatives of the Lodge, he is liable to removal for malfeasance in office, and it is the Master's duty to prefer charges of un-Masonic conduct against him.

The grass is growing over the grave of many a Secretary, who died broken-hearted as the result of this neglect in financial matters. Retaining the funds in his own hands from month to month, instead of paying them promptly to the Treasurer; tempted to employ the money temporarily in his own business, under the delusive hope of being able to repay; unable to meet the demand of the Lodge when made; defaulting in this most sacred trust known to man, he is removed from the South-east with disgrace; he is disciplined with expulsion; he goes down to his grave dishonored, and the money of the widow and orphan is lost through a breach of duty.

It has been asked why the money cannot as well remain in the Secretary's hands as the Treasurer's seeing that in either case the Lodge is liable for defalcation? In reply, waiving the natural response that "one officer must not encroach upon the business of another," we answer that the qualifications for which the Treasurer is elected are altogether of a different class from those sought for in the Secretary. In the latter *business expertness* is the one merit; in the former a *good financial standing* is the one merit.

A word concerning payment for the Secretary's services. He is one of two officers to whom a money reward is made. But this is not for sitting a couple of hours at the Secretary's desk. Such service is trifling and merits trifling wages. It is for writing up the books carefully, drawing off and forwarding the accounts of members for quarterage, acting as the clerk of committees at trials, preserving the books and records with scrupulous care, in short, performing with fidelity all the duties herein specified. Such service merits good wages.

Upon another page we have used a term, scarcely known in this country, but common in British Lodges, "Agenda paper." It simply refers to business *due at the Communication,* and is such a memorandum as the Secretary prepares from the records, for the use of the W.M. This is such a convenient reminder that we may wonder it has not more generally entered into use. Here is a copy of one used some twenty years since:

AGENDA PAPER

Tuesday, March 15

1. Report on A/c Jones, Littlebury & Co.
2. Report of Committee on Petition for Charity, Mrs. Laura S. Hopkins.
3. Standing Quarterly Report on Finance.
4. Examination of Charles Covell, for F.C.
5. Petition George Jakes, for Initiation.
6. Petition John Holmes, for Affiliation.
7. Fire Insurance Policy.

A glance at this Agenda paper enables the W.M. to view *the unfinished business* before him, and thus to make space for what *new business* may come up. It is worth all the "Rules of Order" ever drafted.

The Secretary should be informed that no rude or undigested matter which is laid upon his table can go before the Lodge; nothing can properly go before the Lodge until it has passed the eye or had, in some way, the approval of the W.M. The two hours given to Masonry at the regular communication are too precious to be wasted. The usages of Masonry specify as well the *manner* as the matter of Lodge business, and nothing can be considered *in the Secretary's hands* that is not germane to Lodge work, and in a form to be presented to the Lodge.

HAIL TO THE PEN!

"The pen is mightier than the sword."

HAIL TO THE PEN! the day is past
    When man is governed by the sword.
    There is a principle abroad
Greater than bayonet or the cannon's blast.

HAIL TO THE PEN! the skillful Scribe
    Wields it, a scepter, o'er the world:
    From thrones of darkness it has hurled
The despot, in spite of threatening and bribe.

HAIL TO THE PEN! perennial youth
    And power be with the hand that wields,
    Drawn from the Fount divine that yields
Impartial Justice and unbiased Truth.

HAIL TO THE PEN! and hail to you
    Illustrious Friend, whose pen has taught
    How light and truth may be inwrought,
And History writ that to all time is true.

THE SENIOR DEACON AND HIS DUTIES

Owing to the peculiar relation sustained by the W.M. to his Lodge, he is not at liberty, except in a very few ceremonies of Mason-making, to leave his station. "To open and govern his Lodge, to set the Craft to work and give them good and wholesome instructions for their labors," expresses a class of duties which require him *to remain stationary*. The dignity of his position, as Master and Ruler, would be impaired by his frequent appearance upon the floor of the Lodge.

This being admitted, it is essential that the W.M., who is responsible to the Grand Lodge for the orderly government of affairs of his Lodge, the accurate performance of ceremonies and the enforcement of discipline, should have a proxy, selected by himself, to be in his place, the active forward personage in the proceedings, while he remains at his station, elevated above the rest to supervise, direct and control whatever is going on. Happy the W.M. who enjoys the assistance of such a proxy. To suggest a worthy selection of the Senior Deacon, and to point out the' manner in which he can best strengthen the hands of the W.M., is the object of the present article.

It is too much the fashion of writers to make light of the position of Senior Deacon. They overlook the fact that in modern times the Deacons fulfil duties which were formerly allotted to the Junior Warden, duties of the highest importance to the welfare of the Lodge. They seem not to be aware that without good Deacons (especially a Senior Deacon), every part of the ceremonials drags, the *minutiae* are neglected, the general effect is lost. In the writings of Mackey and others this low estimate of the Senior Deacon is evident, and the only one writer who has appreciated the dignity of this officer at his proper value is SIMONS, ("Principles of Masonic Jurisprudence," p. 136). In dwelling upon "the legitimate exercise of the functions of the S.D.," he describes a man of suavity, one who warms the heart of the visiting brother by his gentlemanly ease, makes him enjoy his visit, etc.; but even Simons overlooks the other duties, so elevated and important, in which the Senior Deacon serves as the proxy of the W.M. of the Lodge.

We shall attempt to fill in these vacant portions, and to show that next to the office of W.M. comes that of Senior Deacon in importance; that instead of selecting a young, inexperienced brother to fill this place, the W.M. should choose from among his best, a member of age and intelligence; because without such a proxy, he cannot, with all his power and influence, govern his Lodge reputably. As a summing up of the topic, we give from the pen of Rob Morris ("Senior Deacon's Special Help," pp. 3 and 4) some prefatory remarks, which express, in the main, our own views:

> In the opening and closing of the Lodge, very much of the beauty and effectiveness depend on the Senior Deacon; if he performs his duties promptly, noiselessly and actively, the participants secure the true effect. In conducting candidates he stands almost alone in making a due impression upon the neophyte, the work fails or proceeds as he *does or neglects to do* the part of *Mercury the Messenger.*
>
> To endeavor to make a Mason without a S.D. were as difficult as to do so without a candidate. In that dramatic business entitled "Advancing to the Middle Chamber," the skilful S.D. is the all-in-all. In the reception and introduction of the visitor, how prominent is his part! how he reflects upon the pleased stranger all the graces of Masonry! In imparting the lectures he is the sponsor of the candidate, designates the emblems as they are successively called out by the W.M., and smooths over the difficult places.
>
> In the public presentations of Masonry, those occasions in which the fraternity is conducted beyond the tyled precincts, and exhibited to the gaze of the profane world, the W.M. will not fail to appoint for the *Marshal of the day* his S.D., His *factotum*, his *alter ego*, who is so thoroughly in his confidence, and knows his wishes. Then the purposes of the W.M. will be regarded, his orders executed, and a perfect unity will cement the proceedings. This is particularly seen in the business of

Masonic Interments, as given in subsequent chapters. None can so well subserve the Master's wishes in forming the procession, conducting the orderly array to the grave, aiding him in grand and solemn observances there, and reconducting the mourning craftsmen to their gathering-place, the Lodge.

In continuing this subject, it is proper to give a synopsis of the duties of Senior Deacon as expressed by himself in his technical response:

1. To carry all orders from the Worshipful Master.
2. To welcome and accommodate visiting brethren.
3. To receive and conduct candidates.

The position of Senior Deacon is one of the most difficult in the entire range of Lodge mechanism, yet the selections for the post are too frequently young, inexperienced Masons, ignorant of the very response peculiar to the office. Well may they take the pledge "to perform their duties to the best of their knowledge and ability," seeing that they have not much of either.

One of the petty annoyances of a person newly installed as Senior Deacon, is that the Lodge will expect him to do his part *exactly as his predecessor did.* The only theory the majority of Masons understand is that "as our Lodge has always done it, *therefore* it is right."

In an answer to this we give from some private notes part of a letter addressed to a Mason recently appointed Senior Deacon:

> The greatest source of annoyance to the Senior Deacon, striving to do his duty conscientiously under orders of his W.M., is that so many of his fellow-members require him to perform his part *just as his predecessor did.* Fortunately for your reputation and security, you are not elected by the Lodge nor responsible to the Lodge. [In those Lodges where he is elected, the Senior Deacon is also responsible to the Lodge as well as to the Worshipful Master.] You are appointed *by the W.M.,* and responsible *to the* W.M., and as long as you have his countenance and support you cannot be impeached or interfered with. If your predecessor was full of those omissions and commissions which render so much of the Masonic ceremonial a farce, the more important that you should supplement his official life by one of fullness. If he never took rod in hand, the more reason you should always be seen with rod in hand. If he cared not where his chair was placed, the more reason you should place yours in the direct line between the N.E. and S.W. corners of the Lodge, and at the proper distance from the Master's station. If he was indifferent where the Holy Scriptures were opened in the various degrees, the more reason why you should open them at the 133d Psalm in the first degree, at the 7th Chapter of Amos in the second degree, at the 12th Chapter of Ecclesiastes in the third degree. If he was negligent (and he probably was) in the welcome and accommodation of strangers, the more reason why you should be vigilant in the performance of that prime duty, introducing and ac-

commodating the humblest as though you might be admitting an angel unawares. If your predecessor was a careless, ignorant Senior Deacon, the more reason why you should do full service to your Master in this behalf, and be thus the life, the energy, the arms and feet of the Lodge.

As a rule, the majority of the members of a Lodge favor *effort* above *sluggishness,* and will follow you with pleased eyes while you go through your part efficiently, skilfully, and conscientiously, and in the end will not fail to reward you according to your merit. That model Grand Master, Judge _____, used to say, that he took his first and best lesson in Masonic service with the rod of the Senior Deacon in his hand, and his private mark as a Mark Master was that very badge—*the wand of a Senior Deacon.*

It follows from the theory already given, that the most perfect harmony must subsist between the Senior Deacon and the W.M. A breach of harmony between the two is disobedience darkened by ingratitude on the part of the former. The perfection of the Senior Deacon's part is *to do the will of his superior.* The stream cannot rise above the fountain. The kindest relations must subsist between them. They should hold frequent conferences together, and the Lodge should understand that what the Senior Deacon does is the echo of what the W.M. *commands.*

THE JUNIOR DEACON AND HIS DUTIES

His appointment usually comes from the Senior Warden, whose proxy he is. [In many Lodges the Junior Deacon is elected; if appointed, it is done by the W.M.] His duties are but few, and comparatively light, and are embodied in the following paragraph:

> "In addition to those duties which appertain to every Mason and those which are purely traditional, and therefore unwritten, the duties of the Junior Deacon are:
> 1. To act as the proxy of the Senior Warden in the active duties of the Lodge; 2. To have special care to the security of the Lodge."

THE STEWARDS AND THEIR DUTIES

These officers are rarely seen, save in City Lodges, but in some portions of Lodge matters they are convenient. They are usually appointed by the Junior Warden [now usually appointed by the W.M.] and are sort of assistants to the Tyler, or Curator of the Lodge hall. This is seen in th following paragraph:

> "In addition to those duties which appertain to the dividual Mason, the duties of the Steward are:

1. To have in charge, subject to the direct orders of the Master, the furniture, jewels, and other property of the Lodge. 2. To provide light, fuel, and refreshments for the comfort of the brethren. 3. To have special care to cleanliness in the hall and ante-rooms."

It will be remembered that the books, records, etc., of the Lodge are in the keeping of the Secretary. The Steward is the custodian of the other property. His duties, however, agree so nearly with those of the Tyler, that in the majority of American Lodges they are appropriated to the latter, and no Stewards are appointed. On the other hand, in the metropolitan Lodges (New York, Philadelphia, Chicago, St. Louis, San Francisco, Cincinnati, New Orleans, and other great cities), considerable work is placed in the hands of Stewards. They are distinguished as *Senior Steward* and *Junior Steward,* placed on the right and left of the Junior Warden, and bear an important part in the circumambulations.

As the Stewards are the proper officers to provide materials for Masonic banquets, and supervise their distribution, we insert here a few toasts and sentiments. In Masonic Festivals (and every Lodge should have at least two annually) the W.M. is expected to be actively foremost, providing the mental *pabulum,* pushing every one forward to his work, according to his merit, encouraging decent mirth, discountenancing dullness, discord, indecency. No matter what "Managers" of the Festival may have been appointed, no matter what committee on viands, committees on invitation, committees on music and what not, the *W.M. is chief,* chairman, and head of the proceedings in every part. As he is responsible to the Grand Master for the good order and decorum of the proceedings, he sways the baton, so to speak, outranking marshals, chairmen, and managers, with easy rule.

In revival of the ancient forms of toasts and sentiments, we append a few of the old-fashioned ones, popular in their day, and as good in this age as a century earlier:

1. May all Masons' Lodges be conducted in peace, love, and harmony.
2. May honor and honesty distinguish the Masonic brethren.
3. May the gentle spirit of love animate the heart of every brother.
4. Honor and influence to every public-spirited brother.
5. The memory of the distinguished three.
6. May every brother have a heart to feel and a hand to give.
7. To the brother who knows the true value and use of the Masonic implements.
8. May Masonry prove as universal as it is honorable and useful.
9. May the foundation of our Lodge be *solid,* its building *sure,* its walls *beautiful,* its members numerous and *happy.*

10. To every true and faithful heart, That still preserves the secret art.
11. The memory of Washington.
12. May peace, concord and harmony subsist among us, and every idle dispute and frivolous distinction be buried in oblivion.
13. To all true Masons and upright,
    Who've seen the East, where rose the light.
14. To each faithful brother, both ancient and young,
    Who governs his passions and bridles his tongue.
15. To all free-born sons of the ancient and honorable craft.
16. To the ancient sons of peace.
17. To the secret and silent.
18. May Masonry flourish till nature expire,
    And its glory increase till the world is afire.
19. Relief to all indigent brethren.
20. The memory of the Tyrian artist.
21. May the frowns of resentment never be known among us.
22. May none of us be called to taste the bitter waters of affliction.
23. Peace and plenty to the universal brotherhood.

THE MASTERS OF CEREMONIES AND THEIR DUTIES

These officers are mainly employed in the preparation and conduct of candidates, and prove convenient when the Lodge is enjoying an influx of applicants. They are appointed by the W.M., and their station is on the right and left of the Senior Warden. In foreign Lodges these officers, also Stewards, Ushers, Masters of Ceremonies, Pursuivants, Marshals, etc., covered with Masonic emblems, glittering in the precious metals, make an attractive display, and add grace and dignity to the proceedings.

THE TYLER AND HIS DUTIES

A considerable portion of the Tyler's duties, as usually understood, has been described under the head of STEWARDS. That he is the proper custodian of the Lodge property, and keeper of the hall during the recesses, is our deliberate conviction. He is one of the two officers who receive a stipend for services, and no one familiar with the business of Tyler will claim that the mere attendance outside the door for a couple of hours gives the Tyler grounds for any payment beyond a trifle. But add to this the duties of Steward and Curator, and the value of his services is great; they occupy business hours. He must supervise the frequent cleansing of the hall and furniture. Lighting and ventilation come under his head.

In some Lodges the Tyler is *elected*, as the W.M., Wardens, etc., perhaps because the place has perquisities, and there is competition for it. [In most Lodges the Tyler is appointed by the W.M.] In city Lodges the same person is often Tyler for several Lodges, occupying the same apartments, and as, in this country, dual membership is not permitted, it follows he cannot be a member of all. [The vast majority of Grand Lodges permit dual or plural membership today.] His duties are expressed by the Junior Deacon at the opening of the Lodge, but being esoteric, cannot be enumerated here. We may, however, make brief comments upon them.

Brother Simons in "Principles of Masonic Jurisprudence" has so well expressed the theory of the Tyler's part that we copy the paragraph.

> The very first duty of the brethren when about to commence their labors, is to be certain that the Tyler is at his post, for, without that, certainly no labor could be felt to be secure from the interruptions of cowans and eavesdroppers. He is the sentinel on the outposts, upon whose sleepless vigilance we depend for security.

> But while he is to be cautious and vigilant in preventing the approach of those who have not the necessary qualifications, he should also be courteous in his demeanor to all who may have occasion to address him. Politeness is not an expensive commodity, and every Tyler may therefore provide himself with an abundant supply, and find his profit in using it freely. The notion which some Tylers seem to entertain, that it is a portion of their duty to imitate the fabled Cerberus, is a fallacy to be explored. Let him "suffer none to pass without permission," but not act as though he were bound to regard every one approaching him as desirous to pass his station at all hazards.

It is a prime duty of the Tyler to serve notices and summonses when ordered by the W.M. or the Lodge. In large Lodges he is also employed to collect quarterage upon accounts placed in his hands by the Secretary. There is no office in which veteran service counts for so much as this. The Tyler is often an aged man, personally acquainted with the members, vigilant at his post, unassuming, not caring to vote upon Lodge propositions, even when a member, intent only upon honest discharge of duty. Such men are greatly missed when the inexorable Summoner searches *them* out and serves upon *them* that rescript which none can refuse or postpone.

GOD BLESS THE OLD TYLER
By ROB MORRIS

God bless the old Tyler! how long he has trudged
   Through sunshine and storm with his summonses due!
No pain nor fatique has the old Tyler grudged
   To serve the great Order, Freemasons, and you!

God bless the old Tyler! how oft he hath led
   The funeral procession from Lodge-room to grave!
How grandly his weapon has guarded the dead
   To the last quiet home where th' acacia-boughs wave!

God bless the old Tyler! how oft he hath knocked
    When vigilant strangers craved welcome and rest!
How widely your portals, though guarded and locked,
    Have swung to the signal the Tyler knows best.

There's a LODGE where the door is *not* guarded or tyled,
    There's a LAND without graves, without mourners or sin,
There's a MASTER most gracious, paternal, and mild,
    And he awaits the old Tyler, to bid him come in!

And there the old Tyler, no longer outside,
    No longer with weapon of war in his hand,
A glorified spirit shall grandly abide,
    And close by the King of His throne he shall stand.

A quiet visit to the Tyler's room of the Lodge will repay our curiosity. Has he the implement of his office, both in hand and on his breast; has he chairs comfortable, cleanly and abundant for brethren in waiting; has he a desk or table for the Visitors' Book; has he convenient books, closets and niches for hats, overcoats and umbrellas; has he suitable toilet-rooms, etc.; has he the means of ventilation in the sultry nights and of warmth in the chilly; do you observe upon his door any peep-hole, sliding panel or other appliance for playing the eavesdropper upon the Lodge. (If so, report it promptly to the W.M. that it may be imperviously covered or immovably screwed in place and used no more!) A Tyler's room, warm, roomy, fresh and sweet, with a genial old man to fill it, is an inviting place, as many a reader of this volume will testify. As the official duties of the Tyler are concentrated in the ante-room, and he claims no share in the work of the Lodge, and no privilege to speak, act or vote in the meetings, it is proper that his apartments should be comfortable to himself and attractive to those who visit him.

The Tyler is the first officer a member or visitor greets. In every respect he should be a gentleman. His manner of greeting will often determine whether or not a visitor will return. The appointment of a Tyler can well be the making or breaking of the Lodge.

> As the ante-room is the first step to entrance into the sanctum, and as early impressions are deepest, the apartment is made to be eminently attractive to the senses. Carpeted, cleanly, warm in the most frigid seasons, cool and airy in the most sultry, and amply supplied at all seasons with wash-rooms, toilets and wardrobes, this is the model in the mind's eye of furnisher. Suitable decorations adorn the walls, likewise portraits, golden maxims, and whatever else will enliven the apartment and give to newcomers an attractive forecast of the pleasant nature of the entertainment to which they have been chosen.

The visiting brother, duly recognized by the Tyler, passes in, by permission of the W.M. How acquired every reader knows, and sees the Junior Deacon immediately at his left hand. Beyond him, toward the north is the Senior Warden, with the Master of Ceremonies, if any, on his right and left, and the two great Pillars of the Lodge. Before him looking to the East, is the Junior Warden, with the Stewards, if any, and the Secretary at his desk. Over the head of the Junior Warden is the emblematical Sheaf of Wheat. In the centre of the hall (if an *American* Lodge, if not, then directly in front of the W.M.) is the *Altar*, covered and surrounded by its appropriate furniture. Beyond that, looking to the north-east, come the Senior Deacon and Treasurer, the latter at his desk.

Directly east of the altar is the station of the W.M. where he sits flanked right and left by Past Masters and the Chaplain. Over his head is the large and ornate letter "G." Upon the wall behind the Secretary are the library shelves; behind the Treasurer in the north-east corner, the Symbolical Chart styled (allusion far-fetched) "the Master's Carpet." The walls on the three sides of the Lodge, South, North and West, are adorned with portraits, symbolical paintings and engravings, models of Masonic objects, etc.

The position of the Tyler gives him a prominent place in the matter of identifying visitors. The *Ancient Charges* warn us "cautiously to examine a strange brother as prudence shall direct you, that you may not be imposed upon by an ignorant, false pretender, whom you are to reject with contempt and derision, and beware of giving him any hints of knowledge." We have observed no less than *eight methods* by which these "ignorant, false pretenders" have passed the Tyler's door:

1. The man points to his name in the catalogue of a Lodge or Grand Lodge, and so gains admission. It is found that he is a pretender, traveling under a name not his own. Or, in another case, it is found that he has been suspended or expelled since the publication aforesaid.

2. The man, impudent and brazen-faced, thrusts himself, duly clothed, in the Masonic procession after it has passed the public gaze. Afterwards he is vouched for as having been seen in such intimacy with Masons, and visits a Lodge. He proves, as might be anticipated, an "ignorant, false pretender," and the Craft is subjected to mortification and loss for their carelessness.

3. The man brings a letter of introduction from a person known to be a Mason. The letter vouches that the bearer is one. He is admitted on the strength of it. He proves to have found, forged or stolen the epistle. He is an "ignorant, false pretender," and the Lodge stands disgraced by the imposition.

4. The man brings a diploma (certificate), regularly drafted and signed by its holder in the margin. Neglecting further methods of examination, he is admitted. The document, like the epistle named in the *third* instance, is forged, and the man proves to be an "ignorant, false pretender."

5. The man secures an examination at the hands of a *very old brother* who has forgotten, or some *very young brother* who never knew the rules for examination, and through them gets a voucher. He proves to be an "ignorant, false pretender."

6. The man is vouched for by brother A., who informs us that Brother B. has sat with him in a Lodge. But the chain of avouchal is too prolonged, and he proves to be an "ignorant, false pretender."

7. The man is regularly vouched for by the Master himself as a Fellowcraft, and his claim to be a M.M. is too loosely accepted. It turns out that he is an "ignorant, false pretender."

8. The man has long been known to *the public* as a Master Mason; and the Lodge too hastily accepts the *vox populi.* It proves to be *vox diaboli,* for the fellow is an "ignorant, false pretender."

CHAPTER 3

CONSTITUTING AND DEDICATING LODGES

The ceremony under consideration in the present chapter is not to be confounded with that of *Dedicating an Edifice*, whether Masonic or Secular.

When a proper number of Masons unite in the good desire of organizing a new Lodge, they join in a respectful petition to the Grand Master, praying for a dispensation to do so. The minimum number of petitioners is, upon such a request, in most jurisdictions, seven, and all must be Master Masons, owing allegiance to the Grand Lodge, whose prerogative is thus invoked. In some jurisdictions, it is requisite that the petitioners be members of Lodges *(affiliated* Masons); in others that they be *demitted* Masons so that they may file their demits with the petition; in others again there is no rule regulating this matter.

The written petition goes regularly through the hands of the Grand Secretary, who submits it for consideration to the Grand Master. Certificates are presented from the contiguous Lodge or Lodges whose jurisdiction will be invaded by the establishment of a new Lodge, and it must be shown in such certificates that at a regular Lodge communication, permission was granted, and the orgainzation of the new Lodge encouraged and recommended. In some jurisdictions, written evidence is required by the Grand Master that the petitioners have control over apartments suitable for Lodge purposes, and that the person designated for W.M. is a Past Master, and competent to act in the position assigned him.

FORM OF PETITION FOR A NEW LODGE

The ordinary form of petition is as follows, but varied according to any peculiarities existing in the jurisprudence of the Grand Lodge:

> They are Free and Accepted Master Masons, are at present (or have been) members of regular Lodges, having the prosperity of the Fraternity at heart, they are willing to exert their best endeavors to promote and diffuse the genuine principles of Masonry; for the convenience of their respective dwellings and for other good reasons, they are desirous of forming a new Lodge in the town of _____, to be named _____ Lodge; in consequence of which desire they pray for LETTERS OF DISPENSATION or a Warrant of Constitution, to empower them to assemble as a legal lodge, to discharge the duties of Masonry in a regular and constitutional manner, according to the original forms of

the Order and the regulations of the Grand Lodge. They have nominated, and do recommend _____ to be the first Master; _____ to be the first Senior Warden; _____ to be the first Junior Warden of the said Lodge. If the prayer of petition shall be granted they promise a strict conformity to all the constitutional laws and regulations of the Grand Lodge.

It will be observed that this petition prays either for *Letters of Dispensation* or a *Warrant of Constitution*. In foreign jurisdictions it is not uncommon to grant the latter without waiting for the intervening stage of a dispensation, but the American Grand Lodges rarely, if ever, do this.

The Grand Master, in his prerogative, orders Letters of Dispensation prepared. He signs them, and requires the Grand Secretary to sign them and impress the broad seal of the Grand Lodge upon them. [In many jurisdictions a dispensation cannot be granted until a majority of Lodges holding concurrent jurisdiction vote favorably for the formation of the new Lodge.] They give authority to the petitioners to assemble as a legal Lodge for a specified time, usually until the day of opening the annual session of the Grand Lodge.

This Lodge Under Dispensation is reckoned as an agent of the Grand Master with limited powers. Its W.M. is not entitled to the Order of Past Master as such. Its officers have no vote or voice in the proceedings of the Grand Lodge. It cannot change its officers without the Grand Master's consent. If it fails to secure a charter at the end of its term, the term of dispensation may be prolonged or the existence of the Lodge terminated; in which latter event all its property, jewels, regalia, library and funds go into the possession of the Grand Lodge.

The term of dispensation being ended, the *Lodge U.D.* sends up its records to Grand Lodge for inspection, and asks either for a charter to be made a full Lodge, or for a renewal of the dispensation. If the former, the Grand Lodge will act upon the report of its own "Committee on Lodges under Dispensation," whose members have considered the subject of territory, inspected the records, and drawn general conclusions, favorable or unfavorable. Should the decision be favorable the new Lodge receives a number upon the Grand Roll of the jurisdiction, and, as soon as formally constituted, possesses in perpetuity all the rights and privileges of the oldest Lodge. The charter being granted, the Grand Master appoints a day and hour for Constituting and Dedicating the new Lodge and Installing the officers thereof.

All the proceedings of Constituting are supposed to be done under the supervision of the Grand Master or his Deputy. If neither of those officials can be present in person, the Grand Master appoints a substitute who is entitled to the same honor and respect ("homaged") as that officer himself when present. If the Grand Master performs the work in person, the Lodge is said to be constituted *in ample form;* if the Deputy Grand Master, *in due form;* if a substitute presides, *in form.* The substitute must be a Master or Past Master. He should be a Mason of age, dignity, and Masonic experience. But in the present chapter we take the presence of the Grand Master for granted.

At the appointed day and hour the Grand Lodge is opened "in extraordinary session for special purposes." All necessary officers, from Deputy Grand Master to Grand Tyler, are named. The Grand Lodge jewels are used for the occasion. The acting Deputy Grand Master, after examining the officers of the new Lodge in the Grand Master's presence, directs them to return to their own apartments. This examination is but *pro forma.* It is already ascertained that these brethren are duly posted in the duties of their respective offices from the experience derived in the *Lodge U.D.* The Deputy Grand Master makes verbal report to the Grand Master that he has performed this duty, and that the examination is satisfactory.

Then the new Lodge sends, by its Marshal, the following message to the Grand Master, in writing:

> MOST WORSHIPFUL GRAND MASTER, the Worshipful Master, Wardens, and Brethren of _____ Lodge, No. _____, now assembled at their apartments, have instructed me to inform you that the Most Worshipful Grand Master of the Grand Lodge of _____, did, on the _____ day of _____, 19___, grant them *Letters of Dispensation,* authorizing them to form and open a Lodge of Free and Accepted Masons [or A.F. & A.M.] in the city of _____.
>
> Since that period they have regularly assembled and conducted the business of Masonry according to the best of their ability. Their proceedings having received the approbation of the Grand Ldoge, they have obtained a Charter of Constitution, and are desirous that their Lodge should be consecrated and their officers installed agreeably to the ancient usages and customs of the Craft.
>
> For this purpose they are now met and await the pleasure of the Most Worshipful Grand Master.

The Lodge Marshal returns to the apartments of the Lodge, with orders from the Grand Master to prepare for the reception of the Grand Lodge. An answer is returned that all is ready, and the coming of the Grand Lodge is expected. The Grand Master orders the procession formed for that purpose. As the Grand Master enters the apartment of the new Lodge he is received, welcomed, and the private grand honors are given him, and then the officers resign their stations to the Grand Officers and take their own places, respectively, on the left of their successors.

If the Worshipful Master of the Lodge has *not* received the Order of

Past Master, the proceedings are stayed until this is done; but such a contingency in modern practice will rarely occur. To keep both assemblies, Masonic and public, waiting while the Master of the new Lodge is placed in the chair of King Solomon, bound to the faithful performance of his trust, and invested with the characteristics of the Chair, would poorly comport with Masonic order and discipline as taught by a modern Grand Master.

The term "Passing the Chair," from which we get our term "Past Master," was in use at least as early as 1744, as we see in a communication of that date from Dr. Fifield d'Assigny, Master of a London Lodge. The expression in those days was written, *"Passed* Master." It had reference only to those who had "Passed into the Oriental Chair of King Solomon," or, in other words, who had taken the degree of Past Master.

The members of the new Lodge are now arranged in line along the south side of the hall. A grand procession is now formed, in three divisions, as follows:

The Visiting Lodges
The New Lodge
The Grand Lodge

The forms of procession are the same as those in a subsequent chapter, and we will only distinguish the third division, i.e.:

> Grand Tyler, with drawn sword
> Grand Stewards, with white rods
> Grand Pursuivant, with sword
> Grand Secretary and Grand Treasurer
> Past Master, bearing the the Holy Writings, Square and Compasses, supported by
> Two Stewards, with black rods
> Two Burning Tapers, borne by Past Masters
> Grand Chaplain and Grand Orator
> Columns of Tuscan and Composite Orders borne by two Master Masons
> Columns of Doric, Ionic, and Corinthian Orders borne by three Master Masons
> Past Grand Wardens
> Past Deputy Grand Masters
> Past Grand Masters
> Celestial and Terrestrial Globes borne by two Master Masons
> Junior Grand Warden bearing the silver vessel of Corn
> Senior Grand Warden bearing the silver vessel of Wine
> Deputy Grand Master bearing the golden vessel of Oil
> Master of the oldest Lodge present bearing the Book of Constitutions
> THE GRAND MASTER supported by

Grand Deacons with white rods
The Grand Standard-Bearer
The Grand Sword-Bearer with drawn sword

The GRAND PROCESSION, thus formed, preceded by bands playing noble marches of established character, governed by a competent Chief Marshal with Assistants, moves slowly and with dignity to the church or other place, where the people are awaiting to witness the ancient Services of Consecration. Halted at the portals, the procession opens and marches by inverted order, so that the last enters *first,* the Grand Master last, and so passes to his place. Platforms, a dais, and suitable seats are supposed to be in readiness that none shall be left standing or neglected. A considerable open space must be left in front of the Grand Master.

The Bible with its furniture, and the Book of Constitutions, are placed on the pedestal immediately in front of the Grand Master. On a larger table, covered with pure white linen, a little more advanced, are deposited successively by their bearers, the burning tapers, and the vessels of corn, wine, and oil. In the centre of these is laid a small box, or casket, oblong in form, covered with white linen, technically styled "The Lodge."

This object is to represent the Masonic Lodge (or Hall of the Lodge) about to be consecrated. In itself it is an emblem of the *Ark of the Covenant,* which was a chest of Acacia wood, 39 inches long, 21 inches high, and the same in breadth. It was overlaid with gold. The Mercy Seat, supporting the two Cherubims, rested on the lid. In it were deposited the tables of stone, the pot of manna and the rod of Aaron. Upon this casket, familiarly known as the LODGE, and representing the Lodge, are sprinkled at the proper times the corn, wine, and oil of the Consecration.

Silence being commanded, and a proclamation made by the Grand Marshal of the presence of the GRAND MASTER and the sublime nature of the proceedings about to be had, the Opening Ode is sung. The air, *Old Hundred,* associated with ten thousand such occasions, is most appropriate.

ODE FOR CONSECRATION

Lo! God is here, our prayers prevail,
    In deeper reverence adore;
Ask freely now, He will not fail
    His largest, richest gifts to pour.

Ask by these emblems, old and true,
    Ask by the memories of the past;
Ask by His own Great Name, for lo,
    His every promise there is cast.

Ask WISDOM, 'tis the chiefest thing—
Ask STRENGTH, such as a God may yield;
Ask BEAUTY from His throne to spring,
And grace the Temple we shall build.

Lord God most high, our Lodge we veil,
To consecrate with ancient care!
Oh, let Thy Spirit ever dwell
And guide the loving builders here!

Following the Ode the Masonic assembly is called up by the gavel of the Grand Master, and the Grand Chaplain offers prayer. It is best that this be extemporaneous, or at least prepared by the Grand Chaplain himself for the occasion. But as the reader may prefer a printed form we offer the following:

Chaplain—Great, Adorable and Supreme Being! We praise Thee for all Thy mercies, and especially for giving us desires to enjoy and powers of enjoying the delights of society. The affections which Thou hast implaneted in us, and which we cannot destroy without violence to our nature, are among the chief blessings which Thy benign wisdom hath bestowed upon us. Help us duly to improve all our powers to the promotion of Thy glory in the world and the good of our fellow-creatures. May we be active under Thy divine light and dwell in Thy truth.

Extend Thy favor to us who are now entering into a fraternal compact under peculiar obligations. Enable us to be faithful to Thee, faithful in our callings in life, faithful Masons in all the duties of the craft, and faithful to each other as members of this society. Take us under the shadow of Thy protection, and to Thy service and glory may we consecrate our hearts. May we always put *faith* in Thee, have *hope* in salvation and be in *charity* with all mankind! AMEN.

Brethren respond—So mote it be.

The Masonic assembly is now seated by the gavel of the Grand Master, and the next step in the proceedings is commenced. The Grand Marshal assembles the officers and members of the new Lodge in front of the Grand Master. Then the Deputy Grand Master addresses that official:

D.G.M.—Most Worshipful Grand Master, a number of brethren, duly instructed in the mysteries of Masonry, having assembled together at stated periods, for some time past, by virtue of *Letters of Dispensation* granted them for that purpose, do now desire to be constituted into a *regular Lodge,* agreeably to the ancient usages and customs of the Fraternity.

The Grand Marshal hands to the Grand Master the charter. Inspecting it for his own satisfaction, he passes it to the hands of the Grand Secretary, with orders to read it aloud, which is done. Then the Grand Master calls up the Masonic assembly and begins the proceedings.

Grand Master—Officers of the Grand Lodge, we will now proceed to constitute these brethren into a regular Lodge agreeably to their request, and the authority contained in the charter, which has been read.

The Marshal of the new Lodge collects the jewels from the officers and delivers them to his W.M., who delivers them to the Deputy Grand Master, and he to the Grand Master. Then the Deputy Grand Master presents by name to that official the W.M. of the new Lodge, thus:

D.G.M.—Most Worshipful Grand Master, I present to you Brother _____, whom the members of the Lodge now to be constituted have chosen as their Master.

The Grand Master asks them if they remain satisfied with their choice. (They bow in assent.)
The W.M. presents severally to the Lodge, by name, his officers, beginning with the Senior Warden. The Grand Master asks them if they remain satisfied with their choice. (They again bow in assent.) The officers and members of the new Lodge are arranged by the Grand Marshal in line in front and facing the Grand Master. The Grand Master with the Grand Lodge officers kneel around "The Lodge" (the casket so called), which is uncovered at this moment by the Deputy Grand Master. Solemn music is introduced. Now follows the first of the two clauses of the Consecration Prayer by the Grand Chaplain.

G.C.—Great Architect of the Universe, Maker and Ruler of all worlds! Deign from Thy celestial temple, from realms of light and glory, to bless us in all the purposes of our present assembly.

We humbly invoke Thee to give us, at this time and at all times, *Wisdom* in all our doings, *Strength* of mind in all our difficulties, and the *Beauty* of harmony in all our communications.!

Permit us, O thou Author of light and life, great source of love and happiness, to erect this Lodge and now solemnly to CONSECRATE it to the honor of Thy name!

The brethren respond—As it was in the beginning, is now and ever shall be! AMEN.

The Grand Officers arise from their knees. The Deputy Grand Master sprinkles, slowly and with deep solemnity, the elements of Con-

secration (*in the order of corn-wine-oil*) *upon "The Lodge" (that is the casket representing it), while solemn music is performed by the instruments.*

Again the Grand Officers kneel and the second clause of the Consecration Prayer is delivered by the Grand Chaplain, as follows:

G.C.—Grant, O Lord our God, that those who are now about to be invested with the government of this Lodge, may be endued with wisdom to instruct their brethren in all duties. May Brotherly Love, Relief and Truth always prevail among the members of this Lodge, and may this bond of union continue to strengthen all Mason Lodges throughout the world. Bless all our brethren, wherever dispersed, and grant speedy relief to all who are either oppressed or distressed.

We affectionately commend to Thee all the members of Thy whole family. May they increase in the knowledge of Thee, and in love for each other.

Finally, may we finish all our work here below with Thine approbation, and then have our transition from this earthly abode to Thy heavenly temple above, there to enjoy light, glory and bliss ineffable and eternal. Glory be to God on high!

The brethren respond.—As it was in the beginning, is now and ever shall be! AMEN.

The Grand Officers arise from their knees. The Deputy Grand Master covers "The Lodge" with its linen enwrapments, while solemn music is performed. Then the Grand Master stretches forth his hands and solemnly pronounces the form of

Dedication

Grand Master—To the memory of the holy Saints John we dedicate this Lodge! May every brother imitate their character and revere their vitues.
The brethren respond—AMEN. So mote it be.

A piece of instrumental music is introduced while the brethren of the new Lodge advance slowly, in perfect order, under the instructions of their own Marshal, and led by their W.M., salute the Grand Lodge with their hands crossed upon their breast (left hand uppermost) and bowing as they pass the place of the Grand Master.

Constitution

The Grand Master now proclaims the consecration complete in these words:

Grand Master—In the name of the Most Worshipful Grand Lodge of
_____, I now constitute you and form you, my good brethren, into a
Lodge of Free and Accepted Masons. From henceforth, you are duly empowered to act as a regular Lodge, constituted in conformity with the
rites of our Order, and the Charges of our Ancient and Honorable Fraternity. And may the Supreme Architect of the Universe prosper, direct and
counsel you in all your doings. AMEN.
The brethren respond—So mote it be.

The Grand Master calls down the assembly with the gavel.
A short recess may be ordered, or a song may be introduced to give
time for rest, and then the ceremonies of Installation proceed.

Much has been said by Masonic writers of late years concerning the true
method of making "The public Grand Honors." It is a sad comment upon
the want of uniformity in American Lodges that radical differences occur
in different parts of this country, in this important ceremony, so much so
that, in the most solemn parts, even at the grave of a departed brother,
the audience is shocked by the awkward and uncouth movements of the
Masonic participants who join in giving "Honors" by gestures neither
symbolical, serious, nor Masonic. The itching for originality has crept into the work of Grand Lecturers, and very serious changes have been introduced, reversing the symbolism on which Mackey's movements are
founded.

Fifty years ago the system of giving the public grand honors in New
York, was as follows:

1. Extend the right hand, palm up, the four fingers of the
   right hand, compressed, striking sharply on the palm of
   the left hand three times.
2. Extend the right hand, palm up, striking with the fingers
   of the left hand in the same manner.
3. The first movement is repeated.

Making in all three times three plaudits. This is the old and popular
method of displaying the public grand honors.

We call attention here to use of the word "Order" in ancient forms of
Installation. Whatever refinements of language may have crept into use
in other societies, the use of words good enough for us two centuries ago is
good enough for us now. To throw out the word Order and substitute
"Fraternity," "Society," "Installation," and other analogies is to open the
way for other word-changes. We have seen our "oblong square," our "So

mote it be," our "irreligious libertine," and other expressions dear to antiquity, thrown out on the same plea, viz: that "the ideas may be better expressed by words more modern." We protest that we want nothing modern in Freemasonry. The land is full of modern societies into which those can go who cannot endure our rugged old Saxon. We contend, ever have contended, ever *will* contend for old forms in old words. The old is better. As the poet has said with force and elegance:

> Oh! guard the venerable relic well;
>   Protect it, Masters, from unholy hand;
> See that its emblems the same lessons tell
>   Sublime, through every age and every land;
> Be not a line erased; the pen that drew
>   These matchless tracings was the PEN DIVINE:
> Infinite wisdom best for mortals knew:
>   God will preserve intact the GRAND DESIGN!

CHAPTER 4

INSTALLATION CEREMONIES

The instructions in the present chapter are necessarily divided into two parts: Installation of officers of *new* Lodges, and Installations of officers of *existing* Lodges. The former is done by the Grand Master, or a Grand Lodge officer selected by him; the latter, by the retiring Worshipful Master, or his proxy. In the former, every officer *must be* installed with the full ceremonial; in the latter (in most jurisdictions), only officers *newly elected* need be installed, those holding over for the current term not requiring re-installation.

INSTALLATION OF OFFICERS OF NEW LODGES

The new Lodge having been Constituted and Dedicated as set forth in the last chapter, the Grand Officers controlling the proceedings, the officers elected (and appointed) are called out for Installation. If the Master-elect has not received the degree of Past Master, a convocation of three or more Past Masters must be held that he may be duly, "Seated in the Oriental Chair of King Solomon," before he can be installed.

In some jurisdictions this is not required. In others it is even required that the *Wardens* receive the degree of Past Master. The Deputy Grand Master now conducts the Worshipful Master to the front of the dais and says:

MASTER

Deputy Grand Master—Most Worshipful Grand Master, I present to you Brother _____, whom the members of this Lodge have elected to serve them as Worshipful Master for the ensuing year, and who now declares himself ready for Installation.

Grand Master—Right Worshipful Deputy Grand Master, have you carefully examined the brother, and do you find him qualified to discharge the duties of the office to which he has been elected?

D.G.M.—Most Worshipful Grand Master, I find him to be a man of good morals, and of great skill, true and trusty; and as he is a lover of the Fraternity, I doubt not he will discharge his duties with fidelity, and with honor.

Grand Master—My brother, previous to your investiture, it is necessary that you should signify your assent to those ancient Charges and Regulations which point out the duty of a Master of a Lodge.

I. You agree to be a good, true man, and strictly to obey the moral law?

II. You agree to be a peaceful citizen, and cheerfully to conform to the laws of the country in which you reside?

III. You promise not to be concerned in plots or conspiracies against the government, but patiently submit to the law and the constituted authorities?

IV. You agree to pay a proper respect to the civil magistrates, to work diligently, live creditably, and act honorably by all men?

V. You agree to hold in veneration the original rulers and patrons of the Order of Masonry, and their regular successors, supreme and subordinate, according to their stations; and submit to the awards and resolutions of your brethren, in Lodge convened, in every case consistent with the Constitutions of the Order?

VI. You agree to avoid private piques and quarrels, and to guard against intemperance and excess?

VII. You agree to be cautious in carriage and behavior, courteous to your brethren, and faithful to your Lodge?

VIII. You promise to respect genuine brethren, and discountenance impostors and all dissenters from the original plan of Masonry?

IX. You agree to promote the general good of society, to cultivate the social virtues, and to propagate the knowledge of the art?

X. You promise to pay homage to the Grand Master for the time being, and to his officers when duly installed; and strictly to conform to every edict of the Grand Lodge that is not subversive of the principles and groundwork of Masonry?

XI. You admit that it is not in the power of any man, or body of men, to make innovations in the body of Masonry?

XII. You promise a regular attendance on the committees and communications of Grand Lodge, on receiving proper notice, and to pay a proper attention to all the duties of Masonry, on convenient occasions?

XIII. You admit that no new Lodge shall be formed without permission of the Grand Lodge; and that no countenance be given to any irregular Lodge, or to any person clandestinely made therein, being contrary to the ancient usages of the Order?

XIV. You admit that no person can be made a Mason in, or admitted a member of, any regular Lodge, without previous notice, and due inquiry into his character?

XV. You agree that no visitors shall be received into your Lodge without due examination, and producing proper vouchers of their having been initiated in a regular Lodge?

These are the regulations of Free and Accepted Masons. Do you submit to these Charges, and promise to support these Regulations, as Masters have done in all ages before you?

The Master answers in the affirmative.

Grand Master—My brother, in consequence of your conformity to the Charges and Regulations of the Order, you are now to be installed Master of this Lodge, in full confidence of your skill and capacity to govern the same.

The Master is then regularly invested with the insignia of his office, and the furniture and implements of the Lodge are placed in his charge. The various implements of his profession are emblematical of his conduct in life, and upon this occasion should be carefully explained as follows:

Grand Master—The *Holy Writings,* that great light in Masonry, will guide you to all truth; it will direct your path to the temple of happiness, and point out to you the whole duty of man.

The *Square* teaches us to regulate our actions by rule and line, and to harmonize our conduct by the principles of morality and virtue.

The *Compasses* teach us to limit our desires in every station, that, rising to eminence by merit, we may live respected, and die regretted.

The *Rule* directs that we should punctually observe our duty; press forward in the path of virtue, and inclining neither to the right nor to the left, in all our actions have eternity in view.

The *Line* teaches us the criterion of moral rectitude, to avoid dissimulation in conversation and action, and to direct our steps in the path which leads to immortality.

The *Book of Constitutions* you are to search at all times. Cause it to be read in your Lodge, that none may pretend ignorance of the excellent precepts it enjoins.

You now receive in charge the *Charter,* by the authority of which this Lodge is held. You are carefully to preserve the same, and duly transmit it to your successor in office.

You will also receive in charge the *By-Laws* of your Lodge, which you are to see carefully and punctually executed.

The new Master is now placed on the right of the Installing Officer, until the other officers are installed.
The other officers are then severally presented by the Grand Marshal to the Grand Master, who delivers to each his appropriate charge.

SENIOR WARDEN

Grand Master—Brother _____, you have been elected Senior Warden of this Lodge. Do you solemnly promise that you will serve the Lodge as Senior Warden for the ensuing year, and will perform all the duties appertaining to that office, to the best of your ability? (*He consents.*) You will now be invested with the insignia of your office.

The *Level* teaches that we are descended from the same stock, partake of the same nature, and share the same hope; "that we are all children of one common father, heirs of the same infirmities, and exposed to the same vicissitudes." It also reminds us, that although distinctions among men are necessary to preserve subordination, no eminence of station should make us forget that we are brethren, and that in the Lodge and our Masonic associations, we are on a level. This implement teaches us that a time will come, and the wisest knows not how soon, when all distinctions but that of goodness shall cease, and death, the grand leveler of all human greatness, reduce us to the same state.

Your regular attendance on the stated and other meetings of the Lodge is essentially necessary. In the absence of the Master, you are to govern the Lodge, and in his presence assist him in the government of it. Hence you will perceive the necessity of preparing yourself for the important duties which may devolve upon you. *Look well to the West*, and guard with scrupulous care the pillar committed to your charge.

He is conducted to his proper station by the Grand Marshal.
In some jurisdictions, all the elected officers are ranged to the west of the altar, where they take a solemn vow and covenant to perform their respective duties to the best of their knowledge and ability.
The following, with the discussions that make up the regular charge, may be given in whole or part, as an explanation of official duties:

The SENIOR WARDEN is the second constitutional officer in the Lodge. He is elected annually, and after installation cannot resign during his term of office. [He can resign in most jurisdictions today.] He pledges himself to perform the duties of his office, and all other duties imposed on him by the Lodge. His prerogatives and duties are:

1. The right to assume the chair, and succeed to all the responsibilities of the Master, in case of his death, inability to serve or absence, while such inability or absence continues.
2. To represent the Lodge, with the Master and Junior Warden, at all Communications of the Grand Lodge.
3. To act on the Standing Committee of Charity.
4. After one year's service, to be eligible to the office of Master.

5. To have the superintendence of the Craft in the Lodge, during the hours of labor.
6. To appoint the Junior Deacon (this rule is not universal).

His station is in the West, upon a dais, reached by two steps; his jewel is a Level—an emblem of the equality and harmony which should ever exist among Masons. Before him, upon a pedestal, is placed, and he carries in processions, a column of the Doric Order—an emblem of Strength. He represents Hiram, King of Tyre, who is also the representative of the column Strength, because he gave aid and strength to King Solomon while erecting the temple at Jerusalem.

JUNIOR WARDEN

Grand Master—My Brother _____, you have been elected Junior Warden of this Lodge. Do you solemnly promise that you will serve the Lodge as Junior Warden for the ensuing year, and will perform all the duties appertaining to that office to the best of your ability? (*He consents.*) You will now be invested with the insignia of your office.

The *Plumb* admonishes us to walk uprightly in our several stations; to do unto others as we would have others to do unto us; to observe the just medium between intemperance and pleasure, and make our passions and prejudices coincide with the line of our duty.

In the absence of the Master and Senior Warden, upon you devolves the government of the Lodge; but to you is especially committed the superintendence of the Craft during hours of refreshment; it is, therefore, not only necessary that you should be temperate and discreet in the indulgence of your own inclinations, but carefully observe that none of the Craft convert the purposes of refreshment into intemperance and excess. *Look well to the South.* Guard with vigilance the pillar committed to your charge, that nothing may disturb the harmony of the Lodge, or mar its *beauty.*

He is conducted to his proper station by the Grand Marshal.

The JUNIOR WARDEN is the third constitutional officer in the Lodge. He is, like other officers of the Lodge, elected annually. In the absence of the Master and Senior Warden, he succeeds to the duties of the Master; to represent the Lodge, in conjunction with the Master and Senior Warden, at the communications of the Grand Lodge; to act on the Standing Committee of Charity; after a year's service, to be eligible to the office of Master; to superintend the Craft during the hours of refreshment; and perform such other duties as the Master or the Lodge may require. He cannot after installation, resign during his term of office. [In most jurisdictions the only officer who cannot resign is the W.M.] His station is in the South, on a platform of one step; his jewel is a plumb, emblematic of the rectitude of conduct which should distinguish the brethren when, during the hours of refreshment, they are beyond the precincts of the Lodge. He has placed before him, and carries in procession, a column of the Corinthian Order, an emblem of Beauty

TREASURER

Grand Master—My Brother _____, you have been elected Treasurer of this Lodge, and will now be invested with the badge of your office.

It is your duty to keep a faithful account of all moneys received for the use of the Lodge, and pay them out to the order of the Worshipful Master, with the consent of the Lodge. [In many jurisdictions the W.M. doesn't need the consent of the Lodge to spend funds for Masonic purposes.] Your own honor, and the confidence the brethren repose in you, will excite to that faithfulness in the discharge of the duties of your office which its important nature demands.

He is conducted to his proper station by the Grand Marshal.

The TREASURER is the fourth constitutional officer of the Lodge, and is elected annually. His duties are to receive whatever moneys may be paid into the hands of the Secretary, in behalf of the Lodge, and pay it out again upon the order of the Master, with the consent or action of the Lodge; to keep just and regular accounts of his receipts and expenditures; to be ready, whenever called upon, to render a statement of the financial condition of the Lodge. His station is in the East, on the right of the Master; his jewel is a pair of keys arranged saltierwise. This is one of the most responsible and important offices known to the Fraternity, and should be confided to a brother known to possess correct business habits and of the strictest integrity. When a Lodge has a "true and trusty" Treasurer, it should not dispense with his services, but continue to elect him so long as he can be prevailed upon to serve the Lodge.

SECRETARY

Grand Master—My Brother _____, you have been elected Secretary of this Lodge, and will now be invested with the badge of your office.

It is your duty to keep the records regularly, fairly and faithfully; to receive all moneys and pay them into the hands of the Treasurer, and to issue summonses at the Master's direction. Your love of the Craft and attachment to the Lodge will induce you cheerfully to fulfil the duties of your office; and in so doing, you will merit the esteem of your brethren.

He is conducted to his proper station by the Grand Marshal.

The SECRETARY is the fifth constitutional officer in the Lodge, and is elected annually. His duties are substantially of a business character, and are of the highest importance to the welfare and prosperity of the Lodge. Punctuality in attendance at the meetings of the Lodge is an indispensable requisite in the Secretary. He should be the first in his place at its meetings, and the nature of his duties is such that he can scarcely avoid being the last to leave the Lodge room. He is particularly charged with the duty of watching the proceedings of the Lodge, and making a complete record of all things proper to be written; to keep the financial accounts between the Lodge and its members; to recieve all moneys due the Lodge, and pay them into the hands of the Treasurer; to prepare the annual reports to the Grand Lodge; to have in charge the seal of the Lodge, and to perform all other clerical duties pertaining to the office, as may be directed by the Master and the Lodge. His position is in the South-east, on the left of the Master; his jewel is two pens crossed. The qualities which should distinguish a Secretary are a quick comprehension, prompt attention to business, a good penman, neatness in the manner of keeping his books, and of sterling integrity in his financial dealings with the Lodge and its members. To be a good and proficient Secretary is worthy of the ambition of any enlightened Mason. He becomes the historian of the Lodge, and his records are the current history of the events as they transpire. The record that he prepares, being the property of the Lodge, will be conveyed to future generations, and may in after days, when the brethren have left their labor on earth, and even the Lodge may cease to exist, remain the only monument by which their work will be remembered. Frequently matters of the highest importance must be settled, as the only reliable evidence, by reference to the Secretary's books of minutes. The Lodge which has secured a brother for this stattion, thoroughly competent for the discharge of the duties of the office, and who feels interested in the work, will do well to value him highly and retain him in office until he "grows gray in the service."

CHAPLAIN

The Chaplain is next brought forward by the Grand Marshal.

Grand Master—Rev. Brother, you are appointed Chaplain of this Lodge, and are now invested with the badge of your office.

It is your duty to perform those solemn services which we should constantly render to our infinite Creator; and which, when offered by one whose holy profession is "to point to heaven and lead the way," may, by refining our souls, strengthening our virtues, and purifying our minds, prepare us for admission into the society of those above, whose happiness will be as endless as it is perfect.

He is conducted to his proper station by the Grand Marshal.

The CHAPLAIN is a recognized officer in many Lodges, appointed annually by the Master to assist him in performing religious services. Notwithstanding the Master possesses all the sacerdotal rights necessary to be used in the ritualistic ceremonies of the Order, yet, it is often advisable to invite a clergyman, who is a Mason, to read the Scriptural lessons incident to the ceremonies using none but the prescribed forms. His station is in the East, in front and on the left of the Master; his jewel is an open Bible.

SENIOR AND JUNIOR DEACONS

Grand Master—My Brethren, you are appointed [or elected] Deacons of this Lodge. It is your duty to attend on the Master and Wardens, and to act as their proxies in the active duties of the Lodge, such as the reception of candidates, and the introduction and accommodation of visitors. These rods, the badges of your office, I entrust to your care in full confidence of your vigilance and attention.

They are conducted to their proper stations by the Grand Marshal.

The SENIOR DEACON is the sixth constitutional officer in the Lodge. The method of obtaining the office varies in different localities. In some the Lodge elects, in others the Master appoints. His special duties are: To act as the proxy of the Master in the active duties of the Lodge; to welcome visiting brethren, and extend the hospitality of the Lodge to them. Nothing in the Masonic institution is more practical or more grateful to the sensibilities of the traveling brother than to find, as he will do in every Lodge wherever dispersed over the globe, an officer whose constitutional duty it is "to welcome and accommodate visiting brethren." This makes the circle of the Order complete, for every well-informed brother has a claim and a right to the hospitalities of Lodges wherever he may travel or work. The Senior Deacon also is to receive and conduct candidates in the different degrees of Masonry. He has charge of the altar and its accompanying lights, and has charge of the ballot-box during the election of candidates for membership and the degrees of Masonry. His station is in the East, on the right and in front of the Master. His jewel is the square and compasses with the sun in the center, and he usually carries a white rod [or staff] as an insignia of office. The Senior Deacon should be a brilliant scholar, a good reader, with some knowledge of elocution. As this officer is the first to meet the candidate on his entrance to the Lodge, it is important that a gentlemanly deportment should characterize his conduct during the circumambulation. Much of the esteem that the neophyte will acquire of the Institution is the result of first impressions. In some classes of processions the Senior and Junior Deacons walk on the right and left of the Master as supporters, with their rods crossed over his head.

The JUNIOR DEACON is the seventh constitutional officer of the Lodge. In some jurisdictions the office is elective; in some the Master appoints; and in others the Senior Warden appoints. His duties are: To act as the proxy of the Senior Warden in the active duties of the Lodge; to have special charge of the door to the Tyler's room; to see that the brethren are properly clothed when they enter; and perform such other duties as may be required by the Master or Senior Warden. His station is on the right of the Senior Warden; his jewel is the square and compasses with a quarter moon in the center. When in processions he carries a white rod [or staff] as the insignia of office. Strict attention to the duties of his office, affability and a gentlemanly deportment toward all who pass his station are the shining characteristics that will commend the Junior Deacon to the love and respect of his brethren and advance him to higher duties.

STEWARDS OR MASTERS OF CEREMONIES

Grand Master—My Brothers, you are appointed Stewards (Masters of Ceremonies) of this Lodge, and will now be invested with the badge of your office. You are to assist the Deacons and other officers in performing their respective duties. Your regular and early attendance at our meetings will afford the best proof of your zeal and attachment to the Lodge.

They are conducted to their proper stations by the Grand Marshal.

The STEWARDS, two officers of the Lodge, are sometimes appointed by the Junior Warden, because of their immediate association with that officer during the hours of refreshment, but more frequently are appointed by the Master. In former times their duties were to introduce visitors and see that they were properly accommodated; to see that the rooms were in proper order for the performance of all the business of the Lodge; to collect subscriptions and other fees, and to keep an exact account of the

Lodge expense. In later days, and particularly since the abolishment of banquets at the regular meetings of the Lodge, the Stewards may assist the Senior Deacon in preparing and conducting the neophyte through the several degrees of Masonry. Their jewel is the cornucopia. Their station is in the South on the right and left, respectively, of the Junior Warden. In processions they are next to the Tyler, and carry white rods.

The MASTERS OF CEREMONIES, are two officers of the Lodge appointed annually by the Master. Their duties are to assist the Senior Deacon in preparing and conducting the candidates. In some Lodges these officers take the place and perform all the duties of the Stewards. Their station is in the West, on the right and left of the Senior Warden. Their jewel is two swords crossed.

In some jurisdictions the Lodges have no Stewards or Masters of Ceremonies.

MARSHAL

Grand Master—My brother, you are appointed Marshal of this Lodge, and will now be invested with the badge of your office. It is your duty to have charge of and conduct the processions of the Lodge, and to assist the Senior Deacon whenever that officer may require your services. On all such occassions the good order that may be displayed mainly depends upon your zeal, knowledge and discretion.

The MARSHAL is an officer appointed by the Master; his duties are principally in public processions, and on such occassions he is the special proxy of the Master. In the Lodge he may assist the Deacons in the reception of Grand Officers and other distinguished visitors. His station is near the Senior Deacon; his jewel is cross-batons. When in charge of a public procession he carries a baton as an insignia of office. Much of the order and beauty of a public procession depends upon his skill and knowledge in managing such proceedings.

TYLER [TILER]

Grand Master—My brother, you are appointed Tyler of this Lodge; and I invest you with the implement of your office. As the *Sword* is placed in the hands of the Tyler to enable him effectually to guard against the approach of cowans and eavesdroppers, and suffer none to pass or repass but such as are duly qualified; so it should morally serve as a constant admonition to us, to set a guard at the entrance of our thoughts; to place a watch at the door of our lips; to post a sentinel at the avenue of our actions, thereby excluding every unqualified and unworthy thought, word, and deed; and preserving consciences void of offence toward God and toward man. Your early and punctual attendance will afford the best proof of your zeal for the Institution.

He is conducted to his station by the Grand Marshal.

The TYLER is the eighth constitutional officer of the Lodge. He must be a Master Mason, and is elected or appointed by the Master. His duties are: to guard the Lodge against the intrusion of improper persons, and to permit no one to pass into the Lodge unless well known to him, or after being properly vouched for, and having the permission of the W.M.; to prepare the Lodge room for its meetings; to arrange the furniture, working tools, regalia, etc., in their proper places; to serve notices, etc., issued under authority of the Lodge, and perform such other duties as may be required. In all processions he takes the lead, armed with a drawn sword. His station is outside of the Lodge room door, and within the Tyler's room. His jewel is the sword, and in addition he bears a drawn sword. Though last in the list of officers, his is far from being the least important. In fact, without him the Lodge cannot proceed to business; nor would it be safe to continue if for a moment should he, after the commencement of labor, desert his post. He should therefore, be a reliable man, and one who will discharge the duties of his position with firmness and courtesy. Special attention should be paid to strangers, when visiting a Lodge, by the Tyler, as much of the pleasure of the visit must begin in the Tyler's room, and from his gentleman-like deportment [Emphatically!] It is his duty to know the business of every person who may remain in the ante-room. If they desire to visit he should make the fact known to the Master in the usual Masonic manner, so that they would be admitted, if known, or examined if not. When the necessities of a poor brother compel him to make application to the Lodge for assistance, the Tyler should exhibit respect and sympathy, and use his best efforts to have the brother's case brought promptly before the Lodge, his wants relieved, and he be permitted to retire at an early hour, rejoicing in his heart that among Masons he had found true and substantial friends. The Tyler should see that every brother enters his name in the Visitor's Book.

The Grand Master now hands the gavel to the Worshipful Master, and resigns the chair to him. He calls up the Lodge. Then is offered by the Chaplain the following or other suitable

PRAYER

Almighty and Eternal God, vouchsafe Thine aid to these solemn rites, and grant that the brother who is now numbered among the rulers of the craft, may be endowed with wisdom to comprehend, judgment to define, and firmness to enforce obedience to Thy law. Sanctify him with Thy grace. Strengthen him with Thy power, and enrich his mind with genuine knowledge, that he may be enabled to enlighten the brethren, and consecrate our meetings to the honor and glory of Thy most holy name. AMEN.

All respond—So mote it be.

Grand Master—Worshipful Master, behold your brethren! Brethren, behold your Master!

> *The Grand Honors are then given the Worshipful Master by the Lodge, the Grand Master leading in the ceremony. A procession is then formed, and the brethren pass around the Lodge, signifying their respect and obedience by the usual distinctive marks in the different degress. During which the following or other appropriate installation ode may be sung:*

> Support to the Master that rules by the Square,
> Let sons of the Light to the East now repair;
> With hearts for his aid, united and free,
> Obedient we labor and kindly agree.

> Support to the Warden, installed in the West,
> Who works by the Level, where sorrows may rest:
> With hearts for his aid, united and free,
> Obedient we labor and kindly agree.

> Support to the Warden, by Plumb still upright,
> Whose sun in the South never hides its fair light;
> With hearts for his aid, united and free,
> Obedient we labor, and kindly agree.

> *The brethren are now seated. Then the Grand Master may deliver an address, or read the following charges in his discretion.*

Grand Master—Worshipful Brother, having been chosen to preside over this Lodge, you cannot be insensible of the obligations which devolve upon you. The honor, reputation, and usefulness of your Lodge will materially depend upon the skill and ability with which you manage its concerns. As Master of this Lodge, it will be your especial duty to attend to the administration of its ceremonies, and preserve the Ancient Landmarks of the Order now committed to your care, and permit no innovation in the principles or rites of the Order.

Upon all suitable occasions remind the brethren that Masonry is founded upon the great moral principals set forth in the Sacred Volume, which we receive as the rule and guide of our faith and practice. Exhort them to govern themselves by these principles, as well with the world at large as with each other. Teach them to reverence the three great lights, comprehending the holy Bible, the perfect square, and the extended compasses, the beautiful symbolism of which is familiar to you, and the explanations of which include some of the most important duties inculcated in our Order.

The leading objects of our Installation are to inculcate sound morality; to make men honest and upright, true to their GOD, and faithful to their country, and to unite them by the strong bonds of charity, friendship and brotherly love. Great care, therefore, should be taken in the admission of members, lest by the introduction of bad materials the Institution should be corrupted. It should be constantly borne in mind, that the respectability and usefulness of a Lodge does not consist in the number, but in the character of its members.

It is better that no workman be added to the roll than even one unworthy foot allowed to cross the threshold of the Lodge. The uninitiated judge of Masonry by the conduct of its individual members. You should be as careful of the reputation of your Lodge as that of your family: and as you would admit none to the society of the latter whose character is bad, so should you carefully exclude such from the former.

As it is the purpose of Freemasonry to create frienship; to make provision for the relief of poor and distressed brethren, and protect the widow and the orphan; to inculcate reverence for Almighty GOD; and to encourage the growth of the social virtues which dignify and adorn human nature, and render mankind peaceful and happy, the doors of the Lodge should be sternly closed against the idle, the profligate, the intemperate, and licentious. If, unfortunately, unworthy members gain admission, it will be your duty to exercise proper discipline to correct abuses, and restrain the refractory. Unruly members must be reduced to order. The first risings of vice must be suppressed, and when kind and affectionate admonitions fail, the unworthy should be removed as a blot upon the Order.

It is also your duty, and will no doubt be your pleasure, to spread light and impart knowledge to the brethren of your Lodge; to preserve the purity of our Order, and maintain unimpaired its ancient rites and ceremonies, instruction is necessary. The mysteries of the Order must be unfolded, and the moral duties inculcated. They are to be frequently reminded of the duties they owe to Almighty GOD, the giver of every good and perfect gift. They must be taught to be good men and true; to be sober, industrious, charitable, upright in their dealings, friendly in their social intercourse, and to live in love and peace, having consciences void of offence, and unspotted from the world. Thus taught and thus acting, they will convince mankind of the value of the Institution.

BROTHERS SENIOR AND JUNIOR WARDENS, to you are committed the pillars of *strength* and *beauty*. It is your duty, therefore, to set before the brethren who surround these pillars the corn of nourishment, the wine of refreshment, and the oil of joy, symbolically inculcated in the moral lessons of our Order, taught from your respective stations in the Lodge. In your own persons you should give evidence that you are governed by the principles of the Order, as it is by a due regard to them in your own lives and conduct, that you can expect obedience in others.

You are to assist the Master in the discharge of his trust, diffusing light and imparting knowledge to all whom he shall place under your care. In the absence of the Master, you will succeed to higher duties; your acquirements must, therefore, be such, as that the Craft may never suffer for want of proper instruction. The spirit which you have hitherto evinced in your attendance to the duties of Freemasonry, whereby the brethren of the Lodge exercised a sound discretion in this selection, leaves no doubt that your future conduct will be such as to merit the approbation of your brethren, and that the just reward which is due for meritorious services will be rendered in your advancement to higher stations.

TO THE BRETHREN OF THE LODGE

Brethren of the Lodge, such is the nature of our Constituion, that some must of necessity rule and teach, others must submit and obey. The officers you have chosen, and who have been solemnly installed, are sufficiently acquainted with the rules of propriety, and the laws of the Institution, to avoid exceeding the powers with which they are entrusted. The harmony of the Lodge will materially depend upon the good order you may preserve in the conduct of its business, and the courtesy and forbearance you may observe toward each other in its deliberations.

I charge you, then, as you shall answer at the last day, that you act worthy of the vocation with which you are called, and suffer no faults, no imperfections on your part, to tarnish the lustre of your jewels, or bring discredit on the craft. Recommend Masonry to the world by the rectitude of your conduct. To this end make yourselves intimately acquainted with all its principles and obligations; and practice in your lives all its duties and requirements. Divest yourselves, brethren, of coldness and apathy, so fatal to your best interests. Shun those affections and groveling passions unworthy of a soul that claims affinity with the "Sons of Light," and put forth all your energies to grasp whatever is noble or elevating in thought, and whatever can reveal new and sublime ideas pertaining to our lofty destiny. Guard against dissensions among yourselves. Let no root of bitterness spring up to trouble you. Use all your exertions to preserve your Lodge pure, and prevent the introduction of vice or error in its thousand forms. If, in the frailty of mortality, a brother falls under the influence of unholy feelings, and wanders into forbidden paths, seek the wanderer out, bring him back to the fold, and show him the superior loveliness of virtue. Much may be accomplished by the force of good example, and by offering good counsel in a friendly spirit, ever remembering that

"To err is human, to forgive divine."

Finally, brethren, be of one mind; live in peace. Let nothing disturb that pure, warm and holy love which our ritual enjoins. Follow these injunctions, and your Lodge will flourish. May the *tenets of your profession* be transmitted through your Lodge unimpaired from generation to generation.

Then the Grand Marshal proclaims the Lodge.

Grand Marshal—In the name of the Most Worshipful Grand Lodge of the State of _____, I proclaim this new Lodge, by the name of _____ Lodge, No. _____, legally consecrated, dedicated, constituted, and the officers duly installed.

The Grand Chaplain then pronounces the BENEDICTION.

ALMIGHTY and everlasting GOD, from Whom cometh every good and perfect gift, send down upon Thy servants here assembled the healthful spirit of Thy grace, that they may truly please Thee in all their doings. Grant, O LORD, power of mind and great understanding unto those whom we have this day clothed with authority to preside over and direct the affairs of this Lodge; and so replenish them with the truth of Thy doctrine, and adorn them with humility of life, that, both by word and example, they may faithfully serve Thee, to the glory of Thy holy name, and to the advancement of our beloved institution. *Amen.*

All respond. —So mote it be.

Then the Grand Lodge returns to its own hall and is closed.

The new Lodge may now proceed to business, and in due time be closed, and the proceedings of the occasion ended.

Considerable criticism has lately been rendered in a portion of American Masonic journals, in regard to the whole subject of *public* installations, and writers have discussed the matter as though it were a new thing, or perversion of the landmarks, etc. This is far from expressing the fact. On the contrary, Masonic records show conclusively that for a century or more it has been the uniform practice of American Lodges to join their installations with their St. John's Festivals, and invite their families and friends to participate in both.

A survey of the preceding pages will show that everything in the ceremonies and instructions we have given can, with the greatest propriety, be made public. It adds to the dignity and practical effect of an installation that intelligent persons *outside the Order* should witness it, and surely no man will be the less inclined to do the duties he has promised to perform when he knows that his family and neighbors have heard his promise, and seen him placed in his station.

[Arguments still continue in this year 1979 concerning public installations. Some Grand Lodges prohibit them; some allow them with restrictions; others believe they are excellent for public relations, which they are, when properly handled. Remember the admonition throughout this book—the law is what *your* Grand Lodge says it is.]

CHAPTER 5

LAYING CORNER-STONES

From time immemorial, it has been the prerogative of the Masonic Society to lay ("plant") corner-stones of edifices, not only such as are intended strictly for Masonic purposes, but all constructions of a public character. The National Capitol in Washington, many State houses, custom houses, colleges, hospitals, asylums, public school buildings, piers of bridges, canal locks, post-offices, public docks, wharves, levees—each in its turn has been the subject of the ancient ceremonial about to be described. To expunge the history of Freemasonry from America would be to draw from twenty thousand edifices the corner-stones planted there by Masonic hands.

This ceremony is conducted by the Grand Master of the jurisdiction, or the Deputy Grand Master. In the absence of both, the Grand Master commissions a Past Master to represent him, and such substitute is entitled and recognized Grand Master for this occasion. [This has caused problems for historians. Many Past Masters have been listed as Grand Masters. Because of this, most Grand Lodges now have the presiding officer listed by his proper title.] It is customary, when practicable, to select a present Grand Lodge officer, or Past Grand Master, or at least some experienced and competent Mason for this place, for nowhere do ignorance and inexperience show more discreditably than in a work like this.

A person accustomed to public speaking is indispensable to a good display, as all will testify who have seen how often the effort results in failure.

Few things exasperate the opponents of Masonry so much as that the corner-stone in so many public buildings is a constant reminder to Freemasons as they pass by to stand square, upright, and true to the emblem of the corner-stone!

The hour announced for the ceremony having arrived, the Lodge to which the ceremony has been instructed is congregated by the Grand Master, and opened in the first degree [usually the Master Mason degree now]. Other Lodges participating may be opened in other apartments, or may all be opened together, under authority of the Grand Master, and afterward separated by the Grand Marshal, for their respective places in the procession. The records of the occasion kept by the Grand Secretary refer to the Lodge under whose auspices the corner-stone is to be laid.

The selection of Grand Marshal, Assistant Marshals, Grand Chaplain, and other officers is now made. The place of Grand Marshal demands qualification but rarely found in one indiscriminate body of Masons. Every officer appointed by the Grand Master for the occasion is entitled "Grand," as "Grand Tyler," etc.

The order of procession is now announced, likewise the rules of government for the day. Then the Grand Marshal, stationing himself near the entrance of the hall, with his assistants around him, orders the door opened (the Lodge being considered *at labor*) and the brethren march out in the Order of Procession previously announced. The Lodge whose charter was *last* granted takes the lead. Templars march according to special orders from the Grand Marshal, either in advance as general escort, or following the Royal Arch Masons in procession, or surrounding the Grand Lodge, etc. The Grand Marshal should be mounted, that he may ride expeditiously along the left of the procession, his assistants being placed at proper distances along the line. If more than one band of music is in attendance, they are arranged in convenient places by the Grand Marshal.

ORDER OF PROCESSION

Tyler of the youngest Lodge with a drawn sword
Band of Music
Deacons with white rods
Entered Apprentices
Fellow Crafts
Master Masons
Treasurer and Secretary
Wardens with their columns.

All other Lodges follow in the same order, according to the dates of their respective charters, the youngest in advance, but in all cases the Lodge under whose auspices the corner-stone is to be laid has the place of honor, which is in the rear of the other Lodges.

Preceding each Lodge is a Tyler, and behind him two Deacons, with white rods, as above. Then come in the other members of the procession as follows:

Stewards with black rods
Past Masters of Lodges
Royal Arch Masons
Knights Templar unless otherwise arranged.

THE GRAND LODGE

in the following order:

The Grand Tyler
The Grand Architect with Assistants bearing the
Plumb, Level and Square

Five Master Masons bearing the five Orders in
Architecture, the Tuscan on the right
The Grand Deacons with rods
Grand Treasurer and Grand Secretary
Past Grand Treasurers and Past Grand
Secretaries
Grand Wardens bearing a silver cup of wine; the
Junior bearing a silver cup of oil
Past Grand Wardens
Deputy Grand Master, bearing a golden cup of
corn (wheat)
Past Deputy Grand Masters

The Chief Magistrate and Civil Officers of the place, if the edifice is
intended for public use. If for a church, etc., the Trustees, Wardens,
etc., of the same occupy this station.

A venerable brother bearing the Book of Con-
stitutions
Grand Bible Bearer bearing the Bible, Square
and Compasses supported by
Grand Stewards with white rods
The Grand Standard-bearer with escort of two
Master Masons
The Grand Chaplain
THE GRAND MASTER supported by
Grand Stewards with black rods.

In this order the procession moves deliberately in moderate time, with
perfect discipline and decorous silence to the place of deposit, which is
usually the northeast corner of the contemplated structure. Arrived there
the procession is halted, then opened, and the Grand Marshal leading in
reverse order, the Grand Master proceeds to the platform and takes his
station. The Grand Officers and civic representatives follow his example;
the constituent Lodges arrange themselves as near as may be in the form
of a hollow square. While these dispositions are making, the bands play
martial music.

After a brief delay the Grand Marshal proclaims silence, announces the
presence of the Grand Master, and reads, in an audible voice, the business
of the occasion. If the proposed structure is for public use, as for example,
a court house, church, etc., a spokesman selected for the purpose will address the Grand Master, stating the purposes of the erection, and requesting that "the corner-stone be laid according to the ancient usages of
Freemasonry." If the edifice is strictly for Masonic purposes, the Master of
the Lodge having precedence will act as spokesman.

It is taken for granted that the corner-stone and the necessary machinery for moving it are in readiness, the stone having upon it the proper date and such other inscriptions as may be preferred. A cavity for the reception of the casket is cut in the stone on the under side. Upon the arrival of the procession, the stone is seen suspended about six feet from the ground.

These matters being perfected, the choir will sing the following, or some other suitable hymn:

ROUND THE SPOT

ROUND THE SPOT, Moriah's hill,
Masons met with cheerful will;
Him who stood as King that day
We as cheerfully obey.
Lord, we love Thy glorious name,
Give the grace Thou gavest him!

ROUND THE SPOT, thus chosen well,
Brothers, with fraternal hail,
Gather in a mystic ring,
Mystic words and joyful sing.
Lord, our hearts, our souls are Thine;
On our labors gracious shine!

ROUND THE SPOT may *Plenty* reign,
Peace, with spirit all benign,
Unity, the golden three—
Here their fulness ever be.
Lord, these jewels of Thy store,
Send them bounteous flowing o'er!

ROUND THE SPOT where now we stand
Soon will meet another band;
We to other worlds must go,
Called by HIM in love below.
Lord, Thy Spirit grant, that they
All Thy counsel may obey!—MORRIS

The Grand Chaplain next delivers the following PRAYER:

Grand Chaplain—Supreme Grand Master of the Universe! bounteous source of every good to the children of men! Thou who didst inspire Thine ancient servant Solomon, to build unto Thee a house, and didst of Thine own infinite grace accept the workmanship of his hands, and didst condescend by Thy spirit to dwell therein, grant to us that grace today that we may make an auspicious commencement of our labors and lay this corner-stone upon the eternal principles of justice, piety, reliance upon God and sacred truth.

Bless our mother-earth to bear firmly upon its bosom the edifice which today we begin to erect. Bless the hands of the bearers of burdens who may bring hither materials for the walls here to rise. Bless the *wisdom* that shall contrive, the *strength* that shall execute and the *beauty* that shall adorn this building, that in the eyes of all beholders it may present a monument of the prosperity of those who follow on to know the Lord.

May words of peace ever resound within its chambers. May the praise of God be its harmony. May its dwellers dwell together in unity, and enjoy the delights of pleasantness and peace.

Keep this edifice from the hands of evil-designing men. Preserve it equally from the lightnings of heaven, from hurricanes, from earthquakes, from conflagrations, from the sword of the invader, from all manner of evil.

May the foliage of many a returning spring open in greenness and beauty about it. May the storms of winter be softened from their wonted rigor and harm it not.

Great God! who hath upheld our nation through generations past, preserve us from the calamities of intestine war, from civil strife, from all the evils and influences of sin.

Supreme Grand Master! omnipotent and omniscient God! who hath kept, from age to age, the *sacred fire* of *Masonry* glowing upon its altars, kindle a brighter flame in the hearts of Freemasons worshipping before Thee today, and be our guide and protector through the wildernesses of life, as with the pillar of fire and cloud Thou didst conduct Thine ancient people.

Holy Father! in all the trials and afflictions we are destined to endure while traveling through this vale of tears, let us ever put our trust in Thee, follow Thy dictates and fear no evil.

And when the work of human life is ended—when we are called up to Thy celestial Lodge to receive the wages for which we have faithfully labored, may we be found prepared, as living stones for that spiritual building, that house not made with hands, eternal in the Heavens. Amen and Amen.

Response from all.—So mote it be.

Then the Grand Master addresses the Senior Grand Warden:

Grand Master—Right Worshipful Senior Grand Warden, it has been the custom among the Fraternity of Free and Accepted Masons, from time immemorial, on invitation, to assemble the Craft and lay with appropriate ceremonies the foundation stones of public edifices. In obedience to that custom, and having accepted the invitation of _____ to lay in due and ancient Masonic form, the corner-stone of this building, now in process of erection, I am here today, with the officers of the Grand Lodge, to perform that duty. It is, therefore, my order, and you will proclaim it to the Right Worshipful Junior Grand Warden, and he to the Craft, and others present, that they, having due and timely notice thereof may govern themselves accordingly.

Senior Grand Warden—Right Worshipful Junior Grand Warden, it is the order of the Most Worshipful Grand Master of Masons of the State of _____, that the corner-stone of this building be now laid in due and ancient Masonic form. This you will proclaim to the Craft and all present, that the proceedings of this occasion may be observed with due and becoming solemnity.

Junior Grand Warden—Brethren of the Masonic Fraternity and all present, take notice that the Most Worshipful Grand Master of Masons of the State of _____, will now cause to be tested and tried the corner-stone of this building, that he may lay the same in due and ancient Masonic form. You will therefore observe that order and decorum which become the dignity and solemnity of the occasion.

The Grand Master then addresses the Grand Treasurer:

Grand Master—Right Worshipful Grand Treasurer, it has ever been the custom of the Craft, on occasions like the present, to deposit in the cavity of the stone placed at the north-east corner of the building, certain memorials of the period in which it was erected, so that if, in the lapse of ages, the fury of the elements, the violence of man, or the slow but certain ravages of time should lay bare its foundation, an enduring evidence may be found by succeeding generations to bear testimony to the untiring industry of Free and Accepted Masons. Has such a deposit been prepared?

Grand Treasurer—It has, Most Worshipful Grand Master, and the memorials are now in the casket before you.

Grand Master—Right Worshipful Grand Secretary, you will read the list of memorials, that all may be informed.

The order is obeyed. The memorials consist in coins of the period, public journals of the day, Masonic periodicals, copies of the latest proceedings and constitutions of the Grand Lodge, town records, a small copy of the Holy Scriptures, and other matters, according to the capacity of the crypt. The list being read, the Grand Master continues.

Grand Master—Right Worshipful Grand Treasurer, you will now deposit the casket in the cavity prepared for it, and may the Grand Architect of the Universe, in His infinite wisdom, grant that ages upon ages shall pass away ere it again be seen by human eyes. Amen.

All respond—So mote it be.

The Grand Treasurer lays the casket upon the basis-stone on which the corner-stone is to descend. Then, by signal from the Grand Marshal, the corner-stone is lowered three feet, while the bands play solemn music. After a pause, by a second signal it is lowered to the surface of the earth, the bands playing as before. After a pause, by a third signal it is lowered, being properly guided to the place prepared for its final reception, so the casket may be exactly coverd and conealed within the double cavities.

Then the choir will sing the following, or some other appropriate piece:

FAITH, HOPE, CHARITY

Master Supreme! to Thee this day,
Our corner-stone with priase we lay;
And resting on Thy word fulfilled,
To Thee, O Lord! our house we build.

Nor build we here with strength alone,
Of carven wood or sculptured stone;
But squarely hewed, and broadly plann'd,
Our lines we raise with ashlars grand.

In *Faith* we toil—in *Hope* we climb
To *Charity*—our arch sublime;
And evermore the key-stone see
Oh Master! Lord! in Thee—in Thee!

The Grand Master descends, followed by his three chief assistants, to the verge of the mason-work in which the stone lies, and there receives from the Grand Architect the Plumb, Level, and Square, successively, with the following observations:

Grand Architect—Most Worshipful Grand Master, the necessary preparations having been made for laying the corner-stone of this building, I present you the Plumb, Level and Square—those useful implements of the Craft—by which you will be able to ascertain that the materials have been properly prepared, and the corner-stone you are about to lay, well formed, true and trusty.

The Grand Master taking the three implements in his hand distributes them successively, the Plumb to the Junior Grand Warden, the Level to the Senior Grand Warden, the Square to the Deputy Grand Master. The following queries and responses are then passed between these four officers:

Grand Master—Right Worshipful Deputy Grand Master, what is the jewel of your office?

Deputy Grand Master—The Square, Most Worshipful Grand Master.

Grand Master—What are its moral and Masonic uses?

Deputy Grand Master—To square our actions by the square of virtue and prove our work.

Grand Master—Right Worshipful Brother, apply it to that portion of the corner-stone which needs to be approved, and make due report.

The order is obeyed.

Deputy Grand Master—Most Worshipful Grand Master, I find the corner-stone to be square. The craftsmen have performed their duty.

Grand Master—Right Worshipful Senior Grand Warden, what is the jewel of your office?

Senior Grand Warden—The Level, Most Worshipful Grand Master.

Grand Master—What are its moral and Masonic uses?

Senior Grand Warden—Morally it is an emblem of equality, and its use is to prove horizontals.

Grand Master—Right Worshipful Brother, apply it to that portion of the corner-stone which needs to be approved, and make due report.

The order is obeyed.

Senior Grand Warden—Most Worshipful, I find the corner-stone to be level. The craftsmen have performed their duty.

Grand Master—Right Worshipful Junior Grand Warden, what is the jewel of your office?

Junior Grand Warden—The Plumb, Most Worshipful Grand Master.

Grand Master—What are its moral and Masonic uses?

Junior Grand Warden—Morally it is an emblem of rectitude of life, and its use is to try perpendiculars.

Grand Master—Right Worshipful Brother, apply it to that portion of the corner-stone which needs to be approved, and make due report.

The order is obeyed

Junior Grand Warden—Most Worshipful, I find the corner-stone to be plumb. The craftsmen have performed their duty.

Grand Master—This corner-stone has been duly tested by the ancient implements of Freemasonry. I testify that the craftsmen have skillfully and faithfully performed their duty, and I declare this corner-stone to be well formed, true and trusty, and accurately laid according to the principles of our art. And may the work thus auspiciously begun be continued and completed by the benign principles of peace, harmony and brotherly love. Amen.

All respond—So mote it be.

> *Then the Grand Master, taking the trowel from the hand of the Grand Architect, spreads mortar freely over the sides and top of the corner-stone and returns the trowel.*

CONSECRATION

Grand Master—The ceremonies of consecration will now proceed.

> *The Deputy Grand Master comes forward with the gold cup of corn (wheat), and sprinkling it profusely upon the corner-stone, he says:*

Deputy Grand Master—This corn I distribute as a symbol of goodness and plenty. May the blessings of bounteous heaven be showered upon us, and upon all like patriotic and benevolent undertakings, and inspire the hearts of people with virtue, wisdom and gratitude. Amen.

All respond—So mote it be.

> *The Senior Grand Warden then comes forward with the silver vessel of wine, and pouring it upon the corner-stone, says:*

Senior Grand Warden—This wine I pour as a symbol of joy and gladness. May the Great Ruler of the universe bless and prosper our national, state, and city governments, preserve the union of States, and may Freemasonry be a bond of friendship and brotherly love that shall endure through all time. Amen.

All respond—So mote it be.

> *The Junior Grand Warden comes forward with the silver vessel of oil, and pouring it upon the corner-stone, he says:*

Junior Grand Warden—This oil I pour as a symbol of peace. May its blessings abide with us continually, and may the Grand Master of heaven and earth shelter and protect the widow and orphan, shield and defend them from all trials and vicissitudes, and so bestow His mercy upon the bereaved, the afflicted, and the sorrowing, that they may know sorrow and trouble no more. Amen.

All respond—So mote it be.

The Grand Master, then standing in front of all, and extending his hands, makes the following

INVOCATION

May the All-bounteous Author of Nature bless the inhabitants of this place with an abundance of the necessaries, conveniences and comforts of life; assist in the erection and completion of this building; protect the workmen against every accident; long preserve the structure from decay; and grant to us all a supply of the corn of *nourishment*, the wine *of refreshment*, and the oil *of joy*. Amen.

All respond—So mote it be.

Then the Grand Master strikes the stone three times with his gavel and says:

Grand Master—Brethren, assist me in giving the grand honors.

The order is obeyed. Then the Grand Marshal steps forward and says:

Grand Marshal—Most Worshipful Grand Master, I present to you the architect of this building, Brother _____ (or Mr. _____). He is ready with his craftsmen for the completion of this work, and asks for the tools that are proper to the undertaking.

The Grand Master delivers to the architect the square, level, plumb, and plan of the building successively, and says:

Grand Master—Worthy brother (or Sir), having thus as Grand Master of Masons, laid the corner-stone of this structure, I now deliver these implements of your profession into your hands, intrusting you with the superintendence and direction of the work, having full confidence in your skill and capacity to conduct the same in such a manner that the building may rise in order, harmony and beauty, and being perfected in strength, that it may answer every purpose for which it is intended, to your credit and the satisfaction and honor of those who have intrusted you with the work.

The bands will discourse martial music.
Then the Grand Master delivers an original or the following

ADDRESS

Men and brethren here assembled, be it known to you, that we be lawful Masons, true and faithful to the laws of our country, and engaged, by solemn obligation, to fear God, the Great Architect of the universe. We have among us, concealed from the eyes of all men, secrets which cannot be divulged, and which have never been found out; but these secrets are lawful and honorable, and not repugnant to the laws of GOD or man. They were intrusted, in peace and honor, to the Masons of ancient times, and having been faithfully transmitted to us, it is our duty to convey them unimpaired to the latest posterity. Unless our Craft were good and our calling honorable, we should not have lasted for so many centuries, nor should we have been honored with the patronage of so many illustrious men in all ages, who have ever shown themselves ready to promote our interests and defend us from all adversaries. We are assembled here today in the presence of you all, to build a house, which we pray GOD may deserve to prosper, by becoming a place of concourse for good men, and promoting harmony and brotherly love throughout the world, till time shall be no more. Amen.

All respond—So mote it be.

An oration may be delivered appropriate to the occasion by the Grand Orator appointed for the purpose.

By order of the Grand Master, the Grand Marshal now makes the following proclamation:

PROCLAMATION

Grand Marshal—In the name of the Grand Lodge of _____, I proclaim that the corner-stone of the structure to be here erected has this day been found square, level and plumb, true and trusty, and laid according to the ancient customs, by the Grand Master of Masons.

The Grand Chaplain then pronounces the following, or other appropriate

BENEDICTION

Glory be to God on high and on earth peace and good will toward men! O Lord, we most heartily beseech Thee, with Thy favor to behold and bless this assemblage; pour down, like the dew that falls upon the mountains, Thy mercy upon Thy servants engaged in the solemn ceremonies of this day. Bless, we pray Thee, all the workmen who shall be engaged in the erection of this edifice; keep them from all forms of accident and harm; grant them in health and prosperity to live; and finally we hope, after this life, through Thy mercy, wisdom, and forgiveness, to attain everlasting joy and felicity in Thy bright mansion—in Thy holy temple—not made with hands, eternal in the heavens. Amen.

All respond—So mote it be.

This completes the Consecration. The Grand Marshal and his assistants arrange the procession as before, and return to the hall. Suitable resolutions are adopted for publication and for record. The Grand Master addresses the Craft, reviewing the proceedings of the day, giving honor where due, and criticizing where demanded. Then the Grand Lodge is closed in ample form.

Among the hundreds of orations at the laying of corner-stones in America, we select a part of the effort of the venerable Judge EZRA GRAVES, of Herkimer, N.Y., delivered 17th June, 1882, at the laying of the corner-stone of a church in that city. We have submitted this fine production to a few excisions and alterations to adapt it to our purpose.

ORATION FOR CHURCH

The established custom of laying with Masonic honors the corner-stones of buildings erected by the Government or by the State, either for legislative, educational, or benevolent purposes, has a beautiful significance. It has awakened inquiry and approval, not only among the intelligent business and philanthropic men in society whose vigilance in all moral and financial matters we highly esteem, but it has entered the calm and sacred retreat with a sentiment akin to religious enthusiasm, and has become a fixed principle among thinking and sincere religionists, that there should exist among us such a concentrated religious duty as would make all who identify themselves with religious and moral orgainzations publicly interested in laying the foundation of every temple and church which is erected for the dissemination of moral truths, being the highest and noblest aim of all teachings.

They are temples and churches sought with due and appreciative reverence, and are dictated in their construction by the will and the wish and in the true spirit of humble adoration to Him, the unchanging Father, who meets the wants of his children in the broad aims of justice and open hands of plenty. The whole world, civilized and semi-civilized, in some form of thought or belief, either through wisdom, intelligence, or tradition, acknowledges the existence of an overruling power, a grand first cause giving life and vitality as well as reverence to all humanity, with a heartfelt adoration and devout worship accordingly to the high and low estimate they have of the being to whom they owe gratitude for the blessings they enjoy.

But no nation, tribe, or clan, whether they sleep under costly drapery or the humble nightly canopy, either in castle, mansion, tent, wigwam but in some form, audible or inaudible, invokes the protecting care of the Being on which they rely. And in a republican form of government like ours, claiming and boasting of religious toleration and sympathy, with mutual love and respect for each and charity for all, it marks, when compared with past ages, almost an enviable national intelligence and honor, when we can with unreserved sympathy meet on common religious grounds where bigotry is unknown and tradition bends in knowledge, and not only contribute, but join with strong hands and willing hearts in building houses of worship where the humble and the great unitedly, arm in arm, though with diversified opinions and religious views, can adore their Creator, each in the form best suited to his or her convictions of duty. ***

The diffusion of knowledge demonstrates the truth that the whole human family are zealously attempting to gather the sheaves of a well-spent life from the common garden of our Heavenly Father, where every herb and plant is scented with his goodness.***

Although this corner-stone is laid as the foundation of a temple dedicated to the worship of our Heavenly Father, yet its doors should always be open to the propagation of all truths which elevate man, and should be closely barred against all dissension, caste, aristocracy and hypocrisy, and its walls should never be the tell-tales of crime or wrongs concealed from public gaze, and virtues lost in the arrogance of church pride.

While its object is the dissemination of the highest possible conception of the wisdom and greatness as well as justice of our Heavenly Father, may it ever be in that noble spirit of kindness exhibited in the life of our Saviour, the world's exemplar. May its teachings be in that same broad, munificent, and independent goodness which gave Him a character that envy could not assail, bigotry could not stain or impeach, or hypocrisy betray or change.

While we know our sister churches here are zealously and devotedly laboring to clothe society with more beautiful garments of temperance, morality, and Freemasonry, may this temple be not only a useful but formidable auxiliary to all their noble efforts in the great work, not only making the worshippers better, but by example diffusing in society a higher moral standard worthy of the most careful limitation when no evil may find an advocate or security within the walls of either of our temples of worship, and with hand joined in hand in friendship, each seeking the welfare of their fellowman, adopt the salutary rule and guide of our Masonic brethren, who have so nobly honored us with their presence today, which is, "Who can best work and best agree."

It not infrequently happens, that owing to the formation of the ground or other cause, the corner-stone is laid in the *southeast angle,* or any save the northeast. In such case the committee of preparation will duly notify the Grand Master that he may make his orders to correspond. In a strictly Masonic edifice the corner-stone is laid in the northeast corner when at all practicable.

CHAPTER 6

PUBLIC DEDICATING CEREMONIES

In the last chapter we gave in considerable detail the rituals for laying the corner-stone of a public construction. In the present chapter we offer the necessary instructions for the dedication of the same edifice when complete and fitted for use. Ancient models for this service may be found in I KINGS viii, and elsewhere, where the far-famed ceremonials practiced at the dedication of King Solomon's Temple are described. In the history of the human race nothing more glorious or affecting to the soul is recorded than the gathering of a great nation around so great and wise a king to consecrate an edifice the most renowned of ancient constructions. The acknowledgement from Jehovah of the divine acceptance is the fitting conclusion of such a narration.

In NEHEMIAH xii, there is a more brief account of the dedication of the walls of Jerusalem, worthy to be studied in the same connection: "At the dedication of the wall of Jerusalem, they sought the Levites out of all their places, to bring them to Jerusalem, to keep the dedication with gladness, both with thanksgiving and with singing, with cymbals, psalteries, and with harps." This affecting ceremony has been paraphrased by a Masonic poet (ROBERT [ROB] MORRIS) in lines that may appropriately make a part of the dedication service.

CROWN THE SACRED HILL

Crown the sacred hill,
  Raise the golden shaft;
God doth bless the cheerful will
  Oh, brothers of the craft!
Long in sleep Moriah lay,
Mourned her desolation-day;
Now awake, in accents clear,
Speaks, and willing Masons hear—
  To crown the sacred hill, etc.

Bring each mystic tool—
  Old and worn they are—
Trowel, gavel, line and rule,
  And level, plumb and square.
Spirits of the ages gone,
Guide us to the corner-stone;
Strangers wait, a loving band,
Westward gazing, yearning stand—
  To crown the sacred hill, etc.

Lo, the ruined shrine!
  Ours that mighty pile;
See on every stone the sign—
  We know and love it well.
Though in dust the builders lie,
Though their works in ruin sigh,
Yon device in whispers read,
Give the lesson earnest heed—

To crown the sacred hill,
  Raise the golden shaft;
God doth bless the cheerful will,
  Oh, brothers of the craft!

DEDICATION OF A MASONIC HALL

At the time appointed for the ceremony of dedication, the Grand Master and his officers, accompanied by members of the Grand Lodge, meet in a room convenient to the Masonic hall which is to be dedicated. The Grand Lodge is opened upon the third degree; if by the Grand Master in person, the opening is said to be in *ample form;* if by the Deputy Grand Master, in *due form;* if by an appointee of the Grand Master, *in form.* The legality of the act is the same in any of the three forms, the expletive referring only to *the dignity of the officer* by whom the act is performed. The officers and members of the Lodge whose hall is to be dedicated are all supposed to be present.

It will be observed that in the ceremonies of constituting and dedicating a new Lodge, and in the ceremonies of installing the officers of a Lodge, and in the ceremonies of planting a corner-stone, *all three classes of Masons participate.* Only in the funeral ceremonies Master Masons alone can take a part.

The W.M. of the Lodge whose hall is to be dedicated now addresses the Grand Master, as follows:

Most Worshipful Grand Master, the brethren of _____ Lodge No., ____, being animated with the desire of promoting the honor and interest of the Craft, have, at great pains and expense, erected a Masonic hall for their convenience and accommodation. They are now desirous that the same should be examined by the Most Worshipful Grand Lodge; and if it should meet their approbation that it should be solemnly DEDICATED TO MASONIC PURPOSES, agreeably to ancient form.

To this request the Grand Master returns a gracious reply, and directs the Grand Secretary to read aloud the order of procession and general exercises, prepared by the committee of arrangements. This is delivered to the Grand Marshal. Then the Deputy Grand Master delivers an appropriate charge to the brethren concerning propriety of behavior. This should embody the following directions:

1. All orders *to the Craft* must come from the Grand Marshal or his assistants. The latter will receive their orders from the Grand Master alone.
2. No person can enter the procession after it passes to the public gaze, save by permission, and under the positive instructions of the Grand Marshal or an assistant. No one may leave the procession without such permission. Every person in procession must be clothed according to the Masonic grade he represents.
3. Brethren march two and two, touching elbows with a light touch.
4. The distance between the files of twos is six feet (the length of the Deacons' rods), and every brother should be careful to *cover his file leader.*
5. No talking or exclamations of any kind can be permitted in the ranks. Laughter, smoking, saluting friends outside the column, etc., are sternly reprehended by the Marshals, and upon a repetition of such disorder the offender may be ordered out of the procession by any one of those officers.
6. Due time must be observed to correspond with the musical rhythm. The first step in the march begins *with the left foot.*

A grand procession is then formed:

GRAND MASONIC PROCESSION

FIRST PART. THE VISITING LODGES

Tyler, with drawn sword
Two Stewards, with white rods
Entered Apprentices
Fellow Crafts
Master Masons
Stewards and Masters of Ceremonies
Junior Deacons
Senior Deacons
Secretaries
Treasurers
Past Wardens
Past Masters
Royal Arch Masons
Royal and Select Masters
Knights Templar, unless otherwise employed as escort to the
    Grand Lodge
The three Great Lights of Masonry, in the hands of a venerable brother
Chaplains
Masters of Lodges

In great processions in large cities it is customary for each Lodge to be formed separately, each having its own Marshal, etc., and arrayed under its proper standard. In such cases the above arrangement is equally proper, save that a Standard-bearer with two supporters must come in behind the Master. The three Great Lights of Masonry (the Scriptures open at the 133d Psalm) are borne upon a handsome cushion suspended from the neck of an old member of the Lodge. The band of music comes in most properly behind the Tyler. If more than one Lodge is thus represented in procession, they take their places according to the dates of their respective charters, the oldest in the rear.

SECOND PART. THE LODGE THAT OWNS THE HALL

The same order as in the first part, save that each number is to be read in the singular, and that behind the Treasurer two brothers bear the casket representing "The Lodge."

THIRD PART. THE GRAND LODGE

Grand Tyler, with drawn sword
Grand Stewards, with white rods
Grand Pursuivant, with sword
Grand Secretary and Grand Treasurer
A Past Master (usually aged and venerable), bearing the Three Great
    Lights of Masonry, supported by
Two Stewards, with black rods
Two Tapers, borne by Master Masons
Grand Chaplain and Grand Orator
Columns of the Tuscan and Composite Orders, borne by
    Master Masons
Columns of the Doric, Ionic and Corinthian Orders, borne by
    Master Masons
Past Grand Wardens
Past Deputy Grand Masters
Past Grand Masters
The Celestial and Terrestrial Globes, borne by two Master Masons
Junior Grand Warden, bearing the silver vessel of Corn
Senior Grand Warden, bearing the silver vessed of Wine
Deputy Grand Master, bearing the golden vessel of Oil
Master of the oldest Lodge present bearing the Book of Constitutions
THE GRAND MASTER, supported by the
Grand Deacons, with black rods
Grand Standard-Bearer
Grand Sword-Bearer, with drawn sword

The grand procession, thus arranged, preceded by musicians playing noble marches of established reputation, and governed by a competent Chief Marshal, with assistants, moves slowly and with dignity to the hall which is to be dedicated. Halted at the portals, the procession opens and marches by inverted order, so that the Grand Sword-bearer enters first and the Grand Master third to his station upon the dais.

The casket representing "The Lodge" is laid upon a small pedestal in front of the Grand Master, and covered with enwrapments of pure white linen, and near it the Three Great Lights and Book of Constitutions. Upon a table a little farther advanced, the Deputy Grand Master and the Grand Wardens place the vessels of corn, wine and oil. The two globes are placed on the floor to the right and left of the last, and grouped near them the five orders in architecture, and the two tapers now lighted. The Grand Standard is set up, high advanced, near the Grand Master, in a conspicuous place. The other Lodges, if separately formed, group around their own banners respectively. The whole Masonic assembly now unite in giving the public grand honors to the Grand Master.

Silence being commanded and a proclamation made by the Grand Marshal of the presence of the Grand Master and the sublime nature of the proceedings, an opening ode is sung, either the following or some other of the numerous pieces that have been composed for the purpose:

OPENING ODE

Master Supreme, accept our praise!
   Still bless this consecrated band;
Parent of light, illume our ways,
   And guide us by Thy sovereign hand.

May Faith, Hope, Charity divine,
   Here hold their undivided reign;
Friendship and harmony combine
   To soothe our cares and banish pain.

May pity dwell within each breast;
   Relief attend the suffering poor;
Thousands by this our Lodge be blest,
   Till worthy souls shall want no more.

The whole assembly is called up by the Grand Master's gavel and a prayer offered by the Grand Chaplain. The assembly is then seated. (It is not thought necessary to introduce forms of prayer here, as the experiene of every clergyman will suggest appropriate invocations.)

A brief exordium is pronounced by the Deputy Grand Master or other well-instructed Mason, in which the general purpose of the proceedings begun is explained to the hearers. Then the architect of the edifice to be dedicated (or some one appointed in his place) will address the Grand Master as follows:

Grand Architect—Most Worshipful Grand Master, having been intrusted with the superintendence and management of the workmen employed in the construction of this edifice, and having, according to the best of my ability, accomplished the task assigned me, I now return my thanks for the honor of this appointment, and beg leave to surrender up the implements which were committed to my care when the foundations of this fabric were laid, humbly hoping, that the exertions which have been made on this occasion will be covered with your approbation and that of the Most Worshipful Grand Lodge.

Grand Master—My brother architect, the skill and fidelity displayed in the execution of the trust reposed in you at the commencement of this undertaking have secured the entire approbation of the Grand Lodge; and they sincerely pray that this edifice may continue a lasting monument of the taste, spirit and liberality of its founders.

A second ode may be sung, and instrumental music introduced.

Deputy Grand Master—Most Worshipful Grand Master, this hall in which we are now assembled and the plan upon which it has been constructed having met with your approbation, it is the desire of the Fraternity that it shall now be dedicated according to ancient form and usage.

The Grand Master giving his consent to this, the Grand Marshal makes proclamation that all save Master Masons shall retire. The responsibility for this rests upon the Master of the Lodge in whose hall they are assembled, and strict rules of rejection and avouchal will be enforced. The purging being carefully performed, and the doors tyled by the local Tyler, a strictly GRAND LODGE PROCESSION *is now formed, the other brethren keeping their places and assisting to execute the ode, which is sung during the various circumambulations. (It may be preferred to introduce instrumental music here. This is in the discretion of the committee of arrangements, provided, that the performers are Master Masons.) The Deputy Grand Master removes the covering from "The Lodge." The procession is then constituted, the respective officers taking up the proper objects as they assume their places:*

> Grand Tyler, with drawn sword;
> Grand Sword-Bearer, with drawn sword
> Grand Standard-Bearer, with standard duly supported
> Past Master, with burning taper
> Past Master, with three Great Lights, displayed at Ecclesiastes xii.
> Two Past Masters, each with burning taper·
> Grand Secretary and Grand Treasurer
> Junior Grand Warden, with silver vessel of corn
> Senior Grand Warden, with silver vessel of wine
> Deputy Grand Master, with golden vessel of oil
> GRAND MASTER
> Two Stewards, with black rods

The first circumambulation brings the Grand Master fronting his first position. A dedication prayer is offered by the Grand Chaplain:

Grand Chaplain—Almighty and ever-glorious and gracious Lord God: Creator of all things and Governor of everything that Thou hast made: mercifully look upon thy servants, now assembled in Thy name and in Thy presence, and bless and prosper all our works begun, continued and ended in Thee. Graciously bestow upon us *wisdom* in all our doings, *strength* in all our difficulties, and the *beauty* of harmony and holiness in all our communications and work. Let *faith* be the foundation of our *hope*, and *charity* the fruit of our obedience to Thy revealed will.

O thou preserver of men, graciously enable us now to dedicate this house which we have erected to the honor and glory of Thy name, and be mercifully pleased to accept this service at our hands.

May all who shall be lawfully appointed to rule herein according to our constitution, be under Thy special guidance and protection and faithfully observe and fulfil all their obligations to Thee and to the Lodge.

May all who come within these consecrated walls have but one heart and one mind to love, to honor, to fear and to obey Thee as Thy majesty and unbounded goodness claim, and to love one another as Thou hast loved us. May every discordant passion be here banished from our bosoms. Here may we meet in Thy presence as a band of brethren created by the same Almighty Parent who are daily sustained by the same beneficent hand, and are traveling the same road through the gates of death. May we have here Thy holy word always present to mind and here may religious virtue, love, harmony and peaceful joy reign triumphant in our hearts.

May all the proper work of our Institution that may be performed in this house be such as Thy wisdom may approve and Thy goodness prosper. And finally, O thou Sovereign Architect of the universe, be graciously pleased to bless the Masonic Craft wherever dispersed, and make them true and faithful to Thee, to their neighbors, to themselves. And when the time of our labor shall draw near to its end, and the pillars of our strength decline to the ground, enable us graciously then, to pass through the valley of the shadow of death supported by Thy rod and Thy staff, to those mansions beyond the skies where love and peace and joy forever reign before Thy throne. Amen.

All respond—So mote it be.

The following or some other suitable Ode is now sung:

WHEN SOLOMON WITH WONDROUS SKILL

When Solomon, with wondrous skill,
A temple did prepare,
Israel with zeal his courts did fill,
And God was honored there.

Celestial rays of glorious light
　The sacred walls contained;
The pure refulgence, day and night,
　With awful force remained.

Oh! may Thy presence, gracious Lord,
　In our assembly be;
Enlighten us to know Thy word
　That we may honor Thee.

And when the final trump shall sound,
　To judge the world of sin,
Within Thy courts may we be found
　Eternally tyled in.

Then the Junior Grand Warden presents to the Grand Master the silver vessel of corn with this explanation:

Junior Grand Warden—Most Worshipful Grand Master, in the dedication of Masonic halls it has been the custom from time immemorial *to pour corn upon the Lodge* as an emblem of *nourishment.* I therefore present you this vessel of corn to be employed according to ancient usage.

Then the Grand Master, striking thrice upon the pedestal with his gavel, pours a portion of the corn (wheat) upon "The Lodge" and thus proclaims:

Grand Master—In the name of the Great Jehovah, to whom be all honor and glory, I do solemnly dedicate this hall to Freemasonry.

Then the private grand honors are given with full accord by the entire assembly.

These forms are of course esoteric. They correspond with those given in all tyled Lodges on the reception of official brethren and distinguished guests. The usage is general in all American Lodges.

The following stanza is sung:

Bring with thee VIRTUE, brightest maid,
　Bring LOVE, bring TRUTH, bring FRIENDSHIP here!
While social mirth shall lend her aid
　To soothe the wrinkled brow of care.

The second circumambulation is made like the first; singing or instrumental music continuing as before. Then the Senior Grand Warden presents to the Grand Master the silver vessel of wine with this explanation:

Senior Grand Warden—Most Worshipful Grand Master, in the dedication of Masonic halls it has been the custom, from time immemorial, *to pour wine upon the Lodge*, as an emblem of *refreshment*. I therefore present you this vessel of wine to be employed according to ancient usage.

Then the Grand Master, striking thrice upon the pedestal with his gavel, pours a portion of the wine upon "The Lodge" and thus proclaims:

Grand Master—In the name of the holy Saints John, I do solemnly dedicate this hall to virtue!

Then the grand honors are given as before and the following stanza sung:

> Bring CHARITY with goodness crowned,
> Encircled in Thy heavenly robe;
> Diffuse Thy blessings all around
> To every corner of the globe.

The third circumambulation is made like the others (that is from east to west by way of the south, the centre of the hall being always at the right hand), singing or instrumental music continuing as before. Then the Deputy Grand Master presents to the Grand Master the golden vessel of oil, with this explanation:

Deputy Grand Master—Most Worshipful Grand Master, in the dedication of Masonic halls it has been the custom from time immemorial *to pour oil upon the Lodge*, as an emblem of *joy*. I therefore present you this vessel of oil, to be employed according to ancient usage.

Then the Grand Master, striking thrice upon the pedestal with his gavel, pours a portion of the oil upon "The Lodge" and thus proclaims:

Grand Master—In the name of the whole fraternity, I do solemnly dedicate this hall to universal benevolence.

Then the grand honors are given as before and the following stanza sung:

> To Heaven's high Architect all praise,
> All praise, all gratitude be given,
> Who deigned the human soul to raise
> By mystic secrets, sprung from Heaven.

The Grand Chaplain pronounces a benediction kneeling and with hands extended and upraised.

*Grand Chaplain—*The LORD bless thee and keep thee.

The LORD make his face shine upon thee and be gracious unto thee.

The LORD lift up his countenance upon thee and give thee peace!
AMEN.

*Response—*So mote it be.

> *Then the Deputy Grand Master covers "The Lodge" with its linen enwrapments, the Grand Master resumes his seat, the officers replace the various objects borne in the procession, and the Grand Master seats the assembly with his gavel.*
>
> *An oration is delivered by the Grand Orator. A collection may be taken by the Grand Stewards for the benefit of all poor and distressed Masons, and the sums thus contributed are handed to the Treasurer of the local Lodge for distribution. Other songs and recitations are introduced at the discretion of the Grand Master, who finally closes the Grand Lodge in ample form.*

DEDICATION OF PUBLIC CONSTRUCTIONS NOT MASONIC

There is no history at our command which gives the ritualistic observances for this sort of dedication. Yet they are not uncommon, nor need the reader of this volume experience any difficulty in preparing a set of forms suitable for the purpose after studying the previous instructions.

In all that has been said concerning the *Public Exercises of Freemasons,* we have omitted any special reference to Knights Templar. The various Monitors, standards in American use, were prepared before the "valaint and magnanimous Order" arrived at its present high state of popularity, and this will account for the scanty notices that Webb, Cross and others of the period, bestow upon them as public escorts. At the present time, however, they rarely, if ever, appear in Masonic processions save as *Guards of Honor* (technically "Escorts"), for which task their brilliant costume, armor and military discipline eminently fit them. So numerous have they become that it is not difficult, in almost any part of the country, to secure the presence of a Commandery of Templars, and often more than one, to give *eclat* to planting a corner-stone or the dedication of a Masonic Hall.

FUNERAL CEREMONIES

CHAPTER 7

FUNERAL CEREMONY - I

[The first of the funeral ceremonies is the one developed by Thomas Smith Webb. Webb is considered the "Father of the American Rite," or more commonly called the "York Rite" of Freemasonry. He adopted the American system of ritual from the works of William Preston of England. Preston was the first Freemason to realize the ritual of Freemasonry must be systematically taught. Webb made Preston's work conform more to the American way of thinking. His *Freemasons Monitor* was widely used, and much of what it contained is still prevalent throughout American Freemasonry. This ceremony is an example.]

The privilege of Masonic interment is highly prized by those who are entitled to it; so much so that many maintain a lifelong affiliation with the Lodge rather than, by demitting, forfeit it. The ceremony of interment is, in itself, striking and impressive. But, more than any other Masonic form, it demands experience and a peculiar gift of oratory to give it due effect. In unworthy hands it partakes of the ridiculous. Close adherence to ritualistic instructions is strongly enjoined upon the W.M. who has so serious a matter in charge as this.

The burial serivce, according to the most approved forms in use, is divided into two sections:

1. THE CEREMONIES IN THE LODGE, which are partly *esoteric*.
2. THE CEREMONIES AT THE GRAVE, which are wholly *exoteric*.

1—THE CEREMONIES IN THE LODGE

When it is announced to the W.M. that a brother has passed that "bourne whence no traveller returns," and he has learned what day and hour the friends of the deceased have set for the interment and he has satisfied himself that all the requirements of the case were fulfilled by the departed brother, he calls his Lodge at a special meeting, by the aid of the Secretary and Tyler, as explained previously. According to American usage a Lodge is at liberty, without dispensation from the Grand Master, to appear in public for this purpose.

The requirements to be fulfilled by a brother to entitle him to Masonic interment are these:

1. He must be a *Master Mason.*
2. He must be in good standing, that is, not laboring under any penalty of suspension or expulsion.
3. He must be affiliated, that is, in membership with some Lodge, but not necessarily the Lodge within whose jurisdiction he dies, for it is one of the most graceful acts of Masonic courtesy to gather as a Lodge and bestow these honors upon worthy sojourning Masons. [Authority to conduct funerals for out-of-state Masons must come through the office of the Grand Secretary, and is easily obtained.]
4. His death must be honorable and in the course of nature, or if by accident, an unavoidable one. Death in a brawl, in a duel, in a fit of intoxication, or by the public hangman, will deprive the departed brother of his title to this honor.
5. It must be known that in his lifetime he desired Masonic interment. This is best entered of record in the Lodge minutes. The evidence of any brother, however, or of the family of the deceased to the same effect, is satisfactory.

A notice for a Masonic interment will suffice if published in a local paper of good circulation. The following form is recommended:

MASONIC FUNERAL NOTICE

The officers and members of _____ Lodge No. ____ F. and A.M., also sojourning Masons, and the members of neighboring Lodges, are hereby notified that the Masonic interment of Brother _____ _____ will take place on _____. The Funeral Lodge will be opened at _____ at the hour of ____ precisely. All Master Masons in good standing are cordially invited.

By order of the Worshipful Master.

_____ _____, Secretary.

The Masonic assemblage had best be *at the Lodge room,* if the distance from the home of the deceased is not too great; but any well-tyled apartment will suffice for the opening of the Funeral Lodge. The Tyler and Steward will be early at the place, to see that the room is in good condition; the aprons fresh-washed and abundant; the jewels brightened; the gavels and symbolical furniture accurately numbered, and a full supply of gloves, sprigs of evergreen and black crape. The Secretary will have in readiness a heavy sheet of paper to represent the Sacred Roll, upon which will be inscribed the name, age, and Masonic history of the deceased. The W.M. will select a suitable brother to be Marshal of the occasion, as much of the success of this public demonstration depends upon the skill and fidelity of that officer. In general, *the Senior Deacon of the Lodge* is the best selection, for he has the confidence of the W.M. and knows his wishes better than the rest.

Visiting brethren not vouched for must be in attendance at least *an hour before the opening* that they may be properly examined by a committee detailed for the purpose, and not admitted upon a hasty and unreliable avouchal. [This length of time is no longer necessary.]

The Marshal of the day uses a baton as his emblem of office, bound at the ends in black crape. If the occasion requires, Assistant Marshals may be appointed. All matters of route, music, directions to the undertaker, etc., appertain to the Chief Marshal, who receives his orders from the W.M., and he alone communicates them to the Craft.

CEREMONIES IN THE LODGE ROOM

The hour having arrived, the *Funeral Lodge* is opened briefly on the third degree, and with the deepest favor and solemnity. A brother accustomed to public prayer should be selected, for it is chilling to the soul to hear the cold-blooded formularies too often palmed upon a suffering circle as Lodge prayers.

Calling up the Brethren, the W.M. says:

Master—What man is he that liveth and shall not see death? Shall he deliver his soul from the hands of the grave?

Response by all—Man walketh in a vain shadow. He heapeth up riches, and cannot tell who shall gather them.

Master—When he dieth, he shall carry nothing away. His glory shall not descend after him.

Response—Naked he came into the world, and naked he shall return.

Master—The Lord gave and the Lord hath taken away, blessed be the name of the Lord.

The W.M. takes the Sacred Roll in his hands and says:

Master—Let me die the death of the righteous, and let my last end be like his.

Response—God is our God forever and ever. He will be our guide even unto death.

The W.M. then reads aloud from the Sacred Roll the details, and hands the document to the Secretary, to be borne by him in the procession and later deposited in the archives of the Lodge.

Master—Almightly God, into Thy hands we commend the soul of our loving brother!

Response—The will of God is accomplished. Amen. So mote it be.

The Private Grand Honors are given. Then the W.M. or the Chaplain repeats the following PRAYER:

Most glorious God, author of all good, and giver of all mercy! Pour down Thy blessings upon us, and strengthen our engagements with the ties of sincere affection. May the present instance of mortality remind us of our approaching end, and draw our attention toward Thee, the only refuge in time of need. That when the awful moment shall arrive that we are about to quit this transitory scene, the enlivening prospect of Thy mercy may dispel the gloom of death; and after our departure hence in peace and in Thy favor, we may be received into Thine everlasting kingdom, to enjoy, in unison with the souls of our departed friends, the just reward of a pious and virtuous life. AMEN.

Response—So mote it be.

The funeral procession is then formed under the direction of the Marshal, which moves forward in following order to the church, funeral parlor, or house of the deceased:

Tyler, with drawn sword
Two Stewards, with white rods
Musicians, if they are Masons. If not they precede
　The Stewards
Master Masons, two and two
Treasurer and Secretary
Two Wardens with their columns
Past Masters, two and two
Three Great Lights of Masonry, borne by an old and venerable
　brother, on a cushion covered with black cloth.

(The oldest member of the Lodge is usually selected for this honor; but none save a religious man is suitable. The Scriptures are open at the 12th Chapter of Ecclesiastes.)

Chaplain
THE MASTER, supported by
Two Deacons, with white rods
[The procession is afterwards completed thus:]

The　　　　　　　　　　Body

Upon the coffin lies　　　a Master Mason's apron

Pall Bearers　　　　　　Pall Beareres

When more than one Lodge is in procession *as a Lodge,* the Lodges go according to the respective dates of their charters, the younger preceding the elder, but the Lodge which has the funeral proceedings in charge occupies the place of honor, in the rear, and the Master of *that* Lodge governs the proceedings of the day. If the Grand Master or Deputy Grand Master is present he of course takes precedence over all, and the same respect is usually shown to any officer of the Grand Lodge present.

Full instructions for marching are given in preceding chapters. The Marshals will exercise special care that no brother be allowed to enter the procession after it goes before the public without special permission, and under no circumstances an Entered Apprentice or Fellow Craft. No brother may permit a friend or a child to march with him. The bandmaster is particularly instructed not to walk too fast, for this is a common and most grievous error.

This completes our instructions for the first part of the proceedings. The Lodge is still supposed to be *at labor,* and the utmost decorum and order are manifested. No loud commands are given, but the Marshals make their wishes known in a subdued tone of voice.

2—THE CEREMONIES AT THE GRAVE

The procession is first directed to the place of the deceased brother, where the coffin, with bearers and pall-bearers, is taken into the procession. Then the movement is to the cemetery and without change of order. The Marshal should be aware of the location of the grave, that he may suitably direct the Tyler at the head of the column. If practicable, the approach is *from the east,* and not *from the west,* if, as is proper, the head of the grave is at the west.

The head of the procession is halted at the foot of the grave, the procession opens and is inverted as follows:

The Chief Marshal

the musicians standing aside, but continuing to play a slow march.
THE BODY

accompanied by pall-bearers and followed by mourners. The coffin is laid directly over the grave upon tressels. The apron is removed. The attendants and mourners are grouped at the foot of the grave.

The Tyler
THE MASTER
The Three Great Lights
Past Masters

Two Wardens
Treasurer and Secretary
Two Deacons
Master Masons

As the W.M. advances he removes his hat, and the brethren do the same. All thereafter remain uncovered until the close of the ceremonies. If, however, the heat of the sun be untolerable, or the weather cold or stormy, rendering it unsafe, they cover by order of the Marshal. The procession circumambulates the grave in ancient order once, and forms a circle or an oblong square, at the discretion of the Marshal. From this all are excluded save the clergy and the mourners. [Rarely do Masons circumambulate the grave any more; it is a disrupting influence and the family of the deceased must be treated with respect.]

The W.M. halts at the head of the grave, the S.W. on his right, the Chaplain on his left. The J.W. stands at the foot. The Three Great Lights are placed open on a pedestal at the head of the grave, the column of the S.W. standing upright in front of it. The column of the J.W. is laid prostrate at the foot of the grave.

Some of these details seem trivial, but they go to make up an admirable whole.

The W.M. orders the Secretary to read resolutions of any of condolence and respect that may have been adopted by the Lodge. The Sacred Roll is opened and read aloud by the Secretary. Brief remarks eulogistic upon the character and standing of the deceased are appropriately introduced here. Then the Funeral Service commenced at the Lodge-room is continued.

Master—Here we view a striking instance of the uncertainty of life, and the vanity of all human pursuits. The last offices paid to the dead are only useful as lectures to the living. From them we are to derive instruction, and consider every solemnity of this kind as a summons to prepare for our own approaching dissolution.

Notwithstanding the various mementoes of mortality which we daily meet; notwithstanding death has established his empire over all the works of nature, yet, through some unaccountable infatuation, we forget that *we are born to die.* We go on from one design to another, add hope to hope, and lay out plans for the employment of many years, till we are suddenly alarmed with the approach of death when we least expect him, and at an hour which we probably concluded to be the meridian of our existence.

What are all the externals of majesty, the pride of wealth, or charms of beauty, when nature has paid her just debt? Fix your eyes on the last scene, and view life stripped of her ornaments, and exposed in her natural meanness; you will then be convinced of the futility of these empty delusions. In the grave all fallacies are detected, all ranks are levelled, all distinctions are done away.

While we drop the sympathetic tear over the grave of our deceased friend, let charity induce us to throw a veil over his foibles, whatever they may have been, and not withhold from his memory the praise that his virtues may have claimed. Suffer the apologies of human nature to plead in his behalf. Perfection on earth has never been attained. The wisest as well as the best of men have erred.

Let the present example excite our most serious thoughts and strengthen our resolutions of amendment. As life is uncertain, and all earthly pursuits are vain, let us no longer postpone the important concern of preparing for eternity, but embrace the happy moment while time and opportunity offer, to provide against the great change, when all the pleasures of this world shall cease to delight, and the reflections of a virtuous life yield the only comfort and consolation. Then our expectations will not be frustrated, nor we hurried, unprepared, into the presence of an all-wise and powerful judge, to whom the secrets of all hearts are known.

Let us, while in this state of existence, support with propriety the character of our profession; advert to the nature of our solemnities, and pursue with assiduity the sacred tenets of our order. Then, with becoming reverence, let us supplicate the divine grace to insure the favor of that Eternal Being whose goodness and power know no bounds; that, when the awful moment arrives, be it soon or late, we may be enabled to prosecute our journey without dread or apprehension to that far-distant country, whence no traveller returns.

This Funeral Oration being completed, the coffin is lowered into the grave. Then the following invocations are made:

Master—May we be true and faithful; and may we live and die in love.
Response by Masons—So mote it be.
Master—May we profess what is good, and always act agreeably to our professions.
Response by Masons—So mote it be.
Master—May the Lord bless us, and prosper us; and may all our good intentions be crowned with success.
Response by Masons—So mote it be.
Master—Glory be to God on high! on earth peace, good-will toward men!
Response by Masons—So mote it be, now, henceforth, and for evermore.

FUNERAL HYMN

AIR : PLEYEL'S HYMN

Solemn strikes the fun'ral chime,
Notes of our departing time,

As we journey here below
Through a pilgrimage of woe.

Mortals, now indulge a tear,
For mortality is here;
See how wide her trophies wave
O'er the slumbers of the grave!

Here another guest we bring,
Seraphs of celestial wing
To our funeral altar come,
Waft this friend and brother home!

Lord of all below, above,
Fill our hearts with truth and love;
As dissolves our earthly tie,
Take us to Thy Lodge on high!

If inconvenient to move about the grave in a circumambulation, owing to the crowd, or the roughness of the ground, or the throng of gravestones, etc., the circumambulation is dispensed with. Three verses of the hymn are all that are usually sung, and a chorister should be engaged to pitch and lead in the singing.

At the close, each brother takes the piece of evergreen (a cedar sprig preferred) which he received in the Lodge room, and drops it solemnly into the open grave. [Again the family must be considered. Too often people have been pushed aside so a Brother could drop his sprig into the grave. In many jurisdictions only the W.M. places his in the grave.]

The funeral honors are now introduced. As these without explanation may excite the public ridicule, the W.M. may, in his dissertation, explain to the bystanders the solemn lessons involved in them.

Then the W.M. delivers the final portion of the service:

Master— From time immemorial it has been a custom among the Fraternity of Free and Accepted Masons, at the request of a brother, to accompany his corpse to the place of interment, and there to desposit his remains with the usual formalities.

In conformity with this usage, and at the special request of our deceased brother, whose memory we revere, and whose loss we now deplore, we have assembled in the character of Masons to resign his body to the earth whence it came, and to offer up to his memory, before the world, the last tribute of our affection; thereby demonstrating the sincereity of our past esteem, and our steady attachment to the principles of the Order.

The Great Creator having been pleased, out of His mercy, to remove our brother from the cares and troubles of a transitory existence to a state of eternal duration, and thereby to weaken the chain by which we are united, man to man, may we who survive him anticipate our approaching fate and be more strongly cemented in the ties of union and friendship, that during the short space alloted to our present existence we may wisely and usefully employ our time, and in the reciprocal intercourse of kind and friendly acts, mutually promote the welfare and happiness of each other.

Unto the grave we resign the body of our deceased friend, there to remain until the general resurrection, in favorable expectation that his immortal soul may there partake of joys which have been prepared for the righteous from the foundation of the world. And may Almightly God, of His infinite goodness, at the great tribunal of unbiased justice, extend His mercy toward him and all of us, and crown our hope with everlasting bliss in the expanded realms of a boundless eternity. This we beg for the honor of His name, to Whom be glory now and forevermore. AMEN.

All the Masons respond—So mote it be.

> *If it is thought best to introduce a public prayer before dissolving the assembly, the following, in general use in the American Lodges, and therefore familiar to all Masons present, is highly recommended. The Chaplain, kneeling and spreading and upraising his hands, delivers the following* PRAYER:

Chaplain—Thou, O God, knowest our down-sitting and our uprising, and understandeth our thoughts afar off. Shield and defend us from the evil intentions of our enemies, and support us under the trials and afflictions we are destined to endure while traveling through this vale of tears.

Man that is born of a woman is of few days and full of trouble. He cometh forth as a flower and is cut down; he fleeth also as a shadow and continueth not. Seeing his days are determined, the number of his months are with Thee; Thou hast appointed his bounds that he cannot pass; turn from him that he may rest till he shall accomplish his day.

For there is hope of a tree, if it be cut down, that it will sprout again, and that the tender branch thereof will not cease. But man dieth and wasteth away; yea, man giveth up the ghost, and where is he? As the waters fail from the sea, and the flood decayeth and drieth up, so man lieth down and riseth not up till the heavens shall be no more.

Yet, O Lord, have compassion upon the children of Thy creation; administer them comfort in time of trouble, and save them with an everlasting salvation. Amen.

All Masons resopnd—So mote it be.

The W.M. gives thanks to the public for their attendance, and to the Craft for their good behavior upon the occasion. The return to the Lodge is done with the same formalities as the departure. Arrived at the Lodge-room, the W.M. thanks the Marshal and other officers for their services. He points out mildly to the brethren what errors he may have observed, and kindly warns them against a repetition. Then the Lodge is closed.

It will be seen that there is no place in a funeral procession for Royal Arch Masons, Templars, etc., *as such;* nor is it good usage to wear any regalia save the plain white apron. If the Templars are engaged as an escort, their own excellent rules of discipline will govern them.

A day's labor in Masonry such as this is good for all concerned. It is better to go to the house of mourning than the house of feasting. It is useful to all to contemplate the ruins made by the arch-destroyer Death. For we *know* that our Redeemer liveth, that at the last day He shall stand upon the earth, and that with our own eyes, we shall see God. In this knowledge lies the best lesson of Masonry, and without it the lesson has little serious import.

It is proper to add that in funeral proceedings Freemasonry admits no partnership with other orders or societies. If other forms are to be employed, the Freemasons finish theirs according to established usage and leaving their dead under the green sprigs, they are not responsible for subsequent proceedings.

Among the various forms that give effect to a funeral service without affecting any Landmark, is the practice by the three principal officers of the Lodge of depositing the first earth in the grave. This gives good effect. After the evergreens are deposited, and the lids placed across the cavity which contains the coffin, the W.M. takes a piece of fresh earth from the heap and divides it into three parts, retaining one and giving one to each of the Wardens. Then the W.M. deposits his piece, saying, with a solemn voice and manner, "Earth to earth." The Senior Warden, depositing his, says, "Ashes to ashes." The Junior Warden, depositing his, says, "Dust to dust." After which the filling of the grave is proceeded with.

CEREMONY OF INTERMENT—II
(By Improved Methods)

It is thought best to detail a method practiced in New York and many other jurisdictions. It will be seen that we follow the ancient rule of dividing the services into two parts:

1. THE CEREMONY IN THE LODGE ROOM

2. THE CEREMONY AT THE GRAVE

The reader will find, in general, that the difference between this form and CEREMONY I lies mostly in the verbiage of the responses, etc. A few of the seventeen rules are given here:

6. Whenever civic societies or the military may unite with Masons in the burial of a Mason, the body of the deceased must be in charge of the Lodge having jurisdiction. The Masonic services should, in all respects, be conducted as if none but the Masons are in attendance.

7. The pall-bearers should be Masons, selected by the Master with the concurrence of the family. If the desceased was a member of a Chapter, Commandery, or Consistory, a portion of the pall-bearers should be taken from those bodies severally.

8. The proper clothing for a Masonic funeral is a black high, hat, black or dark clothes, black necktie, white gloves, and a plain, square white linen or lambskin apron, with a band of black crape around the left arm above the elbow, and a sprig of evergreen on the left breast. [Rarely will the high hat and black crape on the arm be seen anymore.] The Master's gavel, the Wardens' columns, the Deacons' and Stewards' rods, the Tyler's sword, the Bible, the Book of Constitutions, and the Marshal's baton, should be trimmed with black crape and neatly tied with white ribbon. The officers of the Lodge *should*, and Past Masters and Grand Officers *may*, wear their official jewels covered with black crape.

9. After the clergyman shall have performed the religious exercises *of the church*, the Masonic services should begin.

10. A Lodge in procession is to be strictly under the discipline of the Lodge-room; therefore, no brother can enter the procession or leave it without express permission from the Master, conveyed through the Marshal.

If the remains of the deceased are to be removed to a distance where the brethren cannot follow, or the weather should be stormy so that the ceremonies cannot be performed at the grave, the following funeral service may be performed at the

CHURCH, OR THE HOUSE OF THE DECEASED

After the religious services have been performed, the Master will take his station at the head of the coffin, the Senior Warden on his right, the Junior Warden on his left; the Deacons and Stewards, with white rods crossed, the former at the head and the latter at the foot of the coffin, the brethren forming a circle around all; when the Masonic service will commence by the Chaplain or Master repeating the following PRAYER, in which all the brethren will join:

Our Father which art in Heaven, hallowed be Thy name. Thy kingdom come. Thy will be done on earth as it is in heaven. Give us this day our daily bread. And forgive us our trespasses, as we forgive those who trespass against us. And lead us not into temptation, but deliver us from evil. For Thine is the kingdom, and the power, and the glory, for ever and ever. AMEN.

Master—Brethren, we are called upon by the imperious mandate of the dread messenger Death, against whose free entrance within the circle of our fraternity the barred doors and Tyler's weapon offer no impediment, to mourn the loss of one of our companions. The dead body of our beloved brother, A_____ B_____, lies in its narrow house before us, overtaken by that fate which must sooner or later overtake us all; and which no power or station, no virtue or bravery, no wealth or honor, no tears of friends or agonies of relatives can avert; teaching an impressive lesson, continually repeated, yet soon forgotten, that every one of us must, ere long, pass through the valley of the shadow of death and dwell in the house of darkness.

Senior Warden—In the midst of life we are in death; of whom may we seek succor but of Thee O LORD, Who for our sins art justly displeased. Thou knowest, LORD, the secrets of our hearts; shut not Thy merciful ears to our prayer.

Junior Warden—LORD, let me know my end, and the number of my days; that I may be certified how long I have to live.

Master—Man that is born of a woman is of few days and full of trouble. He cometh forth as a flower, and is cut down; he fleeth also as a shadow, and continueth not. Seeing his days are determined, the number of his months are with Thee; Thou hast appointed his bounds that he cannot pass; turn from his that he may rest, till he shall accomplish his day. For there is hope of a tree, if it be cut down, that it will sprout again, and that the tender branch thereof will not cease. But man dieth and wasteth away; yea, man giveth up the ghost, and where is he? As the waters fail from the sea, and the flood decayeth and drieth up, so man lieth down, and riseth not up till the heavens shall be no more.

Senior Warden—Our life is but a span long, and the days of our pilgrimage are few and full of evil.

Junior Warden—So teach us to number our days, that we may apply our hearts unto wisdom.

Master—Man goeth forth to his work and to his labor until the evening of his day. The labor and work of our brother are finished. As it hath pleased Almighty GOD to take the soul of our departed brother, may he find mercy in the great day when all men shall be judged according to the deeds done in the body. We must walk in the light while we have light; for the darkness of death may come upon us at a time when we may not be prepared. Take heed, therefore, watch and pray; for ye know not when the time is; ye know not when the Master cometh; at eve, at midnight, or in the morning. We should so regulate our lives by the line of rectitude and truth, that in the evening of our days we may be found worthy to be called from labor to refreshment, and duly prepared for a translation from the terrestrial to the celestial Lodge, to join the Fraternity of the spirits of just men made perfect.

Senior Warden—Behold, O LORD, we are in distress! Our hearts are turned within us; there is none to comfort us; our sky is darkened with clouds, and mourning and lamentations are heard among us.

Junior Warden—Our life is a vapor that appeareth for a little while, and then vanisheth away. All flesh is as grass, and all the glory of man as the flower of grass. The grass withereth, and the flower thereof falleth away.

Master—It is better to go to the house of mourning than to go to the house of feasting; for that is the end of all men; and the living will lay it to his heart.

Response by the Brethren—So mote it be.

Then may be sung an appropriate Hymn

HYMN

NAOMI.—C.M.

Here death his sacred seal hath set
  On bright and by-gone hours;
The dead we mourn are with us yet,
  And—more than ever—ours.

Ours, by the pledge of love and faith,
  By hopes of heaven on high,
By trust, triumphant over death
  In immortality.

The dead are like the stars by day,
  Withdrawn from mortal eye;
Yet holding unperceived their way
  Through the unclouded sky.

By them, through holy hope and love,
  We feel, in hours serene,
Connected with the Lodge above,
  Immortal and unseen.

The MASTER or CHAPLAIN *will repeat the following* PRAYER:

MOST GLORIOUS GOD! author of all good, and giver of all mercy! pour down Thy blessings upon us, and strengthen our solemn engagements with the ties of sincere affection. May the present instance of mortality remind us of our approaching fate, and draw our attention toward Thee, the only refuge in time of need, that when the awful moment shall arrive that we are about to quit this transitory scene, the enlivening prospect of Thy mercy may dispel the gloom of death; and after our departure hence in peace and in Thy favor, we may be received into Thine everlasting kingdom, to enjoy, in union with the souls of our departed friends, the just rewards of a pious and virtuous life.

Response—So mote it be.

  After the service, the procession will return to the Lodgeroom or disperse, as most convenient.

SERVICE AT THE GRAVE

When the solemn rites of the dead are to be performed at the grave, the procession is formed, as previously described.

When the procession has arrived at the place of interment, the members of the Lodge will form a circle around the grave, as previously described, when the Master, Chaplain and other officers of the acting Lodge, take their positions at the head of the grave, and the mourners at the foot.

After the clergyman has performed the religious service of the church, the Masonic service should begin.

The Chaplain repeats the following PRAYER:

Chaplain—Almighty and most merciful Father, we adore Thee as the God of time and eternity. As it has pleased Thee to take from the light of our abode one dear to our hearts, we beseech Thee to bless and sanctify unto us this dispensation of Thy providence. Inspire our hearts with wisdom from on high, that we may glorify Thee in all our ways.

May we realize that Thine all-seeing eye is upon us, and be influenced by the spirit of truth and love to perfect obedience, that we may enjoy the divine approbation here below. And when our toils on earth shall have ended, may we be raised to the enjoyment of fadeless light and immortal life in that kingdom where faith and hope shall end, and love and joy prevail through eternal ages. And Thine, O righteous Father, shall be the glory forever. AMEN.

Response—So mote it be.

The following exhortation is then given by the Master:

Master—Brethren, the solemn notes that betoken the dissolution of this earthly tabernacle have again alarmed our outer door, and another spirit has been summoned to the land where our fathers have gone before us. Again we are called to assemble among the habitations of the dead, to behold the "narrow house appointed for all living." Here, around us, in that peace which the world cannot give, sleep the unnumbered dead. The gentle breeze fans their verdant covering, they heed it not; the sunshine and the storm pass over them, and they are not disturbed; stones and lettered monuments symbolize the affection of surviving friends, yet no sound proceeds from them save that silent but thrilling admonition, "Seek ye the narrow path and the strait gate that leads unto eternal life."

We are again called upon to consider the uncertainity of human life; the immutable certainty of death, and the vanity of all human pursuits. Decrepitude and decay are written upon every living thing. The cradle and the coffin stand in juxtaposition to each other; and it is a melancholy truth, that as soon as we begin to live, that moment also we begin to die. It is passing strange that, notwithstanding the daily mementoes of mortality that cross our path, notwithstanding the funeral bell so often tolls in our ears, and the "mournful processions" go about our streets, that we will not more seriously consider our approaching fate. We go on from design to design, add hope to hope, and lay out plans for the employment of many years, until we are suddenly alarmed at the approach of the messenger of Death, at a moment when we least expect him, and which we probably conclude to be the meridian of our existence.

What, then, are all the externals of human dignity, the power of wealth, the dreams of ambition, the pride of intellect, or the charms of beauty, when Nature has paid her just debt? Fix your eyes on the last sad scene, and view life stripped of its ornaments, and exposed in its natural meanness, and you must be persuaded of the utter emptiness of these delusions. In the grave, all fallacies are detected, all ranks are levelled, all distinctions are done away. Here the sceptre of the prince and the staff of the beggar are laid side by side.

While we drop the sympathetic tear over the grave of our deceased brother, let us cast around his foibles, whatever they may have been, the *broad mantle of Masonic charity,* nor withhold from his memory the commendation that his virtues claim at our hands. Perfection on earth has never yet been attained; the wisest, as well as the best of men, have gone astray. Suffer, then, the apologies of human nature to plead for him who can no longer plead for himself.

Our present meeting and proceedings will have been vain and useless if they fail to excite our serious reflections, and strengthen our resolutions of amendment. Be then persuaded, my brethren, by this example, of the uncertainty of human life and the unsubstantial nature of all its pursuits, and no longer postpone the all-important concern of preparing for eternity. Let us each embrace the present moment, and while time and opportunity permit, prepare with care for that great change, which we all know must come, when the pleasures of the world shall cease to delight, and be as a poison to our lips; and while we may enjoy the happy reflection of a well-spent life in the exercise of piety and virtue, will yield the only comfort and consolation.

Thus shall our hopes be not frustrated, nor we hurried unprepared into the presence of the all-wise and powerful Judge, to whom the secrets of all hearts are known.

Let us resolve to maintain with sincerity the dignified character of our profession. May our *faith* be evinced in a correct moral walk and deportment; may our *hope* be bright as the glorious mysteries that will be revealed hereafter; and our *charity* boundless as the wants of our fellow-creatures. Having faithfully discharged the great duties which we owe to

GOD, to our neighbor, and to ourselves when at last it shall please the Grand Master of the universe to summon us into His eternal presence, may the *trestle-board* of our whole lives pass such inspection that it may be given unto each of us to "eat of the hidden manna," and to receive the "white stone with a new name," that will insure perpetual and unspeakable happiness at His right hand.

The Master then (presenting the apron) continues:

The lambskin, or white apron, is the emblem of innocence and the badge of a Mason. It is more ancient than the Golden Fleece or Roman Eagle; more honorable than the Star and Garter, when worthily worn.

The Master then deposits it in the grave.

This emblem I now deposit in the grave of our deceased brother. By it we are reminded of the universal dominion of Death. The arm of Friendship cannot interpose to prevent his coming; the wealth of the world cannot purchase our release; nor will the innocence of youth or the charms of beauty propitiate his purpose. The mattock, the coffin, and the melancholy grave admonish us of our mortality, and that, sooner or later, these frail bodies must moulder in their parent dust.

The Master (holding the evergreen) continues:

This *evergreen*, which once marked the temporary resting-place of the illustrious dead, is an emblem of our faith in the immortality of the soul. By this we are reminded that we have an immortal part within us, that shall survive the grave, and which shall never, *never*, NEVER, die. By it we are admonished that, though, like our brother, whose remains lie before us, we shall soon be clothed in the habiliments of DEATH, and deposited in the silent tomb, yet, through our belief in the mercy of GOD, we may confidently hope that our souls will bloom in eternal spring. This, too, I deposit in the grave, with the exclamation, "Alas, my brother!"

> *The brethren then move in procession around the place of interment, and severally drop the sprig of evergreen into the grave, exclaiming, "Alas, my brother!" after which, the funeral honors are given.*
>
> *The following figures represent the manner in which the funeral honors should be given: No. 1 represents the first movement, by extending the hands toward the grave with the palms up; all the brethren will say:*

"To the grave we consign the mortal remains of our deceased brother."

No. 2 represents the second movement, by crossing the arms over the breast, the left above the right, the fingers touching the shoulders; the brethren will say:

"We cherish his memory here,"

No. 3 represents the third and last movement, by raising the hands above the head, looking upward, and say:

"His spirit we commend to God, Who gave it."

Then drop the hands to the sides

It is proper to give the funeral honors only once. *[In some jurisdictions where these movements are used, they are reversed along with the words: "His spirit to God—His memory in our hearts—His body to the earth."]*

The Master then continues the ceremony:

Master—From time immemorial, it has been the custom among the Fraternity of Free and Accepted Masons, at the request of a brother, to accompany his remains to the place of interment, and there to deposit them with the usual formalities.

In comformity with this usage, and at the request of our deceased brother, whose memory we revere, and whose loss we now deplore, we have assembled in the character of Masons to offer up to his memory, before the world, the last tribute of our affection; thereby demonstrating the sincerity of our past esteem for him and our steady attachment to the principles of the Order.

The Great Creator has been pleased, out of His infinite mercy, to remove our brother from the cares and troubles of this transitory existence to a state of endless duration, thus severing another link from the fraternal chain that binds us together.

May we who survive him be more strongly cemented in the ties of union and friendship, that during the short space allotted us here we may wisely and usefully employ our time, and in the reciprocal intercourse of kind and friendly acts, mutually promote the welfare and happiness of each other.

Unto the grave we have consigned the body of our deceased brother, earth to earth (*earth being sprinkled on the coffin*), ashes to ashes (*more earth*), dust to dust (*more earth*), there to remain till the trumpet shall sound on the resurrection morn. We can cheerfully leave him in the hands of a Being, Who has done all things well, Who is glorious in holiness, fearful in praises, doing wonders.

To those of his immediate relatives and friends who are most heart-stricken at the loss we have all sustained, we have but little of this world's consolation to offer. We can only sincerely, deeply and most affectionately sympathize with them in their afflictive bereavement. But we can say that HE who tempers the wind to the shorn lamb, looks down with infinite compassion upon the widow and fatherless in the hour of their desolation; and that the Great Architect will fold the arms of His love and protection around those who put their trust in Him.

Then let us improve this solemn warning that at last, when the sheeted dead are stirring, when the great white throne is set, we shall receive from the Omniscient Judge the thrilling invitation, "Come, ye blessed, inherit the kingdom prepared for you from the foundation of the world."

The following, or some other suitable ode, may be sung:

PLEYEL'S HYMN

Solemn strikes the fun'ral chime,
Notes of our departing time,
As we journey here below
Thro' a pilgrimage of woe.

Here another guest we bring;
Seraphs of celestial wing,

To our funeral altar come,
Waft our friend and brother home.

LORD of alll below—above—
Fill our hearts with truth and love;
When dissolves our earthly tie,
Take us to thy Lodge on high.

*The service may be concluded with the following or some other
suitable PRAYER.*

Most glorious GOD, author of all good and giver of all mercy, pour
down Thy blessings upon us and strengthen our solemn engagements with
the ties of sincere affection. May the present instance of mortality remind
us of our own approaching fate, and, by drawing our attention toward
Thee, the only refuge in time of need, may we be induced so to regulate
our conduct here that when the awful moment shall arrive at which we
must quit this transitory scene, the enlivening prospect of Thy mercy may
dispel the gloom of death; and that after our departure hence in peace
and Thy favor, we may be received into Thine everlasting kingdom, and
there join in union with our friend, and enjoy that uninterrupted and
unceasing felicity which is allotted to the souls of just men made perfect.
AMEN.

Response—So mote it be.

Master—The will of God is accomplished.

Response—So mote it be.

Master—From dust we came, and unto dust we must return.

Response—May we all be recompensed at the resurrection of the just.
AMEN.

*Thus the service ends, and the procession will return in form to the
place whence it set out, where the necessary business of Masonry
should be renewed. The insignia and ornament of the deceased, if an
officer of a Lodge, are to be returned to the Master, with the usual
ceremonies, and the Lodge will be closed in form.*

Having three forms of Masonic interment, both in large use and favor,
it is proper to say that almost every Grand Lodge has set forth a Ritual of
Burial for its own subordinates, each differing in some respects from
these.

It is warmly advised, therefore, that all who join in a ceremony of this
sort be furnished *with the same forms,* having the same designs upon the
trestle-board. Thus a mortifying confusion is avoided, and that due im-

pression is made upon the minds of the public and family of the deceased, which is so winning and so conducive to the future growth of the Lodge, whose missing link is thus honorably and affectionately commemorated.

BURIAL OF THE DEAD—III

BY EDWARD M. L. EHLERS, P.G.M.

Grand Lodge of New York

On arriving at the place of interment the brethren will form parallel lines, the Master, Wardens, and Chaplain at the head, and the family and mourners at the foot of the grave. The coffin having been deposited in the grave, the Master will say:

Master—Man that is born of a woman is of few days and full of trouble. He cometh forth like a flower, and is cut down: he fleeth also so a shadow, and continueth not. In the midst of life we are in death. Of whom may we seek succor but of Thee, O Lord, who for our sins art justly displeased?

PRAYER

Chaplain—Most glorious and merciful Lord God, author of all good, and giver of every perfect gift; vouch-safe, we implore Thee, Thy blessing; and under the solemnities of this occasion bind us closer in the ties of brotherly love and affection. May the present example of mortality sensibly remind us of our approaching end; and may it tend to wean our affections from the things of this transitory world, and to fix them more devotedly upon Thee, the only sure refuge in time of need.

And, at last, Great Architect of the universe, when our journey shall be near its end; when the silver cord shall be loosened and the golden bowl be broken: oh, in that moment of mortal extremity, may the "lamp of Thy love" dispel the gloom of the dark valley; and may we be enabled to "work an entrance" into the Celestial Lodge above, and in Thy glorious presence, amid its ineffable mysteries, enjoy a union with the souls of our departed friends, perfect in the happiness of Heaven, and durable as eternity. Amen.

Response—So mote it be.

The following ode may be sung.

Solemn strikes the fun'ral chime,
Notes of our departing time,
As we journey here below
Through a pilgrimage of woe.

Here another guest we bring:
Seraph of celestial wing,
To our funeral altar come;
Waft this friend and brother home.

LORD of all! below—above—
Fill our hearts with truth and love;
When dissolves our earthly tie,
Take us to Thy Lodge on high.

Master—"The hand of the LORD was upon me, and carried me out in the Spirit of the LORD, and set me down in the midst of the valley which was full of bones,

"And caused me to pass by them round about: and, behold, there were very many in the open valley: and, lo, they were very dry.

"And he said unto me, Son of man, can these bones live? And I answered, O LORD GOD, thou knowest.

"Again he said unto me, Prophesy upon these bones, and say unto them, O ye dry bones, hear the word of the LORD.

'Thus saith the LORD GOD unto these bones: Behold, I will cause breath to enter into you, and ye shall live.

"And I will lay sinews upon you and will bring up flesh upon you, and cover you with skin, and put breath in you, and ye shall live; and ye shall know that I am the LORD.

"So I prophesied as I was commanded: and as I prophesied there was a noise, and behold a shaking, and the bones came together, bone to his bone.

"And when I beheld, lo, the sinews and the flesh came up upon them, and the skin covered them above; but there was no breath in them.

"Then said he unto me, Prophesy unto the wind: prophesy, son of man, and say to the wind, Thus saith the LORD GOD: Come from the four winds, O breath, and breathe upon these slain, that they may live.

"So I prophesied as he commanded me, and the breath came into them, and they lived, and stood up upon their feet, an exceeding great army."

Brethren, we are again called upon, by a solemn admonition, to regard the uncertainty of human life, the certainty of death, and vanity of all earthly ambitions. Decrepitude and decay are written on every living thing. But a span—a heart-beat—a breath—divides the cradle from the grave; and it is a melancholy truth that so soon as we begin to live that moment also we begin to die. Imperfection is an incident of our earthly condition; the Almighty fiat has gone forth—"Dust thou art, and unto dust shalt thou return." What an eloquent commentary is here exhibited of the instability of every human pursuit; and how touchingly does it echo the sentiment of the great preacher, who wrote for our perpetual warning the immortal maxim, "Vanity of vanities, all is vanity."

The city of the dead, my brethren, has a devout emphasis in its solemn silence. It tells us of the gathering within its embrace of parents' fondest hopes; of the severance of all earthly ties which bound us to the departed ones who gave us birth; of the darkness which has enshrouded the bright prospects of the loving husband and the devoted wife; of the unavailing grief of the affectionate brother and tender sister; and of the sleep of death which here envelops many an early, many an instantaneous, call into eternity, given in the midst of health, of gayety, and of brightest hopes.

The last offices we pay to the dead are useless except as they constitute lessons to the living. The cold, marble form enclosed in the "narrow house" before you is alike insensible to our sorrows and our ceremonies. It matters not to him whether two or three gather around the grave to perform these funeral rites, or that hundreds have assembled, with the banners an dinsignia our Fraternity, to deposit his remains in their final resting-place. It is of little moment how, or in what manner, these obsequies are performed; whether the wild winds chant his requiem, or it be accompanied with rare and costly music and the minstrelsy of many voices. His spirit has gone to accomplish the destiny of all our race, while his body, in the slumber of the grave, will be resolved into its original elements. Our faith teaches

> "Corruption, earth, and worms,
> Shall but refine his flesh
> Till his triumphant spirit comes
> To put it on afresh.
>
> "Array'd in glorious grace
> Shall our vile bodies shine;
> And ev'ry hope, and ev'ry face,
> Look heavenly and divine."

What, then, are all the externals of human dignity, the power of wealth, the pride of intellect, or the charms of beauty, when nature has paid her just debt? Look on the last scene and view life stripped of its ornaments, and you must be persuaded of the utter emptiness of all human delusions. The monarch at whose bidding a nation pays obeisance, and the beggar at the gate, are equals in death. The one is obliged to part with his sceptre and his crown—the other with his staff and his rags. Both are indebted to their mother earth for a common sepulchre. In the grave all fallacies are forgotten, all ranks levelled, and all distinctions obliterated.

It is of record, in the volume of Eternal Truth, that perfection on earth has never been attained. The best of men have erred, and the wisest of our race have gone astray. Suffer, then, the apologies of human nature to plead for him who can no longer plead for himself.

While we drop the sympathetic tear over the grave of our departed brother, let us not withhold from his memory the commendation that his virtues claim at our hands.

Master, presenting the Apron, continues:

The lambskin or white apron is an emblem of innocence and the badge of a Mason. It is more ancient than the Golden Fleece; more honorable than the Star and Garter.

This emblem I now deposit in the grave of our deceased brother. By this we are reminded of the universal dominion of death. The arm of friendship cannot interpose to prevent his coming; the wealth of the world cannot purchase our release; nor will the innocence of youth or the charms of beauty propitiate his purpose. The mattock, the coffin, and the melancholy grave admonish us of our mortality; and that, sooner or later, these frail bodies must moulder in their parent dust.

Master (holding the Evergreen) continues:

This evergreen is an emblem of our faith in the immortalty of the soul. By this we are reminded of our high and glorious destiny beyond the "world of shadows," and that there dwells within our tabernacle of clay an imperishable, immortal spirit, over which the grave has no dominion, and death no power.

Master then drops the sprig into the grave exclaiming "Alas! My Brother!"
And likewise each brother in turn, beginning at the right of the Master.
The funeral honors are given by extending the hands toward the grave with the palms up, the brethren repeating in unison:

"To the grave we consign the mortal remains of our deceased brother."

The arms are then crossed over the breast, the left above the right, the fingers touching the shoulders, the brethren repeating in unison:

"We cherish his memory here."

The hands are then raised above the head, and looking upward, all repeating in unison:

"His spirit we commend to God who gave it."

The hands are then dropped to the side.

Master—Forasmuch as it has pleased Almighty God, in his inscrutable providence, to take out of the world the soul of our deceased brother, we therefore commit his body to the grave—earth to earth (*casting a handful of earth in the grave*).

Senior Warden—Ashes to Ashes (*casting more earth in the grave*).

Junior Warden—Dust to Dust (*casting more earth in the grave*).

Master—Looking for the general resurrection in the last day, when the earth and the sea shall give up the dead.

We consign him to the grave—to the long sleep of death; and so profound will be that sleep that even the giant tread of the earthquake shall not distrub it. There will he slumber until the Archangel's trump shall usher in that eventful morn, when, by our Supreme Grand Master's Word, he will be raised to that blissful Lodge which no time can remove, and which to those worthy of admission will remain open during the boundless ages of eternity. In that Heavenly Sanctuary the Mystic Light, unmingled with darkness, will remain unbroken and perpetual. There, amid the sunbeam smiles of Immutable Love, under the benignant bend of the All-Seeing Eye—there, my brethren, may Almighty God, in His infinite mercy, grant that we finally meet to part no more.

> There is an hour of peaceful rest,
> To mourning wanderers given;
> There is a home for souls distressed,
> A balm for every wounded breast,
> 'Tis found alone in heaven.

From time immemorial it has been the custom among the Fraternity of Free and Accepted Masons, upon request, to accompany the body of a deceased brother to the place of interment, there to deposit it with the usual formalities.

In conformity to this ancient usage, we have assembled at this time in the character of Masons to offer before the world the last tribute of our affection; and thereby to demonstrate in the strongest manner the sincerity of our past esteem for him, and our steady attachment to the principles of the Fraternity.

To those of his immediate relatives and friends who are most heart-stricken at the loss we have all sustained, we have little of this world's consolation to offer. We can only sincerely, deeply, and most affectionately sympathize with them in their afflictive bereavement, and commend them to the Infinite Father who looks down with compassion upon the widow and fatherless in the hour of their desolation: He will fold the arms of His love and protection around those who put their trust and confidence in Him.

Then let us each, in our respective stations, so improve this solemn warning, that, at last, when the volume of record of our life is opened, we may receive from the Omniscient Eternal Judge the thrilling invitation, "Come, ye blessed of my Father, inherit the kingdom prepared for you from the foundation of the world."

PRAYER

Chaplain—Almighty and most merciful God, in whom we live and move and have our being, and before whom all men must appear to render an account for the deeds done in the body: we do most earnestly beseech Thee, as we now surround the grave of our deceased brother, to impress deeply upon our minds the solemnities of this hour. May we ever remember that "in the midst of life we are in death," and so live and act that we shall be fittingly prepared to die when the hour of our departure is at hand.

And oh, Gracious Father, vouchsafe to us, we pray Thee, divine assistance to redeem our misspent time; and in the discharge of the duties Thou has assigned us in the erection of our moral edifice, may we have wisdom from on high to direct us, strength commensurate with out task to support us, and 'he beauty of holiness to adorn and render all our labors acceptable in Thy sight. And, at last, when our work on earth is done, when the messenger of death shall call us from our labors, may we obtain an everlasting rest in that Spiritual House not made with hands, eternal in the Heavens. AMEN.

Response—So mote it be.

The Master then approaches the head of the grave (or the entrance to the tomb) and says:

Soft and safe to thee, my brother, be this earthly bed! Bright and glorious be thy rising from it! Fragrant be the acacia sprig that here shall flourish! May the earliest buds of spring unfold their beauties o'er this thy resting place, and here may the sweetness of the summer's last rose linger longest! Though the cold blasts of winter may lay them in the dust, and for a time destroy the loveliness of their existence, yet the destruction is not final; and in the spring-time they shall surely bloom again. So, in the bright morning of the world's resurrection, thy mortal frame, now laid in the dust by the chilling blast of Death, shall come again into newness of life, and expand in immortal beauty in realms beyond the skies. Until then, dear brother—until then—farewell!

The grave will now be filled with earth, and the service closed with the following benediction:

The peace that passeth all understanding rest and abide in you now and forever. Amen.

Response—So mote it be.

TO LIVE BEYOND THE GRAVE

To live beyond the grave—to leave a name
That like a living sun shall hold its way
Undimmed through ages—to be hailed hereafter
As first among the spirits who have gifted
Their land with fame—to dwell amid the thought
Of all sublimer souls or deities,
As treasures in their shrines—to lead the tongues
Of nations, and to be uttered in the songs
And prayers of millions—he who bears *such hope*
Fixed in his heart, and holds his lonely way,
Cheered by this only, and yet keeps himself
Unwavering in the many shocks that push
His purpose from its path—he was not cast
In nature's common mold. *Such hope itself*
Is greatness.

FUNERAL HYMNS

I—L.M.

UNVEIL thy bosom, faithful tomb!
  Take this new treasure to thy trust,
And give these sacred relics room
  To slumber in the silent dust.

Nor pain, nor grief, nor anxious fear,
  Invade thy bounds; no mortal woes
Can reach the peaceful sleeper here,
  While angels watch the soft repose.

II—8's AND 7's

BROTHER, rest from sin and sorrow!
  Death is o'er, and life is won;
On thy slumber dawns no morrow;
  Rest! thine earthly race is run.

Fare thee well! though woe is blending
  With the tones of early love,
Triumph high and joy unending
  Wait thee in the realms above!

III—8's AND 7's

SAD and solemn flow our numbers,
   While disconsolate we mourn
The loss of him who sweetly slumbers
   Mouldering 'neath the silent urn.

To the exalted Power Almighty,
   Softly breathe an ardent prayer;
On his sacred mound tread lightly,
   While we wipe the falling tear.

IV—C.M.

WHY do we mourn departing friends,
   Or shake at death's alarms?
'Tis but the voice the Master sends,
   To call us to his arms.

Why should we tremble to convey
   Their bodies to the tomb?
'Tis but the consecrated way
   To the eternal home.

MEMORIAL SERVICE

OR

LODGE OF SORROW

From an old wood cut showing a Catafalque

CHAPTER 8

MEMORIAL SERVICE OR LODGE OF SORROW

AMONG French and other continental Lodges, it is the custom at stated periods to hold *Lodges of Sorrow,* for the purpose of commemorating the loss of brethren deceased during the interval. These occasions are very strongly marked. One of the most prominent of which we have minutes is the Lodge of Sorrow held in Paris, Nov. 28, 1778, by the *Lodge of Nine Muses (Loge des Neuf Soeurs),* of that city, in honor of the poet and philosopher, Voltaire, who had received the three degrees of the Lodge, February 7, of the same year. Upon his death, May 30, following, they resolved to honor his memory to the utmost. Benjamin Franklin, then the American Ambassador to the Court of France, and a devoted friend of Voltaire, took an active part in the proceedings. Lalande presided as Master, Franklin and Itroganoff assisted as Wardens. The eloquent Lechangeaux was Orator. The hall was heavily draped with black cloth, and lighted dimly by lamps. The walls were hung with passages selected from the prose and poetry of the talented poet, whose death was the subject of these lamentations. A mausoleum stood in the background of the hall.

During the delivery of the eulogy the mausoleum slowly disappeared by the aid of machinery, and in its place there rose up a representation of the apotheosis of Voltaire.

Brother Roucher recited a poem of much merit, of which one passage was so splendidly declaimed as to call for a repetition of the entire piece. This was:—*Où reposé un grand homme un dieu doit habiter* ("where a truly great man lies buried there a deity should dwell"). At the point in the memorial service, where it is required to deposit the mystic sprig of Acacia upon the cenotaphium, Brother Benjamin Franklin stepped forward and laid an elegant wreath upon it, in token of fraternal sorrow. An *Agapé,* or love-feast, concluded the proceedings.

It is becoming the usage in many cities in America to introduce this practice. Grand Lodges, smarting under the loss of a brother peculiarly eminent and useful, are giving expression to their grief by *memorial services.* For the best model we are indebted to Brother JOHN W. SIMONS, Past Grand Master of New York, who prepared a "Ritual for a Lodge of Sorrow" that has become a national standard of reference.

The reader will easily draw the distinction between the matters of burying the dead and this of honoring them, often months and years afterward, by memorial services. "The latter are intended to celebrate their memory, and while we thus recall to our recollection their virtues, and temper anew our resolutions so to live that when we shall have passed the silent portals, our memories may be cherished with grateful remembrance, we learn to look upon death from a more elevated point of view, to see in it the wise and necessary transition from the trials and imperfections of this world, to the perfect life for which our transient journey here has been the school and the preparation. We learn that 'the soul is the whole of man; that for it *to be born* is really to die; that earth is but its place of exile, and heaven its native land.' "

The rules laid down by this veteran and widely known writer (SIMONS), are worthy of acceptation:

1. Dark clothing must be worn. No insignia are admissible save white aprons and white gloves.

2. Music, vocal and instrumental, is absolutely essential to the successful conduct of this memorial service.

3. No secrecy is necessary. Lodges of Sorrow are best held in churches and public halls, where *all persons interested* can witness the proceedings.

4. The apartment must be draped in black, and the stations particularly marked with badges of mourning.

5. A skull and lighted taper should mark the station of the W.M.

6. In the centre of the room is placed the catafalque, which consists of a rectangular platform, about six feet long by four wide, on which are two smaller platforms, so that three steps are represented. On the third one should be an elevation of convenient height, on which is placed an urn. The platform should be draped in black, and a canopy of black drapery may be raised over the urn.

7. At each corner of the platform will be placed a candlestick, bearing a lighted taper, and near it, facing the East, will be seated a brother, provided with an extinguisher, to be used at the proper time.

8. During the first part of the ceremonies the lights in the room should burn dimly.

9. Arrangements should be made to enable the light to be increased to brilliancy at the appropriate point in the ceremony.

10. On the catafalque will be laid a pair of white gloves, a lambskin apron, and, if the deceased brother has been an offier, the appropriate insignia of his office.

11. When the Lodge is held in memory of several brethren, shields bearing their names are placed around the catafalque.

OPENING THE LODGE

The several officers being in their places, and the brethren seated, the Master will call up the Lodge, and say:

Master—Brother Senior Warden, for what purpose are we assembled?

Senior Warden—To honor the memory of those brethren whom death hath taken from us; to comtemplate our own approaching dissolution; and, by the remembrance of immortality, to raise our souls above the consideration of this transitory existence.

Master—Brother Junior Warden, what sentiments should inspire the souls of Masons on occasions like the present?

Junior Warden—Calm sorrow for the absence of our brethren who have gone before us; earnest solicitude for our eternal welfare, and a firm faith and reliance upon the wisdom and goodness of the Great Architect of the Universe.

Master—Brethren, commending these sentiments to your earnest consideration, and invoking your assistance in the solemn ceremonies about to take place, I declare this Lodge of Sorrow opened.

The Chaplain or Master will then offer the following or some other suitable PRAYER:

Grand Architect of the Universe, in whose holy sight centuries are but as days, to Whose omniscience the past and the future are but as one eternal present, look down upon Thy children, who still wander among the delusions of time, who still tremble with dread of dissolution, and shudder at the mysteries of the future; look down, we beseech Thee, from Thy glorious and eternal day into the dark night of our error and presumption, and suffer a ray of Thy divine light to penetrate into our hearts, that in them may awaken and bloom the certainty of life, reliance upon Thy promises, and assurance of a place at Thy right hand. AMEN.

Response—So mote it be.

The following or some other appropriate ode may be sung:

> Brother, thou art gone to rest;
> We will not weep for thee,
> For thou art now where oft on earth
> Thy spirit longed to be.

> Brother, thou art gone to rest;
> Thy toils and cares are o'er;
> And sorrow, pain, and suffering, now,
> Shall ne'er distress thee more.

Brother, thou art gone to rest;
And this shall be our prayer,
That when we reach our journey's end,
Thy glory we shall share.

The Master (taking the skull in his hand) will then say:

Master—Brethren, in the midst of life we are in death, and the wisest cannot know what a day may bring forth. We live but to see those we love passing away into the silent land.

Behold this emblem of mortality, once the abode of a spirit like our own. Beneath this mouldering canopy once shone the bright and busy eye; within this hollow cavern once played the ready, swift, and tuneful tongue; and now, sightless and mute, it is eloquent only in the lessons it teaches us.

Think of those brethren who, but a few days since, were among us in all the pride and power of life; bring to your minds the remembrance of their wisdom, their strength, and their beauty, and then reflect that "to this complexion have they come at last." Think of yourselves; thus will you be when the lamp of your brief existence has burned out. Think how soon death, for you, will be a reality. Man's life is like a flower, which blooms today, and tomorrow is faded, cast aside, and trodden under foot.

The most of us, my brethren, are fast approaching, or have already passed the meridian of life; our sun is setting in the West, and oh! how much more swift is the passage of our declining years than when we started upon the journey, and believed—as the young are too apt to believe—that the roseate hues of the rising sun of our existence were always to be continued.

When we look back upon the happy days of our childhood, when the dawning intellect first began to exercise its powers of thought, it seems but as yesterday, and that, by a simple effort of the will, we could put aside manhood, and seek again the loving caresses of a mother, or be happy in the possession of a bauble; and could we now realize the idea that our last hour had come, our whole earthly life would appear but as the space of time from yesterday until today.

Centuries upon centuries have rolled away behind us; before us stretches out an eternity of years to come; and on the narrow boundary between the past and the present flickers the puny taper we term our life. The cradle speaks to us of *remembrance*—the coffin of *hope*, of a blessed trust in a never-ending existence beyond the gloomy portals of the tomb.

When God sends his messenger to us with the final summons, let us look upon it as an act of mercy, to prevent many calamities of a longer life, and lay down our heads softly and pass into the sleep that knows no waking. For this at least man gets by death, that his calamities are not immortal. To bear grief honorably, temperately, and to die nobly, are the duties of a good man and true Mason.

A solemn piece of music will now be performed, or the following ode may be sung:

MUSIC—*Naomi*—C.M.

When those we love are snatched away,
  By Death's relentless hand,
Our hearts the mournful tribute pay,
  That friendship must demand.

While pity prompts the rising sigh,
  With awful power imprest;
May this dread truth, "I, too, must die,"
  Sink deep in every breast.

Let this vain world allure no more;
  Behold the opening tomb!
It bids us use the present hour;
  To-morrow death may come.

At its conclusion Chaplain will read the following passages:

Chaplain—Lo, he goeth by me and I see him not. He passeth on also, but I perceive him not. Behold, he taketh away, who can hinder him?

Man that is born of a woman is of few days, and full of trouble. He cometh forth like a flower, and is cut down; he fleeth also as a shadow, and continueth not. Seeing his days are determined, the number of his months are with Thee; Thou hast appointed his bounds that he cannot pass; turn from him that he may rest, till he shall accomplish his day. For there is hope of a tree if it be cut down, that it will sprout again, and that the tender branch thereof will not cease. But man dieth and wasteth away; yea, man giveth up the ghost, and where is he? As the waters fail from the sea and the flood decayeth and drieth up, so man lieth down and riseth not; till the heavens be no more they shall not awake nor be raised out of their sleep.

For I know that my Redeemer liveth, and that He shall stand at the latter day upon the earth. And though after my skin worms destroy this body, yet in my flesh shall I see God. Whom I shall see for myself, and mine eyes shall behold, and not another.

For Thou hast cast me into the deep, in the midst of the seas; and Thy floods compassed me about; all Thy billows and Thy waves passed over me. Then I said, I am cast out of Thy sight; yet will I look again toward Thy holy temple. The waters compassed me about, even to the soul; the depth closed me round about, the weeds were wrapt about my head.

Are not my days few? Cease then, and let me alone, that I may take comfort a little, before I go whence I shall not return, even to the land of darkness, and the shadow of death. A land of darkness, as darkness itself; and of the shadow of death, without any order, and where the light is as darkness.

An interval of profound silence will be observed. The general lights of the hall, if there be convenience, will be turned low, and the four brethren will extinguish the tapers near which respectively they are placed.

PRAYER BY THE CHAPLAIN

OUR FATHER Who art in heaven, it hath pleased Thee to take from among us those who were our brethren. Let time, as it heals the wounds thus inflicted upon our hearts and on the hearts of those who were near and dear to them, not erase the salutary lessons engraved there; but let those lessons, always continuing distinct and legible, make us and them wiser and better. And whatever distress or trouble may hereafter come upon us, may we ever be consoled by the reflection that Thy wisdom and Thy love are equally infinite, and that our sorrows are not the visitations of Thy wrath, but the result of the great law of harmony by which everything is being conducted to good and perfect issue in the fulness of Thy time.

Let the loss of our brethren increase our affection for those who are yet spared to us, and make us more punctual in the performance of the duties that Friendship, Love and Honor demand. Be with us now, and sanctify the solemnities of this occasion to our hearts, that we may serve Thee in spirit and understanding. And to Thy name shall be ascribed the praise forever. AMEN.

Response—So mote it be.

The Wardens, Deacons and Stewards, will now approach the East and form a procession, thus:

Two Stewards, with rods
Two Wardens, with columns
Deacon,   THE MASTER   Deacon,
with rod   with rod

Which will move once round the catafalque to slow and solemn music.
On arriving at the East, the procession will halt and open to the right and left. The Junior Warden will then advance to the catafalque, and, placing upon it a bunch of white flowers, will say:

Junior Warden—In memory of our departed brethren I deposit these white flowers, emblematical of that pure life to which they have been called, and reminding us that as these children of an hour will droop and fade away, so, too, we shall soon follow those who have gone before us, and inciting us to fill the brief span of our existence that we may leave to our survivors a sweet savor of remembrance.

The Junior Warden will now return to his place, and an interval of profound silence will be observed.
The procession will again be formed, and move as before, to the sound of slow music, around the catafalque.
They will open as before, and the Senior Warden, approaching the catafalque, will place upon it a wreath of white flowers, and say:

Senior Warden—As the sun sets in the West, to close the day and herald the approach of night, so, one by one, we lie down in the darkness of the tomb, to wait in its calm repose for the time when the heavens shall pass away as a scroll, and man, standing in the presence of the Infinite, shall realize the true end of his pilgrimage here below. Let these flowers be to us the symbol of remembrance of all the virtues of our brethren who have preceded us to the silent land, the token of that fraternal alliance which binds us while on earth, and which we hope will finally unite us in heaven.

The Senior Warden returns to his place, and an interval of silence will be observed.
The procession will again be formed, and move around the catafalque to slow music, as before.
Arrived at the East, the Master will advance and place upon the urn a wreath of evergreen, and say

Master—It is appointed unto all men once to die, and after death cometh the resurrection. The dust shall return to the earth, and the spirit unto God Who gave it. In the grave all men are equal; the good deeds, the lofty thoughts, the heroic sacrifices alone survive and bear fruit in the lives of those who strive to emulate them.

While, therefore, nature will have its way, and our tears will fall upon the graves of our brethren, let us be reminded, by the evergreen symbol, of our faith in immortal life, that the dead are but sleeping, and be comforted by the reflection that their memories will not be forgotten. And so, trusting in the infinite love and tender mercy of Him without whose knowledge not even a sparrow falls, let us prepare to meet them where there is no parting, and where, with them, we shall enjoy eternal rest.

The Master will return to his place, and a period of silence will follow.
The Chaplain will now be conducted to the altar, where he will read:

Chaplain—But some man will say: How are the dead raised up? and with what body do they come? Thou fool, that which thou sowest is not quickened except it die. And that which thou sowest, thou sowest not that body that shall be, but bare grain. It may be of wheat or of some other grain, but God giveth it a body as it hath pleased him, and to every seed his own body.

Now this I say, brethren, that flesh and blood cannot inherit the kingdom of God; neither doth corruption inherit incorruption.

Behold, I shew you a mystery: we shall not all sleep, but we shall all be changed; in a moment, in the twinkling of an eye, at the last trump: for the trumpet shall sound, and the dead shall be raised incorruptible, and we shall be changed. For this corruptible must put on incorruption, and this mortal must put on immortality. So when this corruptible shall have put on incorruption, and this mortal shall have put on immortality, then shall be brought to pass the saying that is written, Death is swallowed up in victory. O death, where is thy sting? O grave, where is thy victory?

As the Chaplain pronounces the concluding words, "O grave, where is thy victory?" the lights in the hall will be raised to brilliancy, the four brethren seated around the catafalque will relight their respective tapers.
The Chaplain will return to his place in the East, and the following ode will be sung, to music of a more cheerful character:

MUSIC—*Simons*

Friend after friend departs;
   Who has not lost a friend?
There is no union here of hearts
   That finds not here an end.
Were this frail world our only rest,
Living or dying, none were blest.

There is a world above
   Where parting is unknown—

> A whole eternity of love
> And blessedness alone,
> And faith beholds the dying here
> Translated to that happier sphere.

Master—Brother Orator, it devolves upon you to rehearse before us the story of the dead. Tell us their good deeds, enlarge upon their virtues, kindle within us the spirit of gratitude and respect, so that we may justly mourn for what we have lost, and strive to imitate their virtues. Freemasonry does not sit in judgment upon the departed. There is no Rhadamanthus here to expose every secret error and defect. On the contrary, we are required to throw around their foibles, whatever they may have been, the broad mantle of Masonic charity, and to suffer the apologies of human nature to plead for those who can no longer plead for themselves.

Nevertheless, I charge you, Brother Orator, that you are to speak nothing of these our deceased friends save what is true. Truth is a divine attribute, and the foundation of every virtue. If you cannot truthfully say good things of the dead, let your lips be sealed.

If the memorial services include a number of brethren, an Orator may be selected for each person.

Then follows an ode:

OLD HUNDRED—L.M.

> Once more, O Lord, let grateful praise,
> From every heart to thee ascend;
> Thou art the guardian of our days,
> Our first, our best, and changeless friend.
>
> Hear, now, our parting hymn of praise,
> And bind our hearts in love divine;
> O, may we walk in wisdom's ways,
> And ever feel that we are thine.

CLOSING

Master—Brother Senior Warden, our recollection of our departed friends has been refreshed, and we may now ask ourselves, were they just and perfect Masons, worthy men, unwearied toilers in the vineyard, and possessed of so many vitures as to overcome their faults and shortcomings? Answer these questions, as Masons should answer.

Senior Warden—Man judgeth not of man. He whose infinite and tender mercy passeth all comprehension, Whose goodness endureth forever, has called our brethren hence. Let Him judge.

In ancient Egypt no one could gain admittance to the sacred asylum of the tomb until he had passed under the most solemn judgment before a grave tribunal. Princes and peasants came there to be judged, escorted only by their virtues and their vices. A public accuser recounted the history of their lives, and threw the penetrating light of truth on all their actions. If it were adjudged that the dead man had led an evil life, his memory was condemned in the presence of the nation, and his body was denied the honors of sepulture.

But Masonry has no such tribunal to sit in judgment upon her dead; with her, the good that her sons have done lives after them, and the evil in interred with their bodies. She does require, however, that whatever is said concerning them shall be the truth; and should it ever happen that of a Mason, who dies, nothing good can be truthfully said, she will mournfully and pityingly bury him out of her sight in silence.

Master—Brethren, let us profit by the admonitions of this solemn occasion, lay to heart the truths to which we have listened, and resolve so to walk, that when we lay us down to the last sleep it may be the privilege of the brethren to strew white flowers upon our graves and keep our memories as a pleasant remembrance.

Brother Senior Warden, announce to the brethren that our labors are now concluded, and that this Lodge of Sorrow will be closed.

Senior Warden—Brother Junior Warden, the labors of this Lodge of Sorrow being ended, it will now be closed. Make due announcement to the brethren, and invite them to assist.

Junior Warden—(Calling up the Lodge) Brethren, the labors of this Lodge of Sorrow being ended, it will now be closed.

Master—Let us unite with our Chaplain in an invocation to the Throne of Grace.

*　　*　　*　　*　　*　　*　　*

Master—This Lodge of Sorrow is now closed.

CHAPTER 9

PARLIAMENTARY LAW IN FREEMASONRY

"WHATEVER is best administered is best," may be truly said of all systems or customs governing men in their deliberative assemblies. To manage the business of the Lodge successfully the Master should be, to some extent, posted in the forms and rules of government known as PARLIAMENTARY LAW. By this term we understand those forms originally collected out of English records and precedents for the government of the British legislature, but adapted by Jefferson and others to American use.

So much is said in works upon Parliamentary Law about English precedents and usages, that it is well to bear in mind that the first and original instrument or organic law in which the principle that *the majority shall rule* is recognized, was conceived and adopted in the earliest days of New England. This principle is at the bottom of Masonic government in all its departments, and underlies all that is offered in the present volume.

All societies which are deliberative in their character must have a fixed system of conducting business and set rules for governing their proceedings, or confusion and discord will take the place of harmony. This is exemplified in the contrast between a noisy, disorderly town meeting, and a deliberative assembly, where all words and actions are controlled by written laws, understood and respected by the members. No association of men can meet together for the discussion of any subject, with the slightest probability of coming to a conclusion, unless its debates are regulated by certain and acknowledged rules.

It has been said, with a considerable show of justice, that, as the Worshipful Master of the Lodge, he holds a power for the time almost unlimited, and for which he is not directly responsible to the members who elected him Master. He needs no minute code of laws or parliamentary usage to control his actions. It may be admitted that in many things the Worshipful Master *is* independent of the votes of his own constituents, and does *not* require such a system to direct him as the chairman of an ordinary deliberative assembly would. But this idea of irresponsiblity may be, and sometimes is, carried much too far.

Is the Worshipful Master the sole judge in these matters? Look at his installing engagements, as given on other pages of this volume, and see how "the by-laws of the Lodge were placed in his hands, with injunctions to have them carefully and punctually executed"; how "he promised to sub-

mit to the awards and resolutions of his brethren when in Lodge convened, and to promote the general good of the society." Consider the esoteric
vows of the Past Master, in which he obligated himself "not to govern his
Lodge in a haughty and arbitrary manner."

While there may not be a necessity for the same amount of parliamentary instruction to the Worshipful Master as to the chairman of another
society, yet, in many things, he must pursue a fixed and rigid rule of action if he would make a successful officer.

It is the universal sentiment of ages and experienced Masters that while
in strictness the governing officer has the fixing of the rules of order, etc.,
it is far better for himself and those he governs that such things be *included in the by-laws*, as well for his direction as for theirs. [Putting such rules
in the By-laws would tie the hands of the W.M. This wouldn't be allowed
in many jurisdictions (see By-laws).] And while he undoubtedly has the
right to deviate from them in the *order of business* at his direction, and
even to waive them temporarily upon occasion, he will find his own
burdens lightened and the friendly sentiments of the Craft towards
himself increased by *adherence to them*. For this reason we begin with a
well-prepared "Order of Business" common to thousands of American
Lodges.

There is another reason why a knowledge of parliamentary law is advantageous to the Master: that from his honorable position as head of the
Lodge, he is subject to calls from the public to act as chairman, president,
moderator, etc., in political, ecclesiastical, and other meetings. The object of parliamentary law is to assist a meeting in accomplishing the work
for which it is held, in the best possible manner; and the man who can
best expedite business by preserving order, decency and regularity in a
dignified public body, is sure of his reward—*the respect of those around
him*.

> *Readers interested in the subject of Parliamentary Law, whether for
> Masonic or general practice, will find the subject practically treated in*
> Robert's Rules of Order, Revised. *It is something every Masonic leader
> should study along with the laws of his Grand Lodge.*

As a young and inexperienced Master is often perplexed with the difficult questions sprung upon him in the heat of debate, he will do well to
heed the general rule laid down by a distinguished writer on parliamentary law: "the great purpose of all rules and forms is to *subserve the will of
the Lodge rather than to restrain it;* to facilitate and not to obstruct the
expression of their deliberate sense."

Lodges ought not to elect their *second*-rate men to the East; much less
their *third*-rate, still less their *fourth*. On the contrary, the Gavel-Wielder

should be among the brightest, best-informed, and most intelligent upon the roll of membership. There are Lodges today containing educated persons, professional men, members of the press, Past Masters of experience, whose acting Masters are men who cannot speak five consecutive sentences grammatically.

Lodge meetings, technically styled "Communications," are either Regular or Called. The REGULAR COMMUNICATIONS are such as are established *in the By-laws,* as monthly, semi-monthly or weekly communications; or *by usage,* as the two St. John's days (June 24 and December 27), or *by Grand Lodge regulations.* The CALLED COMMUNICATIONS are such as the W.M. designates to complete unfinished business, or for funeral or other emergent occasions, as may seem to him good. For this he has unlimited power, as explained in other parts of this volume.

As no Lodge meeting can be *adjourned* beyond the day or night in which it is held, but must be regularly *closed* and its record made up, it follows that when the work of a REGULAR COMMUNICATION is unfinished (as for instance, Trials of Offences, Discussions upon Reports, Conferring Degrees, etc.), there may be CALLED MEETINGS. All this is strictly in the prerogative of the Master.

ORDER OF BUSINESS

The following is a well-digested arrangement, equally convenient to the W.M. and the members:

1. Opening the Lodge.
2. Calling the roll of officers.
3. Reading minutes of last regular and special communications.
4. Sickness and distress.
5. Reports on petitions previously referred.
6. Balloting on petitions.
7. Presenting and referring petitions.
8. Reports of committees, regular and special.
   Annual elections of officers.
9. Unfinished business.
10. New business.
11. Work—(conferring degrees).
12. Reading minutes of present communication.
13. Closing.

PARLIAMENTARY RULES

We give, in alphabetical form, a considerable number of decisions upon topics most likely to come up in Lodge practice. The practical application of many of these is seen in the subsequent chapter, where we have given the full history of a Lodge debate of complicated character.

COMMITTEES

The business of the Lodge is expedited and placed in more perfect form by dividing it among committees. These are either *standing* committees or *special*. The former are appointed annually, in accordance with the by-laws; the latter are designated from time to time, to attend to the particular business committed to them. A special committee having performed the business intrusted to it, is discharged by that fact; but the Lodge upon motion may recommit the business to the same committee.

Members of special committees are appointed by the W.M., unless the Lodge, upon motion, otherwise ordains, and the number composing it is three. [In most jurisdictions only the W.M. is empowered to appoint committees. This he *may* choose to do at the request of the Lodge.] The first person named upon the committee usually acts as chairman. In selecting the members of a committee, the majority should be such as are known to favor the proposition under consideration. [Not necessarily. See Committees and Their Duties.]

The majority of the committee must agree upon a report, but the minority may present a counter report, if it so desires.

When a committee is unable to agree upon a report, or cannot complete its labors, it should ask to be discharged, and a new committee appointed. But if, in case of captiousness, or inefficiency, it refuses or neglects to report, the W.M. may discharge it and appoint a new committee.

The chairman of the committee informs the Lodge that the committee, to whom was referred such a subject or paper, is ready to report. The report is then read by the chairman, or more properly from the Secretary's desk, when action may be taken thereon.

The powers and functions of committees depend chiefly upon the general authority and particular instructions given them by the Lodge at the time of their appointment. When no directions are given, a committee may select its own time and place of meeting, and may adjourn from day to day or otherwise, until it has gone through with the business committed to it.

When a committee consists of a large number of persons, a majority of the members is necessary to constitute a quorum for business, unless a larger or smaller number is fixed. A vote taken in committee is as binding [for its report] as a vote of the Lodge itself.

A committee is restricted to the consideration and investigation of the proposition with which it is charged. It has no authority to act upon or participate in other matters. The purpose of its appointment must be closely adhered to, or the object sought to be obtained will fail.

DIVISION OF A QUESTION

A proposition containing more than one part may be divided at the request of a member, or by order of the W.M., who will decide, upon inspection, whether the proposition is susceptible of such division, and if so, into how many and what parts it may be divided. When the matter is thus divided, after the question is taken on one part the remaining parts are successively open to amendment and debate.

The W.M. will know that a question is divisible when its respective parts are so entire and distinct that if one or more of them are taken away, the others will stand entire and by themselves.

MOTIONS

Every member of the Lodge has the equal privilege to make and second motions, rising to his feet for that purpose, and addressing the East in Masonic manner. [A "second" is not allowed in many jurisdictions; the W.M., by accepting the motion, in theory, seconds it.] If required by any member, a motion must be *in writing*, and read aloud by the Secretary. The W.M. may find it convenient to read motions before they are handed to the Secretary, that, if necessary, he may pronounce them out of order, and so suppress them. For this the mover has no redress, as there can be no appeal from the W.M.'s decision. If, however, the ruling of the W.M. should be arbitrary and unreasonable, an appeal may be taken to the Grand Master, who would justly set the decision of the W.M. aside, and action would be had upon the motion.

QUORUM

The quorum for the meeting of a Lodge is set by order of Grand Lodge. It is usually seven Master Masons, together with the Tyler, making, in all, eight; but in some jurisdictions three, five, or seven, according to the degree.

A Lodge to be capable of doing work and transacting business must be just, perfect and regular. A "perfect" Lodge is understood to be one that consists of the requisite number of brethren, and the ordinary usage demands seven exclusive of the Tyler.

RECONSIDERATION OF A QUESTION

A motion to reconsider a question which has been adopted, must be made by one who voted with the successful party, and at the same meeting at which it was adopted.

There may be questions where the majority are not the successful party. Thus, on a motion to amend the by-laws, where a two-thirds or three-forths vote is required, a majority of the members may vote for the amendment and yet there may not be enough to make the requisite majority of two-thirds or three-forths. Here the minority are evidently the successful party, and a motion for reconsideration must be made by one of them. It is always the successful side that must make the motion.

The motion for reconsideration can only be made in reference to matters that remain within the control of the meeting.

A motion for reconsideration is debatable, even though the question proposed to be reconsidered is not. The motion for reconsideration may be postponed definitely or indefintely, or laid upon the table. [Nothing can be "laid upon the table" in many jurisdictions. The proposition may be postponed, however, to a definite date.] If the motion to reconsider is adopted, it places the original proposition in precisely the position it occupied before its adoption. No motion can be twice reconsidered.

RECONSIDERATION OF AN UNFAVORABLE BALLOT

A motion for the reconsideration of an unfavorable ballot, on a candidate, after the result of the ballot has been announced, would be at all times out or order, and the presiding officer would not, therefore, be justified in entertaining a motion for such a purpose. This apparent contradiction to the ordinary operations of parliamentary law is due to the peculiarly sacred and binding force of the secret ballot.

REFERRING TO COMMITTEES

When motions are made to refer a pending question to more than one committee (as to the Committee on Charity, a special committee, etc.), the question must be taken in the order in which the motions were made. [The wise W.M. will refer questions to the committee of *his* choice, or none at all.]

Subsidiary Questions are motions intended to change the character of a proposition by adding to it, taking from it, or essentially modifying its purpose. There are, in general, seven of these, as generally accepted in parliamentary bodies, and they take their place in the order here stated. Supposing a motion before a deliberative assembly for any purpose, its opponents may prevent or delay its adoption thus:

1. By moving to adjourn; or,
2. A motion to lay on the table; or,
3. By moving the previous question; or,
4. By moving to postpone to a day certain; or,
5. By moving to refer the question to a committee; or,
6. By moving to amend; or,
7. By moving to postpone indefinitely.

We will consider these subsidiary questions in their order.

1. *Moving to adjourn*—This is not admissible in the business of a subordinate lodge. We have pointed out, as one of the prerogatives of the W.M., the right to close the Lodge at his discretion. (See arguments at the proper place.)

A motion to adjourn is frequently, by Masonic parliamentarians, pronounced inadmissible even in the Grand Lodge, yet it is the common practice to accept and adopt a motion to adjourn, and no one finds fault with it.

2. *A motion to lay on the table [if permitted in your jurisdiction.]*—This is admissible but not debatable. The Master puts it at once to the Lodge, and, if carried, the matter, for the time, is disposed of. But the subject may be taken up at any future time, whenever it may suit the convenience of the Lodge.

The proper motion for proceeding with a matter that has been ordered to lay on the table, is that: "*Resolved*, That the Lodge do now proceed to consider that matter;" or that "The subject named be now taken .up for consideration." If agreed to, the business, with all its amendments and train of procedures, comes up again exactly in the position it occupied when laid upon the table. If the motion to lay on the table is not agreed to by the Lodge, such motion cannot be renewed until after some other business, or some new matter, or some alteration of the question, shall have been introduced. A motion to lay on the table, if adopted, may be reconsidered.

3. *Moving the previous question*—This motion is not admissible in a Masonic Lodge. Yet in some Grand Lodges the previous question is in use. If this is to be tolerated or admitted in a Masonic body, it must be only in the *Grand Lodge*, that being purely a deliberative assemblage.

If the friend of a measure in Grand Lodge desires to bring the question to an immediate decision, he *moves the previous question*. This motion is not debatable. The Grand Master at once rises and inquires, "Shall the main question be now put?" If the Grand Lodge vote affirmatively, the Grand Master proceeds to put the question, successively upon the amendments, if any have been introduced, and then upon the measure itself. No question save that of adjournment can be interposed, until the final vote is had upon the business.

Any motion that has been introduced during the debate may be withdrawn after the previous question is ordered, provided it has been amended, or in any other way taken out of the control of the mover.

If the Lodge decides that the main question shall *not* be put, the business goes on as though no such motion had been entertained.

4. *Moving to postpone to a day certain*—The forth plan to delay action upon the business before the Lodge is to move to postpone to a day certain. This motion takes precedence of a motion to commit (No. 5), to amend (No. 6), and to postpone indefinitely (No. 7). This motion is debatable within small limits, the merits of the subject matter not being considered here. It is further limited in Masonic matters, as "the day certain" must fall on some regular communication of the Lodge, unless by order of the Master, a call of the Lodge is made to consider the unfinished business.

It is said in manuals of Parliamentary Law, that "business taken up on postponement has precedence over all other business for every part of the day, until disposed of." But this does not apply to Lodge matters, where business for the most part is regulated by RULES OF ORDER, and the postponed business can only come in at its proper place. The effect of the motion, if adopted, is to postpone the whole subject to the time specified, but the motion itself may be amended as all other motions.

5. *By moving to refer the motion to a committee [if the W.M. agrees to accept the motion].*—When the subject matter of a question is regarded with favor, but the form in which it is introduced is so defective that a more careful and deliberate consideration is necessary than can conveniently be given to it in the Lodge itself, the proper motion is made to refer it to a committee—either one of the regular committees of the Lodge (as "Charity," "Library," "Complaints," etc.), or a special committee appointed for the purpose.

If the matter has already been considered by a committee, the motion may be to *recommit*, either to the same or a new committee. Or the number of the members of the committee may be increased or reduced; or it may be accompanied by instructions to the committee to introduce some particular amendment. If this latter motion be carried in the affirmative, the main question, and everything pertaining thereto, is placed in the hands of the committee, who will report according to the directions given. In all other cases the committee may make such report as it judges best.

6. *By moving to amend the motion*—When a proposition is before the Lodge it is competent for any member *to propose an amendment* thereto, which amendment takes precedence over the original motion.

When an amendment has been moved and seconded, the W.M. should always state the question distinctly, so that everyone may know exactly what is before them, reading first the paragraph which it is proposed to amend, then the words to be struck out, if there be any; next, the words to be inserted, if any; and finally, the paragraph as it will stand if the amendment is adopted.

Any member who has spoken to the main question may speak to the amendment.

It is also in order to amend an amendment, but such amendment cannot be amended beyond the second degree. That is to say: if an amendment is moved, an amendment to that amendment is admissible, but nothing beyond in that direction. If the amendment to the amendment is agreed to, it becomes a part of the amendment first moved, and the last named is then susceptible of a new attempt to amend; and so, if the amendment to the amendment is negatived. And this process may be repeated, unless the will of the assembly intervenes by the previous question, or in some other way.

Amendments come in the order they are moved, unless the subject be considered by sections.

An amendment assumes the form of a substitute when it becomes a new proposition, though relating to the subject under consideration.

To summarize: "An amendment may be made to a proposition by either of five methods:

First—By adding to the proposition.

Second—By striking out something from the proposition.

Third—By striking out certain words and inserting others.

Fourth—By substituting a different motion on the same subject.

Fifth—By dividing the question into two or more questions, as specified by the mover, so as to get a separate vote on any particular point or points.

7. *By moving to postpone indefinitely*—This motion, for all practical purposes, is equivalent to rejection. "A question indefinitely postponed cannot be acted upon again," says a parliamentarian of renown. "Its effect," says another writer, "is to entirely remove the question before the Lodge for that meeting." It cannot be amended, but opens to debate the entire question which it is proposed to postpone.

In relation to the above question, we think that the fair Masonic way to settle any question presented by a fellow member of the Lodge is *to take a square vote upon it.* All the tricky and roundabout methods justified in political assemblies, such as indefinite postponement and the like, are strangely out of place in the Masonic Lodge. As all debates among Masons are aimed *to elicit truth* and give effect to the will of the Lodge, the strictest courtesy is demanded among the members; furthermore, as those ungracious methods of stifling debate called the *previous question* and *adjournment* are admittedly unmasonic, the W.M. may well use his friendly influence, if not his power, to require a real vote of the Lodge upon a question that has been lawfully introduced, properly debated, and fairly presented to his fellow members upon its merits.

Dr. Mackey elegantly observes here, that "no means of stifling debate and silencing the voice of the minority, such as are so frequently resorted to by parliamentary strategists, are admissible in the Lodge. The discourtesy which such motions exhibit on the part of the majority, and their evident object to prevent inquiry, make them entirely antagonistic to the benignant principles of the Masonic Institution."

Furthermore, in the great number of questions that spring up during the discussion of any important proposition, harmony and brotherly feeling must be maintained at every cost. This is the first consideration with the W.M. No mere parliamentary victory in the Lodge will compensate a Mason for wounding the feelings of a brother. No speaking can be allowed in the Lodge unless a motion is regularly before it (made and seconded), or the speaker is prepared to make one, and it is always better that the motion be *first read and seconded* before he speaks in any way in its advocacy. Nothing is so wearisome and unfruitful in Lodge business as "making remarks" without a target, yet nothing is more common. Perhaps there is no better characterization of a good W.M. than that "he makes no desultory remarks."

WITHDRAWAL OF A MOTION—The mover of a motion may withdraw it (by consent of his second) if the Lodge permits, but not after it has been acted upon affirmatively or negatively by the Lodge. A motion being withdrawn, the matter stands as though it had never been presented to the Lodge.

FULL REPORT OF A LODGE DEBATE

We proceed to show every movement in opposition or advocacy of a proposed measure. In this report we design to make the whole subject of Parliamentary Law practical and easy of application to the W.M.

Tuscan Lodge, No. 587, having some funds in the treasury, and there being a crying need of a more commodious and secure Lodge room than the one in use, *undertakes to build one.* A small but influential minority opposes the measure. There is much difference of opinion also, as to the locality. It is finally carried after a discussion which continued from meeting to meeting for several months, and in which the various obstacles of parliamentary law are brought to bear in opposition. We give the various stages of the proceedings *by numbers*, for convenience of reference, and give some convenient explanations. It is proper for us to add that names and dates are fictitious.

1. At the regular communcation of April, 1883, under the head "New Business" Brother A sends to the Secretary, in writing, a resolution to the effect that the Lodge proceed to the erection of a Masonic hall. It is duly seconded by Brother B.

Brothers A and B being the movers of the resolution, should be prepared to take the lead in the advocacy of the measure, until it is fully adopted or lost. All important proposals of business on which the Lodge is expected to act should be *in writing*. It is the prerogative of any member to demand this. An experienced Secretary will *always* demand it, and the W.M. will require it.

2. The Secretary hands the resolution to the W.M., who peruses it, returns it to the Secretary, and orders it read to the Lodge.

It is incumbent on the W.M. that nothing shall be introduced into the Lodge that infringes upon the landmarks. He is responsible to the Grand Lodge for this, and his personal reputation as an intelligent and conscientious officer depends upon it.

3. The resolution is in the following form:
"*Resolved*, That Tuscan Lodge, No. 587, do proceed to the erection of a suitable hall in an eligible part of the village of LaGrange."

We have given this in the briefest form. It is better, however, to begin with a preamble reciting the necessity of the proposed measure, thus: "*Whereas*, the hall in which we are now meeting is small, insecure, and poorly adapted to the workings of the Lodge; and, *Whereas*, the prospective increase of our membership and the condition of our finances justify us in meeting the demand for a commodious, attractive, and secure place of assembly. Therefore, *Resolved*," etc., etc.

4. Brother C moves to amend by substituting the word "Brentford" in place of "LaGrange." Seconded by Brother D.

For several years there has been a difference of opinion in Tuscan Lodge, as to the *best location* for the hall, and permission has already been given by the Grand Master to remove the Lodge to Brentford, three miles distant, provided a majority of the members favor it. Hence motion No. 4. Brothers C and D are known to be the strongest advocates for the removal of the Lodge to Brentford.

5. Brother E moves to lay the resolution (No. 3) and amendment upon the table. Seconded by Brother F. [We are assuming a motion to "table" is permissible and "seconds" are required.]

Brother E is opposed to going into the measure of building, lest the Lodge incur undue indebtedness. He favors renting a hall temporarily.

The form of the motion is simply, "I move to lay the question upon the table." The effect of such a motion is to postpone the subject in such a way that at any time after it can be taken up, either at the same or a future meeting. This cannot be accomplished by a motion *to postpone*, either definitely or indefinitely. To order a question *laid upon the table* carries everything with it in the way of amendments. For instance, if the motion of Brother E (No. 5) is adopted, it will carry the motion of Brother C (No. 4) with it, and, in fact, remove the whole business from the consideration of the Lodge.

6. Brother E commences to advocate his motion (No. 5), but is forbidden by the W.M., and seated by the ordinary signal, one knock from the gavel.

A "motion to lay upon the table" is not debatable, and the W.M. was bound to forbid Brother E from advocating his proposition in the way proposed.

7. Upon the question, "Shall the resolution be laid upon the table?" 13 vote *aye,* 21 vote *no.* The W.M. declares the motion lost, and the question then recurs upon Brother C's amendment (No. 4).

The proportion 13 to 21 does not necessarily show the sentiment of the members. Some are in favor of the resolution of Brother A (No. 3), but opposed to acting on it *at this time.* Some do not understand the effect of "laying on the table." In fact, these technical terms of parliamentary usage are "puzzles to many members," and rarely understood by the mass. Had motion No. 5 been carried, it would have been in the power of Brother A to renew his resolution (No. 1), by moving that "the Lodge do now proceed to consider it." But, in general, when a matter is ordered *to lay on the table* it is not considered prudent in its advocates to attempt to revive it at the same communication.

8. Brother G moves to postpone action upon the resolution (No. 3) until the next regular communication of the Lodge. This motion is carried.

This places the business upon the record to come up at the May communication, under the head of "Unfinished Business." The Secretary will take care that the business is inserted in the *Agenda Paper,* to be laid before the W.M. It would perhaps have been more systematic had Brother G moved to refer it to a committee with instructions to report at the next communication.

9. At the May communication, the night being stormy, only twelve members are present, and the W.M., by virtue of his prerogative, orders that resolution (No.3) *be passed over* for that occasion, to come up at the June communication. He instructs the Secretary further, to issue a notification to the members to that effect, that all may attend.

This should always be done in the management of important questions, like the one now before Tuscan Lodge. The notification may be made through the Tyler, or by a written or printed notice mailed to each member, or in the advertising columns of the local press, according to the custom of Tuscan Lodge. But no W.M. has the power to issue a *summons* for such a purpose, save by special order of the Lodge.

10. At the June communication the attendance is large, and the contending forces, as between LaGrange and Brentford, come fully armed for the contest. Considerable feeling is manifested; both parties are in favor of building a hall, but they are radically divided *as to location.* In the *Order of Business,* at "Unfinished Business," the W.M. announces the question before them. He reads from the by-laws of Tuscan Lodge the regulation that "no brother shall speak the second time upon any question until every other brother has spoken who desires to do so, nor shall any speech be extended over five minutes without special permission of the Lodge." He warns the Lodge kindly and dispassionately, that "all debate

must be conducted with respect to the East and fraternal regard to opponents," and that all observations must be directed to the subject matter. The Secretary then reads the resolution (No. 3) offered by Brother A, and the proposed amendment (No. 4) by Brother C, and the W.M. declares that "the question is on the amendment."

It is well, in a complicated matter like this, for the W.M. to remind the Lodge from time to time, *what is the immediate business before them.* Too much attention cannot be given to this. In the intricacies of Masonic trials, etc., the members particularly need constant reminders of this sort, that they may vote understandingly.

11. Brother E moves to lay the whole matter upon the table.

This is a repetition of his course at the April meeting, and is designed as a feeler. The motion is at once put and negatived 8 to 26 (See Nos. 5, 6 and 7). It is evident by this that the members are disposed to proceed with the business. No debate can be permitted upon the question to lay on the table.

12. Brother G moves the previous question.

This is for the purpose of securing a decision on the resolution of Brother A (No. 1) without further debate. But as the previous question is not admissible in a Masonic Lodge, the W.M. promptly pronounces it "out of order."

Dr. Mackey says that he never knew the previous question to be put in a Masonic Lodge. But it is *often attempted,* and the W.M. should be well fortified against so insidious a method of stifling debate. The object of the motion, as already stated, is to dispose at once of the pending question, permitting no further consideration of it by the Lodge. Benj. B. French, an old Mason and a bright parliamentarian, long Clerk of the National House of Representatives, declares that "Masonry cannot endure the previous question, and no Lodge may tolerate it." We have seen its evils sufficiently in Grand Lodges to be warned against a method well termed "the tyrant's trick to silence the minority."

13. Brother G takes an appeal from the decision of the W.M.

This is not so much intended as a rebuke or fault-finding of the W.M. under the impression that his ruling (No. 12) is unparliamentary. The

W.M. pronounces the appeal of order, and warns the brethren not to make further motions infringing upon the law of Masonry and the Landmarks of the Order. He explains to the Lodge the distinction between ordinary deliberative assemblies and the Masonic Lodge. A decided but fraternal spirit marks this piece of instruction.

The W.M. should be earnest to learn *the minds* of his brethren, and in all things where Landmarks and great Masonic principles are not infringed, be anxious to defer to it. No Master need fear the loss of dignity and respect by giving way, in ordinary cases, to the evident sentiment of the Lodge. All his personal interests lie in giving content to his fellow members. Peace and harmony rest at the basis of Masonic history. The arbitrary power entrusted to the W.M. is only to preserve the Landmarks from popular inroads.

14. Brother H moves to postpone action upon the resolutions until the regular communication of May, 1888.

In other words, he would stifle the whole business by delaying action for *four years*. The W.M. pronounced this motion obstructive and out of order, and refused to entertain it. He is justified in this upon the theory of his prerogative and duties, stated earlier in this volume.

15. Brother H moves to postpone action until the regular communication of July next.

It is not necessary to repeat, in every instance, that "the motion was duly seconded." This is always understood, and the W.M. will never put a question until assured that it has a second, [if it is required].

Upon the motion of Brother H (No. 15), the motion is put by the W.M. as follows: "The question is, Shall the business before us be postponed till the next regular communication of the Lodge? As many as are in favor of the motion, say *aye*. Those of contrary opinion, say *no*." The count is made by the Senior Deacon, and announced to the W.M. who declares, "The motion is *lost* (or *carried*)," as the case may be.

In many Lodges the order is: "So many as are in favor of the motion, raise your hands." In other Lodges the sense of the brethren is shown by rising to the feet. Either of these two methods is better than the first, especially where precision is demanded, or where the vote is likely to be close. The voting by *ayes* and *noes* is sometimes vitiated by the most reprehensible habit of visitors and non-members joining in the vote. Upon the whole, the method of voting *by rising to the feet* is preferable in a discussion like this.

An experienced Mason says, upon the manner of voting, "This depends upon the subject on which the vote is to be taken. In elections of officers, ballots are used, which are slips of paper on which the voter writes his preference; and in elections of candidates, white and black balls (or black cubes) are used. On all other questions the vote should be taken by the ancient custom of the fraternity for the members to express their opinions by each one holding up *one of his hands,* which uplifted hands the Senior Deacon shall count unless the number of hands be so unequal as to render the counting unnecessary."

There is a peculiarity in Masonic work (copied by modern affiliations, but originally Masonic), that of voting upon delicate questions by ballot. While the sense of the Lodge may be gathered upon ordinary questions by *viva voce* vote, or uplifitng the hand, or rising, yet in matters of discipline, as well as in the reception of candidates, etc., the more secret method prevails.

Upon the motion of Brother H (No. 15), the vote is lost—6 to 28. This implies that the members purpose to continue the consideration of the business in hand.

16. Brother H moves that the Lodge now adjourn.

Every other measure to delay action upon the business in hand having failed, there is but one more obstructive course that occurs to the mind of the brother: to *adjourn the Lodge.* This being unmasonic and out of order, the W.M. refuses to entertain it. He gives a rebuke to Brother H from the chair, and, repeats his injunction against the brethren consuming the time of the Lodge by merely obstructive motions.

17. The resolution of Brother A (No. 3) being again read, the W.M. announces that the amendment by Brother C (No. 4) is in order: to substitute "Brentford" for "LaGrange."

18. Brother K moves to amend the resolution of Brother A by substituting, after the words "suitable hall," the words "Afton Springs."

"Afton Springs" is at a medium point between LaGrange and Brentford.

19. Brother L presents a paper in advocacy of proposition No. 18. No objections being offered, the paper is sent to the Secretary and read. It contains proposals from neighbors in the vicinity of Afton Springs to aid in the erection of a Masonic Hall, provided that location is selected, and offers various reasons for preferring that place to others.

20. Brother A asks leave to withdraw his resolution (No. 3). Brother L objects.

After a question has been stated by the W.M., the mover can neither withdraw nor modify it, if anyone objects, except by obtaining leave from the Lodge. A learned parliamentarian puts it in this form: "When a motion is regularly before the Lodge, and the mover wishes to withdraw or modify it, or substitute a different motion in its place, if no one objects, the presiding officer may grant the permission; but, if an objection is made, it will be necessary to obtain leave to withdraw, etc., on a motion for that purpose. This motion cannot be debated or amended. Permission to withdraw a motion may be made at any state of the proceedings before the final vote is declared, by a motion, and, if adopted or granted, it removes the proposition as if it had never been made. The withdrawal of a motion, as above referred to, is not intended to apply to petitions for initiation, which in most of Masonic jurisdictions cannot be withdrawn after having been presented to a Lodge and referred to a committee. A motion for the withdrawal of such a proposition would be out of order.

21. The W.M. puts the quesiton, "Shall Brother A have leave to withdraw his motion?" Negatived.

To grant permission to withdraw is equivalent to a complete quashing of the affair. There would then be *nothing before the Lodge.* It is plain that the members are in favor of a Lodge hall, and are not disposed to lose the time already expended in discussing the questions.

22. The W.M. informs the Lodge that the question is on the amendment of Brother K (No. 18), to substitute the place "Afton Springs."

No time should be lost between the various stages of business, but the moment a decision is made on one point, the W.M. should state the question next under consideration.

23. Brother M moves that the whole subject be referred to a committee.

A debate follows, in which various subjects are discussed as to Who shall appoint the committee? Of what number shall the committee consist? When shall the committee report? etc. The motion of Brother M then takes this shape:
"*Resolved,* That the resolution to erect a Masonic hall, together with the amendments, be referred to a committee of five, to be appointed by

the W.M., the W.M. to be chairman; report to be made at the regular communication of October next." Carried. [The W.M. is actually the head of all committees, so he doesn't have to appoint himself chairman. The decision to refer a question to a committee is the Master's alone.]

As Lodge matters languish during the summer months, it is well to remove this important business over to October. As the W.M. is an experienced and disinterested man, not a resident of either of the three contending localities, it is well to make him chairman of the committee. In selecting the other four members he will look for brethren indifferent as to locality, Masons of age and standing, past officers of the Lodge.

24. At the October communication a large gathering of the members is present. At the proper time, according to the rules of order ("No. 6, Reports of Committees"), the W.M. announces the business, and orders the Secretary to read the majority report of the committee. It is signed by four of the members. It endorses the resolution of Brother A (No. 3), literally. A minority report is also offered to the effect "That it is inexpedient for Tuscan Lodge to engage in the erection of a Masonic hall at the present time." On motion, the reports are received, and the committee discharged.

25. Brother E moves the adoption of the minority report. Negatived; it has only five advocates.

This implies that the members favor, as before, a Lodge building at the present time, though they may differ in details of shape, cost, and locality.

In regard to minority reports in general, they are not recognized as reports of the committee, or acted on as such. They are received only by *courtesy*, and allowed to accompany the report as representing the opinions of the minority. Instead of the method suggested in No. 25, the motion of Brother E should have come in *as an amendment* to the report, and so considered. But the contrary custom in American Grand Lodges has become so fixed that we place it here.

26. Brother A moves the adoption of the majority report. The W.M. announces: "The question is on the adoption of the majority report."

27. The W.M. now selects an experienced Past Master to preside, and vacates the East. [It should be a rare case, indeed, when the W.M. vacates his station. He should remain in his position to control all debate.

It is he, and he alone, to whom the Grand Lodge looks for the conduct of his Lodge. This is another reason he should not appoint himself chairman or a member of any committee.]

This is done for two reasons: *First,* As the W.M. is chairman of the committee, he may be required to advocate or otherwise explain the adoption of his report; and, *Secondly,* There is an indelicacy in his acting as W.M. while the report made by himself is under discussion. The reader may think he should not have consented to serve as chairman of the committee at all. In general this is correct. But it is a matter of which he is the best judge. In the interests of peace and harmony the W.M. will sometimes assume a paternal relation toward the Lodge which would be absurd in a presiding officer of another society.

28. Brother C moves to amend the motion of Brother A (No. 26), and recommit the report to the committee with instructions to report "Brentford" in place of "LaGrange" (No. 4). Whereupon a debate ensues, and various motions follow, which the reader should examine carefully.

29. Brother G moves the previous question (as in No. 13).

The presiding officer pronounces this motion *out of order,* and admininsters a reprimand to Brother G. He shows his misconduct in this, that after the various warnings and instructions given in regard to obstructive and unmasonic motions, he should persist in making one. Brother G expresses his regret at the occurrence, and promises hereafter to keep within the rules of order, to the best of his knowledge.

The presiding officer may, of his own motion, order a recusant brother to retire from the room, who persists in violating the decorum of the Lodge by unmasonic motions or any other method of delaying the proceedings. This code of parliamentary practice affords an abundance of methods for retarding hasty actions upon propositions without resorting to unmasonic methods.

30. Brother L asks that the paper which he presented at the June communication (No. 19) be again read for information. The presiding officer decides that "As the paper has already been once read, and does not directly refer to the pending motion, it constitutes no part of the proceedings, and need not be read at this time unless the Lodge so order."

This was right. The paper alluded to was an argument for the erection of the hall at "Afton Springs," while the question before the Lodge (No.

26) is of a different nature. Had Brother L made *a motion* to have the paper read, the Lodge would have said by vote whether or not they wished to hear it.

31. Brother H moves to amend the motion before the Lodge by postponing further action until the regular November communication. Negatived.

This implies that the Lodge is resolved to pursue the business to some conclusion *at the present meeting,* and will not postpone it.

32. Brother N moves to divide the report into two parts: *first,* the proposition to erect a Masonic hall, *second,* the location. Agreed to.

This is done to expedite the business, and is a laudable act. It is plain that the Lodge is determined to erect an edifice somewhere, and the one question upon which the members seem divided is *the location.*

33. The presiding officer again announces the question, "to recommit the report to the committee with instructions to insert 'Brentford' in place of 'LaGrange' " (No. 26). Negative.

The question of location is now narrowed by the dropping of "Brentford." The Lodge has shown they will have none of Brentford. The presiding officer announces "The question is on the adoption of the majority report," and orders it read by the Secretary (No. 24).

34. Brother A moves as an amendment, that the first part of the report be considered as a separate question: "That Tuscan Lodge, No. 587, do proceed to the erection of a suitable hall," etc. Agreed to. Now the question as stated by the presiding officer is, "Shall a suitable hall be built in an eligible part of LaGrange?"

35. Brother K moves to amend the resolution by inserting "Afton Springs" in place of "LaGrange," and asks for the reading of the paper presented (No. 19) by Brother L. This is granted because, although the paper was read at the June communicaiton, yet as it presents arguments in advocacy of Afton Springs, it is pertinent to the matter in hand. Upon the motion to insert, "Afton Springs," the Lodge votes *no.*

It is an ordinary practice and a good one, by persons unskilled in public speaking, to write out or have others write out the arguments they would offer. The Lodge will always regard such requests as that in No. 35 with favor.

36. Brother O moves to amend the resolution by inserting "Johnsonville."

As there is a Lodge already at work in Johnsonville, the presiding officer rules the motion *out of order*, and again cautions the brethren against making motions merely dilatory and thus contrary to Masonic law.

37. Brother P moves to amend the resolution by inserting "Bennet's School House." Defeated.

38. Brother Q moves to amend the resolution by inserting "Lorrens' Cross Roads." Negatived. This closes the propositions, and the presiding officer, after inquiring if any further amendments are offered, prepares to put the question, "Shall the second part of the report be adopted?" If necessary he states the question to be, "*Resolved.* That a Masonic hall shall be erected in an eligible place in LaGrange." Agreed to. Then he presents the whole report as in No. 24, thus: "As many as are of opinion that the report of the committee be adopted, say *Aye.*". . . "As many as are of a different opinion, say *No.*" The report is adopted.

These thirty-eight paragraphs give in sufficient detail the parliamentary management of the case. The circumstances of cost, size and form of hall, exact locality, etc., form subjects for future discussion. But as the Lodge has now fairly committed itself to the main question, and launched forth upon the work of erection, and it is the duty of the minority fraternally to come into the views of the majority, it may be presumed that by submitting the various matters to skilful committees, a harmonious work will be accomplished, and by the 27th of December succeeding the corner-stone may be laid, and by the 24th of June succeeding the new hall dedicated, according to the directions given in the appropriate chapters of this volume.

The reader will not accept the foregoing "full report of a Masonic debate" applicable to town meetings, church meetings, etc., without considering the peculiar nature of Freemasonry. Dr. Mackey properly suggests "that Masonry has an organization peculiar to itself. Wherever it comes in conflict with that of other associations, the parliamentary law will not be applicable. Where, on the contrary, it agrees with other deliberative assemblies, the rules of order are the same." A thoughtful Mason, familiar with the Landmarks and laws of his Grand Lodge will not materially err.

CHAPTER 10

MASONIC DISCIPLINE

THERE are no subjects that can be presented for the consideration of the Worshipful Master more interesting, more important, and, we may add, more difficult than this. The very definitions of the word "Discipline" (*rules of government; subjection to laws; correction; chastisement*), suggest the difficulty of application. The theory of Masonic initiation is that an applicant is already "a good man and true"; "worthy and well qualified"; chosen by strict ballot from the mass of mankind; a believer in a written and inspired law of God; no blasphemer; no thief; charitable; affectionate. As such he is not supposed to need the pressure of harsh and strict discipline, like others. Court houses, judges, jails, scaffolds, are not for good Masons, nor do codes of Masonic law have any attraction of repulsion for them.

Yet discipline is a thing that every Lodge should understand, and with its application every W.M. should be familiar. Masons, however, "good men and true," have their weaknesses. Under the excitement of passion they are sometimes violent, and trespass against the laws that govern the Craft. Then they must submit to discipline, as they promised to do while yet candidates in the preparation-room they solemnly declared upon their honor, in the presence of Masonic witnesses, that "they would cheerfully conform to all the ancient established usages and customs of the Fraternity." This declaration is the foundation of Masonic discipline exercised by the Lodge over those who have voluntarily come under its laws.

In the covenants of the second and third degrees the pledge of obedience is made impressive, the candidate being obligated "to stand to and abide by the laws, rules, and regulations of the Lodge." He learns, upon inquiry, the Holy Scriptures, the Ancient Constitutions, and the Lodge by-laws are the sources from which he may certainly derive the whole body of Masonic law and he discovers the character of the penalties due to the recreant Mason who wilfully and persistently violates it.

The first question for consideration, then, is, "What are those offences which demand Masonic discipline?"

WHAT ARE MASONIC OFFENCES?

The range of misconduct known as "Masonic offences," is broad. In the *Proceedings* of various American Grand Lodges since 1800 or thereabouts, the following are generally recognized as the greater offences: assault, blasphemy, contumacy, disobedience, gambling, homicide, intoxication, libertinism, murder, perjury, robbery, Sabbath-breaking, secret-breaking, slander, theft. Minor offences are reckoned as including non-payment of dues, neglect of social and domestic duties, etc.; but the greater include the less. Some Grand Lodges have sententiously expressed the subject in this form: "A Masonic offence is an act which contravenes: 1. The constitutional rules and edicts of the Grand Lodge, or the by-laws of the Lodge having jurisdiction; 2. The unwritten laws of Masonry; 3. The laws of the land; 4. The laws of God." This is an excellent summary, and recognizes the definition of the word "offence" in the English dictionary: *Any transgression of laws divine or human; a crime; a sin; act of wickedness, or omission of duty.*

From the by-laws of the Lodge of Antiquity, London, England, the oldest Masonic organization in the world, we take this quaint synopsis of unmasonic practices:

> "If any brother swear, or say anything irreligious, obscene or ludicrous, hold private committees, dispute about religion or politics, offer to lay wagers, or to sell, give away, or show any tickets or shop bills, interrupt another brother while speaking to the Master, or hiss at about what has been said, be not on his legs when addressing the Master, sit down unclothed, sup or smoke in the Lodge room, be disguised in liquor during Lodge hours—such offending brother shall be immediately fined, by a private ballot, for each offence, any sum a majority of the members then present shall think proper—not under one shilling (twenty-five cents) nor above five shillings—which fine or fines, if such brother refuse to pay, he shall be immediately expelled, and never again be admitted into the Lodge as a member or visitor, until he shall have made proper submission in open Lodge, and paid the said fine or fines, exclusive of a new admission fee, should he apply to be reinstated, which shall all be terminated by ballot, according to the by-laws."
>
> [Today he would have charges preferred against him, then stand trial for un-Masonic conduct.]

WHO SHALL BE THE ACCUSER?

Any member of the Lodge. A non-affiliate, or a non-Mason having no standing in the Lodge, cannot act as the prosecutor. Information coming from such may be received, and serve as the foundation of charges, but the charges themselves must be brought *by a member.* The Masonic writer, Rob Morris, as early as 1846, was the first to suggest the *Junior Warden* should be the official accuser, in which suggestion he was followed in 1855 by the distinguished Masonic jurist, A.G. Mackey. This theory has been since adopted by many persons who, with more or less skill, have written upon Masonic jurisprudence. It is said of the Junior Warden: "he superintends the Craft during the hours of refreshment (that is, during the intervals between the Lodge communications), and sees that they do not convert the purpose of refreshments into intemperance and excess." Reading this symbolical language by the esoteric key, it suggests plainly enough that the Junior Warden is the supervisor of morals, and if supervisor, then certainly the accuser of such of his brethren as may violate the "law of Masonry," and so subject themselves to discipline.

The above theory is confirmed in Simons' excellent *Principles of Masonic Jurisprudence:* "The first step in a Masonic trial is the presentation of charges, which must be done in open Lodge, at a regular communication, by a brother in good standing (usually the Junior Warden), non-affiliated Masons, and profanes not being competent to prefer charges."

WHAT IS THE FORM OF THE ACCUSATION?

The accusation (officially termed the *charges* or *complaint*) must invariably be in writing and signed by the prosecutor. A general and flexible form of charges is the following:

"To the W.M., Wardens, and Brethren of _____ Lodge, No. _____:

"This undersigned, Junior Warden of the Lodge, in pursuance of his duty, defined in Chapter _____, Section _____ of the By-laws, does hereby charge against Brother _____ _____, a member of this Lodge, the following unmasonic conduct, viz:
First _____
Second _____
Third _____, etc.

"And the undersigned, as the official prosecutor, prays that the honor and dignity of the Craft may be vindicated by the exercise of Masonic discipline upon the aforesaid offender, or that his innocence may be brought to light and endorsed by the Lodge.
                    (Signed),   _____ _____, *Junior Warden.*
    (Date)

If the accusation is brought by any other than the Junior Warden, the wording may be made to correspond. If the accused is a non-affiliate Mason, or member of another Lodge residing within the jurisdiction, the verbiage is changed to show it.

The charges having been read to the Lodge by the Secretary, a motion is made by the prosecutor to receive them. If lost, the subject is dropped, and the accusation falls to the ground. In such case, if the offence is notorious, and the scandal open and large, any member may appeal to the Grand Master, stating the circumstances of the scandal, and the refusal to the Lodge to bring the offender to trial, and the Grand Master will promptly take the case in hand, ordering the Lodge to proceed to the examination of the case, or upon refusal, suspending the functions of the Lodge until the Grand Lodge can investigate the matter. It is a part of the darker side of Masonic history that Masons, wielding large influence, have violated the laws of Masonry in matters of licentiousness, physical violence, profanity, etc., and the Lodge, actuated either by fear or favor, has refused to bring them to trial. For the credit of the Masonic Fraternity, it must be hoped that such instances are not common.

On the other hand, the chronicles of the Order show that in some Lodges an opposite feeling has prevailed. Charges based upon the most frivolous pretexts have been presented, received, submitted to trial, and the peace and harmony of the Lodge thereby disturbed and even destroyed. Extremists in religious and temperance enterprises have endangered the very existence of Masonry by pressing their sectarian and one-sided views upon the Lodge. But the W.M. will be wise to draw the line between extremes. "True charity is long-suffering and kind, and seeks to exhaust the influences of brotherly love before resorting to sterner proceedings." The duty of every brother to warn his fellow of approaching danger is of the same class as the duty to whisper good counsel in his ear, remind him of his faults, and endeavor to aid his reformation. On the other hand, there are offences so open and scandalous that there is no room for warning or counsel. The limb must be *amputated*, for it is *past cure.*

The defendant will enter his plea of guilty or not guilty, before further proceedings.

HOW SHALL THE EVIDENCE BE TAKEN?

[Laws have been established in many jurisdictions providing for trial commissions. These are composed of Past Masters of Lodges not connected with the one involved. The mechanics follow, in many respects, what was outlined by Robert Macoy in 1885.]

The Lodge having decided to try the charges, the question arises, In what manner shall they proceed to secure the evidence? To do this *in open Lodge*, is, of course, impracticable; the fact that the witnesses are not necessarily Masons, is sufficient to show that. A committee of some sort is needed, but whether it shall be a standing committee, as in some jurisdictions, or a special committee appointed for the purpose, is a question for the Lodge to decide. The latter is preferable. In some jurisdictions this committee is termed a *Commission,* but this is only another name for the same thing. The sole object of the committee is to elicit the truth, without curtailment, coloring, or exaggeration. The committee is in no sense *a jury,* nor does the performance of this function affect their right to vote *as a jury* when the question comes before the Lodge for decision. It may also be said here that the sole object of a Masonic trial is *to arrive at the truth,* so that the guilty may be punished, the innocent acquitted, and the honor of Masonry vindicated before the public.

It must be carefully borne in mind that the accused has in no manner lost his standing in the Lodge by the fact that he is under charges. No matter what the accusation may be, he is to be considered innocent until judicially pronounced guilty and the grade of punishment affixed by the Lodge. It is only at the close of the trial, and just previous to taking the question upon his case, that he is ordered to retire from the Lodge.

As all Lodge committees are appointed by the W.M., so with this, and he will particularly designate the chairman. The committee may consist of any (uneven) number, but, in general, *three* will suffice. In selecting them the W.M. will exercise careful thought and discretion. Men of age and Masonic experience are suggested—Past Masters, if convenient; men who will give time and patient consideration to the case; men not connected by ties of relationship and business with the accused; men who are not known to be unfriendly to the accused; men of moral standing. Every Lodge affords a choice more or less close to this standard.

The Secretary of the Lodge is the proper clerk to attend all meetings of the committee and report the proceedings and the evidence. If he cannot attend, the committee will appoint a substitute. Bear in mind that the appeal cases before Grand Lodges, that occupy so much time, and lead often to such confusion and injustice, grow out, for the most part, of the neglect of Secretaries to record the evidence properly. The Lodge may always take it for granted that *an appeal to the Grand Lodge will be taken.* Upon this theory everything should be conducted according to rule. In any question of doubt or uncertainty the chairman may inquire, "Will the Grand Lodge sustain us in this, on appeal?"

The committe being appointed and the chairman designated, the time and place of the first meeting are set and the defendant notified. The *place* best appointed is, for various reasons, the Masonic hall. The *time* must be set far enough in advance to insure that the defendant shall have opportunity to secure counsel (if desired) and be in attendance. Any affiliated Master Mason may serve as counsel, and the defendant need not attend the committee in person if he prefers to be represented by proxy; but it is better that he attend the meetings. If the defendant is absent he is notified by mail. If he has absconded, the trial should nevertheless proceed, the W.M. appointing a brother to defend him and to cross-examine witnesses, and see not only that justice is done him, but done *judicially*, according to Masonic law. The committee also is privileged to engage counsel, if deemed necessary. The *time* and *place* being set, the committee, acting upon the written charges presented them by the prosecutor, send notifications to the witnesses, for which they have plenary powers. The defendant may also present a list of witnesses to be called upon his part, and these should be equally notified. Should the trial demand more than one meeting of the committee, which is highly probable, the chairman of the committee must report progress to the Lodge at each regular communication. Under no circumstances may any portion of the proceedings of the committee be made public until the final decision of the case.

> It should be remembered that the world at large has no right to know that a brother is under trial; and the W.M. should caution the brethren to this effect, and take such other steps to prevent public scandal as truth, honor and justice may require—H.B. GRANT.

If the witnesses are Masons, they are required under their Masonic obligations to attend the trial, and true answers to make to all questions pertinent to the case. Failure in these will subject them to severe penalties. But if the answers tend to criminate the witness, he may be excused from making reply.

Witnesses who are not Masons are under no compulsion to wait upon the committee or respond to their questions, and many an offender fails to receive merited punishment on this account. Testimony [by non-Masons] should be given under the sanction of a judicial oath or affirmation, being first reduced to writing and signed by the attestants.

The committee having exhausted the evidence presented, it is held, in some jurisidictions, that "the accused shall have permission to take evidence in his own behalf, at such time and place as *he* may select, upon giving reasonable notice to the W.M. of the Lodge." However, the *place* must be an accessible one, and the *time* near at hand, and convenient to the committee, and the evidence must be regularly attested as in the case of the other, or this privilege may be forfeited. There cannot be many instances where justice demands so irregular a course.

HOW SHALL THE CASE BE DECIDED?

The W.M. will see the propriety of bringing the decision before a regular (not called) communication of the Lodge, even though the by-laws may be silent upon the subject. Nor will it be deemed an undue extension of prerogative if he orders the Secretary to notify the members to attend, as upon emergency.

The regular proceedings of the Lodge being had, and the subject of unfinished business approached, the report is called for and read by the Secretary. This includes all evidence taken, *pro* and *con*. It brings the question to the point of guilt or innocence. Yet it is in order, both for the prosecution and defence, to present their views, strengthening or softening the character of the evidence by judicious remarks. The defendant has full liberty, restrained only by the law of courtesy, to speak of himself, his previous character, etc., avoiding charges against other brethren, the accuser, the witnesses, or the committee. His counsel will be granted the same privilege, being kept by the gavel of the W.M. strictly under the law of decorum. The debate being closed, the defendant is ordered to retire, but his counsel may remain.

Now the W.M. puts the question, "Is Brother _____ _____ guilty of unmasonic conduct as stated in the charges?" The decision is had through the ballot-box, white balls expressing *innocence,* black balls (or cubes) *guilt.* The W.M. will carefully explain this before passing the box, lest the method may mislead the minds of the voters. Every member of the Lodge is bound to vote, unless specially excused by order of the Lodge.

The ballot-box having returned to the hand of the W.M., he instructs the Senior Deacon to count the number of voters. He himself counts the ballots, to see that the numbers correspond. He then announces the number of black balls, and of white balls. If the former exceed the latter by a certain proportion, the decision is "guilty." That proportion in the majority of jurisdictions is two-thirds; in some, four-fifths; in some, three-fourths, etc. In general this matter is settled in the by-laws, or is made the subject of a constitutional provision by the Grand Lodge.

It is scarcely necessary to say that the trial must be had in the highest degree of the Lodge attained by the defendant, for otherwise he could not enter the Lodge at all.

Should the number of white balls exceed the others, or the majority of black balls fall below the proportion necessary to convict, the W.M. announces the fact, the record of *not guilty* is entered, the defendant is invited to return, and the trial is closed.

But, on the other hand, if the decision of the Lodge sustains the guilt of the accused, the record of *guilty* is entered, and the W.M. announces the second quesiton, "Shall Brother _____ _____ be expelled?" This is decided precisely as the first question. If the result is in the negative, and he is

not to be expelled, the third question at once follows, "Shall Brother
_____ _____ be reprimanded?" This question may be deemed
superfluous, as the accused has been pronounced "guilty" and *some*
discipline is necessary, if only as a warning to offenders. But for form's
sake the fourth question is always put, and if, as is possible, this too is
answered in the negative, the W.M. will do well to communicate the fact
to the Grand Master, and ask his official *dictum* upon this question, "the
Lodge has declared that the member is guilty, but refuses to inflict a
penalty."

If the third question is decided in the affirmative, viz: that the accused
shall be *suspended,* the W.M. states the next question as to the *time,* commencing with twelve months, or some period more protracted. If he
prefers it, he may order each brother to write upon a slip of paper *a time
of suspension,* and so gather the sentiments of the Lodge.

From the moment the decision is announced the accused is virtually
dead to Masonry, and the case is closed.

Should the Lodge decide to inflict only a reprimand, the accused is
ordered to return to the Lodge at once, and receive it. The reprimand is
administered by the W.M., or by some brother deputed by him for the
purpose, and done in a manner which conveys a clear idea of the offence,
thus reprehended, and at the same time holds out in full measure pardon
and love to the erring, repentant brother.

A member refusing to come forward and receive the reprimand ordered
by the Lodge is liable to summary expulsion for *contumacy.* This offence
is technically understood to be the refusal to obey a due summons from
the Lodge or Grand Lodge, and subjects the offender to condign punishment.

There is no principle more frequently or more strongly enforced in the
Masonic code than *obedience,* and the sin diametrically opposed to that is
contumacy; for if a Mason will not obey a *due summons,* there is nothing
for it but to expel him from a society whose fundamental principle he has
so shockingly violated.

It happens not unfrequently, that the accused pleads *quilty* upon *the
accusation,* that is, upon the presentation of the charges. Or he may plead
quilty before the committee ere the evidence is complete, or before the
Lodge when the case is up for trial. In either of these cases the Lodge may,
by vote, pardon him, or proceed with the questions, "Shall Brother
_____ _____ be expelled," etc., in due order as before. But it is held,
that after he has been ordered to retire from the Lodge preparatory to
voting, and a ballot has been taken, his proxy cannot enter a plea of *quilty,* but the matter must take its due course.

In regard to offences in general, where the guilt proven is in direct violation of Masonic vows, as against a Mason, or a Lodge, or the female relative of a Mason, the case is an aggravated one, and the penalty more severe than in others.

On the other hand—in cases of intemperance, profanity,etc.—if it is proven that such faults have been allowed to go unchecked among the members, and that the defendant was never counseled or warned, or his reformation sought, as the covenants of Freemasonry require, there may be a mitigation of the penalty, especially if the offener is young in Masonry and inexperienced. A frank and speedy acknowledgment of the fault will usually soften the punishment; a solemn pledge of reformation goes to the heart of every member.

It is well to bear in mind while considering this question of Masonic discipline, that the duties and privileges of Freemasonry do exactly balance each other. DE WITT CLINTON, a name as famous in Freemasonry as in statesmanship, wrote as early as 1793, the following synopsis of Masonic duties:

> A Mason is bound to consult the happiness and promote the interests of his brother; to avoid everything offensive to his feelings; to abstain from reproach, censure, and unjust suspicions; to warn him of the machination of his enemies; to advise him of his errors; to advance the reputation and welfare of his family; to protect the chastity of his house; to defend his life, his property, and, what is dearer to the man of honor, his *character* against unjust attacks; to relieve his wants and his distress; to instil into his mind proper ideas of conduct in the department of life which he is called to fill; and, let me add, to foster his schemes of interest and promotion, if compatible with the paramount duties a man owes to the community.

We think the grand platform of Masonic action has never been better described by another.

It has been a mooted question among Masonic authorities whether charges can be twice brought against a brother for one offence, of which, upon the first trial, he was acquitted. The burden of opinion is that where large and important additions have been made to the evidence criminating the accused, he *may be subject to a second trial*. But the W.M. will always have his Grand Master to counsel with when rare questions of this class arise.

Nothing can deprive the defendant of his right of appeal to the Grand Lodge, and, as before intimated, the committee and the Lodge should act all the time with the shadow of an appeal impending, and shape their course accordingly. The appeal must be in writing, and addressed in respectful terms to the W.M. In some jurisdictions the time within which an appeal may be taken is specified. This should be understood in every case. Upon reception of this demand from the accused, the W.M. will order the Secretary to copy the full record of the Lodge proceedings in the case from the commencement, also the records of the committee and the evidence taken, so far as these things may lawfully be committed to writing. These papers, duly authenticated by the Secretary under the Lodge seal, must be promptly forwarded to the Grand Secretary in time to be reviewed by the Committee on Complaints and Appeals of the Grand Lodge, at its next communication.

We repeat that the penalities of expulsion, suspension and reprimand begin their effect *immediately upon the decision of the Lodge,* and are in no wise affected by the demand of the accused for an appeal. If the penalty is only a reprimand, he must come forward at once and receive it, or be subject to the *penalty of expulsion* for contumacy (disobedience).

The term for which the accused has been condemned to suspension having expired, he regains his membership without action of the Lodge. [Not so in most jurisdictions now. The man expelled or suspended must pass a unanimous ballot to be restored to the rights and benefits of Freemasonry, and to membership in the Lodge.] Should the Grand Lodge pronounce the trial irregular and order a new trial, he is placed upon his former footing, *but under charges,* and subject to the same round of discipline as before. If the Grand Lodge simply restores him to Masonry, he becomes a non-affiliated Mason, and may solicit membership as any other Mason in that condition. [If reversed by the Grand Lodge, he remains a member of the Lodge.]

No brother can be demitted from the Lodge while under charges, and the W.M. is justified in postponing action upon an application for a demit if he believes there are reports out prejudicial to the character of the applicant, until such reports are inquired into. [Under the trial commission system, the Lodge has nothing to do with the determination of guilt or innocence. The trial commission makes this decision. If the defendant is found quilty, the commission sets the penalty. Both the defendant and the Lodge have the right to appeal the verdict to the Grand Lodge. This appeal must be taken during a period established by the Grand Lodge.]

TRIAL OF AN OFFENDER

In an endeavor to give you a clear idea of Masonic justice at work, we will follow a Masonic trial from beginning to end. Where a trial commission conducts the trial, substitute it for what takes place here in the Lodge.

One of two things must exist in a community: a crippled, disgraced Lodge, or the rigid enforcement of Masonic discipline. The *former* no true Mason can consent to. A society so ancient, so broad-spread, so honorable as the Masonic, must and shall be maintained intact. The latter, therefore, is the only conclusion.

This is an unpleasant subject for discussion—a theme altogether disagreeable to the writer. Many topics are delightful. The dissemination of true light; the evidences that God's favor is and has been with us from remote times; tales of Masonic attachment; the poetry of Freemasonry; instances of fidelity to the Craft; the progress of the great Order around the globe—all these are topics pleasant to discuss, pleasant to peruse. But the method of ejecting unworthy material, the denouncing, the casting out of the excrements of Masonic digestion—nothing can be more unpleasant to one who loves and respects the institution.

To draw the flawy and unworthy stone from the wall in which it ought never to have been laid, and to cast it back to its proper place among the rubbish, is, of all duties, the most disagreeable; and this discussion is done only as a matter of duty.

THE FORM OF COMPLAINT

In preparing the charges the Junior Warden or brother should introduce nothing save what he expects to sustain. The charges should exactly cover the alleged misconduct. In civil and criminal courts it is customary to frame the complaint at great length, and often with a great number of allegations and specifications. This is highly improper in Masonic trials, and if the Junior Warden or brother extends the charges in this manner we may presuppose personal malice on his part. *Let the complaint correspond with the offence,* and nothing more.

We now give a correct form of complaint. The reader will understand that all names of persons and places, etc., here introduced are fictitious.

The undersigned, Junior Warden (or member in good standing) of Robert Burns Lodge, No. 84, Allerton, Nevada, in the performance of his official duties, specified in Part VI, Chapter 8, of the Constitutional Regulations of the Grand Lodge of Nevada, and in Chapter IV., paragraph 3, of the By-laws of this Lodge, CHARGES Brother Henry Larrabee, a Master Mason and member of this Lodge, with UNMASONIC CONDUCT, according to the following specifications, to wit:

First—Uttering abusive language to and concerning Brother Thomas L. Freeman, a Master Mason and member of this Lodge, on the 5th day of March, 188-, in the village of New London, Nevada.

Second—With striking the aforesaid Brother Thomas L. Freeman, at the time and place named in the first specification.

And the undersigned, as the official prosecutor of the Lodge, prays that the honor and dignity of Freemasonry may be vindicated by the due exercise of Masonic discipline upon the aforesaid brother, Henry Larrabee.

(Signed)   LABAN CARROLL,

April 12, 188-   Junior Warden.

As this is the first paper which would be examined by the Committee of Grand Lodge in event of appeal, great care should be taken that in matters of names, dates, and essential facts, the strictest accuracy is observed. Sometimes the whole proceedings of a Masonic trial, conducted at much expenditure of time, toil, and money, are pronounced void by Grand Lodge, not because injustice has been done the accused, but because the proceedings are had without regard to regularity of form. Injustice *seems* to have been done because the record of the trial is imperfect.

If, instead of the Junior Warden, the prosecution is conducted by a *Committee*, the verbiage is varied accordingly. If the accused is an Entered Apprentice or Fellow Craft (instead of Master Mason), the form of charges must show it. Suitable variations must be made where the accused is a non-affiliating Mason or a member of another Lodge. On the other hand, if the aggrieved party is a member of some other Lodge, the charges must show it. A non-alliliating Mason, while he is as much subject to Masonic discipline as any other Mason, has no claim upon the Lodge for redress, no mater what the aggravation may be. This seems unjust, but the injustice grows out of the choice of the party himself. To save a few dollars per annum he has volunatrily placed himself in a condition awkward indeed, and possibly embarrasing, but for which he will thank no one but himself.

Having given one form of "Charges" as presented by the Junior Warden, we offer a number of variations. It is understood that the same caption is pursued in each, so far as the words "following specifications, to wit:"

1. Uttering blasphemous expressions in the village of New London, Nevada, on the 5th day of March last.
2. Uniting with a mob to release a prisoner from the hands of the sheriff at New London, Nevada.
3. Uttering expressions of contempt and defiance of the laws of the land.

4. Violating the solemnity of the Sabbath day.

5. Stealing the property of Joseph Summerson, to wit, one horse.

6. Uttering falsehood to Brother Charles Mothen, relative to the value of one ox team, sold by him to the said Mothen.

7. Uttering falsehoods to Mr. William Wyman, relative to the title of a horse sold by him to said Wyman.

8. Contumacy, in refusing to obey a lawful summons issued by Robert Burns Lodge, No. 84, and served by Brother Aaron Badger, Tyler of said Lodge.

9. Uttering slanderous, abusive and insulting expressions against Robert Burns Lodge, No. 84; against Worshipful Brother Richard Pyles, Master; against Brother Aaron Badger, Tyler of the same Lodge; and against the Masonic Order in general, its principles and practices, and especially its treatment of him, the said Brother Henry Larrabee.

10. Violating the secrecy of the ballot-box, in exposing his ballot upon the application of George Handy, for initiation; in informing Brother Charles Smith, a member of this Lodge, that he cast a black ball upon the petition of George Handy, as aforesaid; in declaring in open Lodge that he had blackballed George Handy, as aforesaid, and would continue to do so upon any future attempt of him (the said George Handy) to enter this Lodge.

11. Committing adultery with Mrs. Adele Bruner.

12. Committing homicide, in shooting to death Mr. Daniel Acton.

13. Wronging Robert Burns Lodge, No. 84, by retaining the funds collected by him as Secretary of this Lodge, and failure to pay them over promptly into the hands of the Treasurer, according to the requisitions of our by-laws.

14. Wronging Robert Burns Lodge, No. 84, by retaining the funds received as Treasurer of the Lodge (and receipted for) by him from the hands of the Secretary, and failing to pay them out by order of the Worshipful Master, with the consent of the Lodge.

15. Repudiating his Masonic covenants openly, and in a most unmasonic manner, before a crowd of hearers.

16. Stabbing Mr. Francis Duval in the heat of political excitement, and while under the influence of alcoholic drink.

17. Being intoxicated.

18. Departing in a clandestine manner from his home, leaving debts unpaid and various engagements unfulfilled, and to the scandal of the Masonic Order.
19. Conversing upon the secret matters of Freemasonry with Mr. James Hodges, a non-Mason.
20. Wronging Robert Burns Lodge, No. 84, by retaining in his hands certain moneys (about $30), intrusted to him as committee of the Lodge, to pay the Grand Lodge dues.
21. Wronging Robert Burns Lodge, No. 84, by withholding and failing to pay over, according to the by-laws of this Lodge (Chapter II., Paragraph 1) the amount of his annual dues.

In these twenty-one formulas we have not attempted to embrace *every possible form of offence*, but those most likely to occur in the workings of an active Lodge. Some of them would not be likely to happen within the lifetime of the reader; some may occur quite frequently. The same general form of charges will suit them all, with such variations in detail as will suggest themselves to the mind of the Junior Warden, or the brother who may prefer the charges. They are each and all "unmasonic acts," no more or less, and are to be presented accordingly. It is not in the option of the brother preferring the charges to characterize any of them as "grossly unmasonic," for that is the function of the Lodge after the verdict of "guilty" has been rendered. A few definite rules may be added for the inexperienced:

1. All evidence taken must have a direct bearing upon the offences charged.
2. Only one brother can be tried in the same indictment.
3. The accused must be allowed every reasonable opportunity to secure counter testimony, to cross-examine the witnesses, to challenge irrelevant testimony, and all prejudicial remarks by the committee.
4. If an appeal is demanded it cannot be refused, but the Lodge must forward to the Grand Secretary of the Grand Lodge full and authenticated copies of all papers, from the "charges" to the record of judgment and penalty.
5. Everything should be conducted from the beginning under the expectation than *an appeal will be taken*, and therefore the records must be lucid and full, and the proceedings of a character to stand the most rigid investigation.

6. All evidence that is proper to be written must be reduced to writing, signed by the witness, and laid up in the archives of the Lodge for preservation.

7. Charges can only be brought against a brother at a *regular communication* of the Lodge, though the trial in all its stages may be conducted at called meetings, due and timely notice being given the members and the accused.

8. All summonses must be issued by order of the Lodge, authenticated by the sign manual of the Secretary and the Lodge seal.

9. If the witnesses are Masons they are regularly summoned, and a refusal to obey will be deemed an act of contumacy for which the highest penalty of Masonry may be inflicted.

THE PROCEEDINGS

The Lodge having by vote decided to take up the case, and the Committee of Investigation having been appointed, summonses for witnesses (if Masons) are sent out in this form:

HALL OF ROBERT BURNS LODGE, NO. 84
Allerton, Nevada, 29th April, 188-.

BROTHER JAMES AINSWORTH:
By order of Robert Burns Lodge, No. 84, you are hereby summoned to attend the Committee of Investigation in the case of the said Lodge against Brother Henry Larrabee, charged with the offence of _____. To meet at the Masonic Hall, at 10 A.M. on Saturday, the 3d of May, 188-.

(Signed), FRANCIS FALES, *Secretary*
(Seal)

If the witness is not a Mason, the citation may be varied;

HALL OF ROBERT BURNS LODGE, NO. 84
Allerton, Nevada, 29th April, 188-.

MR. JAMES AINSWORTH:
By order of Robert Burns Lodge, No. 84., you are hereby requested to attend the Committee of Investigation in the case of the said Lodge, against Brother Henry Larrabee, charged with the offence of _____.

To meet at the Masonic Hall, at 10 A.M. on Saturday, the 3d of May, 188-

                    (Signed),   FRANCIS FALES, *Secretary.*
(Seal)

The hour having arrived, the chairman calls the meeting to order, none being present save the committee and Secretary and Junior Warden.

The Secretary of the Lodge being present, or the Secretary selected by the committee, the order of the Lodge appointing the Committee of Investigation is read and filed. The charges are read and filed, all papers being lettered A, B, C, D, etc., in the order of their introduction. A list of witnesses is read and filed. The accused is invited in, together with his counsel, if he has selected any. The committee invites their own counsel in, if any other than the Junior Warden has been chosen. No persons are allowed present at any stage of the proceedings save as above, and the witnesses one at a time. It is the grossest of errors in a Lodge trial to permit the crowd to attend upon the investigation. Should the accused not appear, either in person or by proxy, the fact is entered upon the journal of the proceedings, and some brother, not of the committee, is invited in to represent him. The chairman should earnestly admonish the committee that they have assembled on a matter of grave importance, and that all remarks of a violent and irrelevant character are interdicted. No insinuations, as against the prosecutor or the accused should be tolerated. The strictest attention must be given to the proceedings by all concerned.

Questions to witnesses are propounded by the chairman, aided, it may be, by the other members of the committee and the Junior Warden. Both questions and replies must be reduced to writing. After the witness has been examined on the part of the Lodge, he (or she) may be cross-examined by the accused or his counsel. This cross-examination being ended, further questions may be asked, and these also subjected to cross-examination until the knowledge of the witness is exhausted.

We have avoided the question whether witnesses should be *sworn* before deposing, because such different rules prevail in the various jurisdictions. Our preference is that an officer authorized to take depositions shall be in waiting in the ante-room, to administer the customary oath to each witness as he enters, and to witness his signature to the evidence as he departs. It is held, however, by good authority, that witnesses *who are Masons,* are already sufficiently bound in the terms of the obligation, and need offer no further security of good faith.

Should questions arise upon the bearing and propriety of testimony, the witness will retire during the discussion. All such questions are to be disposed of by the majority of the committee. Protests by the accused or his counsel against any part of the proceedings are to be entered upon the record and form a portion of the history of the case.

The opening of the record by the Secretary may be in manner and form like this:

HALL OF ROBERT BURNS LODGE, NO. 84,
Allerton, Nebraska, 3d May, 188-

The Committee of Investigation appointed by the Lodge to take evidence in the case of Robert Burns Lodge, No. 84, *vs.* Brother Henry Larrabee, charged with unmasonic conduct, assembled at 10 A.M.

Present:—Brother Amos Morris, *Chairman,*
  ''   Thomas Mostyn,
  ''   Hiram A. Hunter
  ''   Francis Fales, *Secretary,*
     Of Robert Burns Lodge, No. 84

The chairman called the committee to order, and announced the business upon which it had assembled.

The record of the Lodge appointing the committee was read, marked A, and ordered to be filed.

The charges preferred against Brother Larrabee by the Junior Warden (or Brother _____), and accepted by the Lodge, were read, marked B, and ordered to be filed.

The accused brother was invited in, together with his counsel, Brother James Lingman, a Master Mason and member of this Lodge.

The list of witnesses was read, and it was found that the following were in attendance: ____, ____, ____. A copy of the summons served upon each Masonic witness was marked C, and ordered to be filed. The Tyler's report upon summoning the various witnesses was read, marked D, and ordered to be filed.

The above is merely designed to show the minuteness essential to a record when prepared upon the theory that *an appeal will be taken.* At each session of the committee the caption should be as full as the form above given, naming the persons present, etc.

As specimens of the style of testimony taken in certain trials that have come under our knowledge, we give the following. It will be seen the charges were two-fold: 1st. For slanderous expressions to a Master Mason;

2nd. For striking a Master Mason. One witness, Caleb Wright, deposed as follows:

Brother Caleb Wright, a Master Mason and member of Robert Burns Lodge, No. 84, testifies and declares, upon his honor as a Master Mason:

Question—Did you hear Brother Henry Larrabee employ abusive language towards Brother Thomas L. Freeman, in the village of New London, on the 5th day of March last?

Answer—I did.

Question—What was the language? State the circumstances, and give the exact words, as nearly as possible.

Answer—I cannot recall the exact order in which the words were used, but the words themselves are deeply impressed upon my memory. Brother Larrabee distinctly called Brother Freeman a d_____d rascal, a sneak, and a spy. He said that Freeman had told the Lodge things that he (Larrabee) never did; that he had sneaked around and listened to catch up his (Larrabee's) words, so as to degrade him in the Lodge; that he had never once warned him of his errors, as a Mason should; that he was a hollow-hearted pretender of Masonry, a hypocrite, and ignorant of the first principles of the Order. He kept on repeating these words until quite a crowd had gathered round. I tried several times to stop him by whispering good counsel in his ear, and other Masons present did the same, but this had no effect. At last the constable came up, and told him to shut up or he would arrest him; then I took my horse and came home.

Question—Do you know anything about the striking of Brother Freeman by Brother Larrabee?

Answer—Only from hearsay. I have been told _____ (Here the counsel of the accused interposed and protested against hearsay evidene being introduced. In this he was sustained by the chairman).

Question—At what time of day was the abusive language employed to which you have testified?

Answer—About two o'clock in the afternoon.

No cross-examination was made.

The foregoing having been read in the hearing of Brother Caleb Wright, he signed it and retired. (It was *not* the custom, in that jurisdiction, to put a witness, who was a Master Mason, *to his oath*.) [Tape recorders usually take the place of reporters, so the signing of testimony is not necessary.]

A second witness was Brother Andew Leigh, who also testified upon his honor as a Master Mason, and replied to questions as follows:

Question—Did you see Brother Henry Larrabee strike Brother Thomas L. Freeman?

Answer—I did.

Question—State the circumstances.

Answer—About three o'clock in the afternoon of March 5 I was in attendance at the Magistrate's Court, in New London, when Brother Freeman approached me to ask a question in reference to some business of his in my hands. We stepped outside the magistrate's office, where we found Brother Larrabee, who instantly began a tirade of abusive and insulting words against Brother Freeman. Being constable, and having heard enough from him on that subject an hour before, I arrested him, and was conducting him before the magistrate to make complaint, when he broke from me, and, before I was aware of his purpose, rushed upon Brother Freeman and struck him violently in the face. I seized him at once, and placed him in the magistrate's keeping. When I returned to Brother Freeman he was sitting on the ground, with the blood running from his mouth and nose.

Question—What reply did Brother Freeman make to the abusive expressions which you describe?

Answer—Only that the charges were not true, and that if he (Brother Larrabee) was sober he would never make such statements. These remarks were made in a pacific and friendly manner.

Question—What is Brother Freeman's calling in life?

(Question objected to by defense. Objection overruled.)

Answer—He is a minister of the gospel and a school teacher.

Question—What is his condition of health?

(Question objected to. Objection overruled.)

Answer—He is a very feeble man in health, and has been sick much of the year.

Question—Do you know the cause of the ill-feeling between Brothers Larrabee and Freeman?

(Question objected to. Vote taken by the committee on the objection, and objection sustained.)

The witness was now cross-examined.

Question—Did not Brother Freeman come that day armed, and with a threatened purpose to do violence to Brother Larrabee?

Answer—The only arms of which I know anything was a cane. I am not aware of any threats made, or of any purpose that Brother Freeman had to do violence.

Question—Describe the heavy bludgeon that Brother Freeman was armed with.

Answer—It was a hickory staff, loaded at the top and bottom with lead.

Question—Is this the deadly weapon that you saw in Brother Freeman's hands that day?

Answer—It is.

(The cross-examination being ended, the prosecution continued.)

Question—Is Brother Freeman not in the habit of carrying that heavy cane as a support? Has he not white swelling in one of his knees, and is he not necessitated to use a heavy cane or crutch?

(This form of questions was objected to as being too much of the nature of leading questions. Objection not sustained by the committee. Notice given that an appeal will be taken to the Grand Lodge on this point. The chairman remarked, that as the eliciting of truth is the sole business of the committee, and the defense has unrestrained privilege of cross-examination, the mere form of question is unimportant. But to avoid future complications, he suggests to the prosecution the presentation of the question in a simpler form. The prosecution assented, withdrew the question last above stated, and substituted the following:)

Question—State what you know about Brother Freeman's carrying a cane, and the reason why he does so.

Answer—Brother Freeman suffers from white swelling in his right knee. For some time he walked with crutches. Latterly he gets along with a cane, made very strong and heavy.

Question—What is the character of Brother Freeman, in relation to assaults and public offences?

Answer—I have known him from boyhood, and have never heard of his engaging in any acts of violence.

Cross-examination waived, and witness allowed to retire again after signing and certifying to the evidence as read before him.

The following form of report of the committee to the Lodge is appropriate:

To the Worshipful Master, Wardens and Brethren of
Robert Burns Lodge, No. 84

The undersigned committee, appointed to take evidence in the case of Brother Henry Larrabee, charged with unmasonic conduct in slandering and striking Brother Thomas L. Freeman, met at the Masonic Hall on the ____ day of ____, 188-, and organized. By regular adjournment we met again on the ____ day of ____, when we concluded the work which had been assigned to us. Neither from Brother Larrabee nor his counsel did we receive any intimation that he wished for further meetings on this subject.

Of the witnesses regularly summoned to appear before us, all responded and were present, save Brother Asa Jenkins, a member of this Lodge, and Mr. George Barnard, a non-Mason.

The full record of the committee's proceedings is herewith presented to the Lodge, the testimony of the various witnesses and the proper papers being regularly labeled, A, B, C, D, etc., to correspond with the entries in the record.

The committee ask to be discharged from further duty in the premises.

(Signed),   ____ ____, *Chairman.*

____ ____,

(Date)   ____ ____,

It has already been observed that a partial report of the committee's proceedings must be made *at each regular communication of the Lodge,* until the full report is offered. At the presentation of the partial report the question comes up in one of these forms:

1. "Moved that the committee be given further time;" or,

2. "Moved that the report be received, and the committee discharged; " or,

3. "Moved that further proceedings in relation to the charges against Brother Larrabee be discontinued."

The ordinary motion would be that marked "No. 1." In case the committee cannot further serve owing to sickness, etc., or in case the committee asks to be excused from further consideration of the subject, for any reason satisfactory to themselves, the motion marked "No. 2" would be appropriate. In case the defendant has acknowledged his guilt, and thrown himself upon the charity of the Lodge for forgiveness, etc., motion marked "No. 3" may properly be made.

We proceed to view this trial under another form. Suppose the accused, Larrabee, refused to appear before the committee either in person or by proxy, and thus defies the authority of the Lodge represented by the committee; there are two methods of procedure open to the committee: (1) To make up the record of the opening meeting as above, and so close their report, in which case the Lodge may order Larrabee tried for contumacy, and then make short work of his expulsion. Or (2), Proceed with the trial in the absence of Larrabee, by appointing some experienced brother as his counsel. It should be borne in mind, that as the Lodge has plenary powers over an erring brother, and may, at short notice, expell him, patience and brotherly charity must not be spared. Do not permit a rash and impetuous brother to commit Masonic suicide through obstinacy and wrong counsel.

Give him time for consideration. Let him be visited by the elder members, and calmly counseled. He may be saved to the Craft and to himself. It is only the obstinate and determined sinner, whom no covenant binds, that the rigor of Masonic law should reach. In this very case of Larrabee's (under assumed names, of course), the power of mercy was strongly exemplified; for, after traversing the evidence by cross-examination, and threats of appeal, he came meekly before the Lodge at last, acknowledged his fault, asked the pardon of the injured Brother Freeman, and cheerfully accepted the penalty (suspension for twelve months) pronounced by the Lodge. Nay, so much was he affected by the peril into which the habit of intoxication had led him, that he made thorough reform, lived for a number of years in the fellowship of church and Lodge, was Master of his Lodge thrice, and died under good report. So much for the forgiving spirit which actuated the proceedings of the Lodge, and the brotherly counsels by which he was pursued and turned into the right path.

In the trial of a delicate case, one in which moral character is involved, it is sometimes best *to close the doors* against all save the members of the Lodge. In one instance, where a very exciting question had run for several months through the Lodge, the affair actually *got into the papers* through the indiscretion of a reporter, and involved an expensive law suit.

To give out friendly notices that "this is a family conference and visitors will not be admitted," can offend no one, and may preserve the Order from damaging remarks. The principle of curiosity, more or less prurient, which will call Masons, affiliated and non-affiliated, for miles around to attend a Lodge trial, is not one that the W.M. is particularly called upon to respect; and he may be confident that the Grand Master will sustain him in his desire to suppress and keep Masonic affairs under the cloak of secrecy. [Another advantage of a Trial Commission is the secrecy of all trials. The more men involved, the greater is the problem of information being spread to unathorized sources.]

The following rules are appropriately set here:

1. The W.M. is as strongly bound to answer the summons of the committee to give testimony, for or against the accused, as any other member.

2. All summonses must be served by the regular Tyler of the Lodge, or by some one regularly appointed by the W.M. to perform that function. In the latter case the substitute must have all the papers duly certified, as though he were Tyler.

3. It is well to furnish the Tyler with two copies of each summons, one to serve upon the brother whose name is therein given, the other to return, properly indorsed, to the Secretary. But if only one copy is made, that must be read to the summoned party, exhibited to him if desired, but returned to the Secretary, as above. The Tyler's indorsement may be in this form:

> Served upon Brother Henry Larrabee on the ____ day of ____, a certified copy of this summons.
> (Signed) ____ ____, Tyler.

[A summons sent by certified mail is approved in most jurisidictions today.]

4. The secretary must not copy into the Lodge records any part of the evidence or of the committee's report until decision of the case is had by the Lodge. Often when an acquital upon the charges is announced, or the Lodge consents to pardon the offender upon confession, it is ordered that the papers be simply filed, and not recorded.

We conclude with some general remarks.

1. A second trial for the same offence has been elsewhere considered. The legality of it is not settled by competent authorities, but each case must stand upon its own merits.
2. A suspension for non-payment of dues works the same penalty as suspension for any other offence.
3. An offence brought to trial ought not to be antiquated. After a year or two an unmasonic act, unless very gross and threatening the good name of the Order may be left to oblivion.
4. A document of any kind, after being offered to and accepted by the Lodge or the committee which is acting *for* the Lodge, cannot be withdrawn save by the consent of the Lodge or committee.
5. The wife of an offending brother may give evidence for or against him if she consents to do so and the committee approve. This is, of course, reserved for extreme cases, and such testimony must be received with caution. Cases will suggest themselves to the mind of the reader in which such

evidence is of the very highest importance, and without which the trial could scarcely proceed.

6. All cases of trial should be disposed of as speedily as circumstances permit. The quiet and harmony of the Order are disturbed during the pendency of such proceedings. It is not of the real nature of Masonry, which studies peace. The first temple was erected without the sound of axe, hammer or any tool of iron, and this fact is constantly (and justly) cited to enforce harmony and good will in the workings of the modern Order. Yet it will be remembered that the historical harmony of the Craft of King Solomon's time was woefully disturbed, more severely, in fact, than that of modern Society. "*Foul murder*, conspiracy and murder" shook the temple-erection and the very existence of the fraternity of temple-builders to the centre, and the principles of Masonic jurisprudence were then first put to test. It was proven that Masonic *law* was as broad and as high as Masonic *harmony*.

[Again it must be emphasized the law of your Grand Lodge must be followed. What has been written here is intended to give you the mechanics of Masonic justice.]

In most jurisdictions Trial Commissions try all cases of un-Masonic conduct. These Commissions are sometimes appointed by the Grand Master following his election. In other cases they are appointed as needed by the District Deputy Grand Master involved, and approved by the Grand Master. Your Grand Lodge law will clearly show the method in use in your jurisdiction. Read it carefully. Follow it to the letter.]

CHAPTER 11

MASONIC LAW

FREEMASONRY enjoys for its foundation that universal law which is best known, always recognized, and generally acknowledged. It is *universal*, because all people understand its force and utility; it is personal and general. The foundation of Masonic ethics is the moral law, dictated by God himself; therefore, it is of superior obligation. It is the basis of all human laws, and is contained in this brief sentence made up of twelve short words—"Do onto others as you would that they should do unto you."

THE JURISPRUDENCE OF FREEMASONRY

JURISPRUDENCE (Lat. *Jurisprudentia*) is from *jus*, a right, the tenor of laws, institutions and customs, insofar as they are binding, and determine what is lawful and what is not; and *prudentia*, a science, a foreseeing, the wise and prudent knowledge of a matter—the SCIENCE OF RIGHT, in accordance with Positive Law. And as law deals with the person and property of individuals, so individuals everywhere are bound to render faithful and submissive obedience to law. Jurisprudence may, therefore, be divided into two parts, and recognized as Universal and Particular.

THE LANDMARKS OF FREEMASONRY

Concerning the Landmarks of Freemasonry, there is some diversity of opinion among writers. One writer (Rob Morris) defines Landmarks to be "those fixed tenets by which the limits of Freemasonry may be known and preserved." A.G. Mackey says, "a custom or rule of action to constitute a landmark is, that it must have existed from time whereof the memory of man runneth not to the contrary." Antiquity is its essential element.

In the preparation of this portion of our work we have gathered useful and valuable material from the various sources at our command, selecting from all the works devoted to the subject.

When opinions are compared, the difference seems more a matter of *enumeration* than of principles. One writer makes two landmarks, or even three, out of that which, by another, is compressed into one. It is fair criticism to say that some writers appear needlessly diffuse, while others have not drawn the lines of distinction clearly between subjects of diverse natures. We will not, however, occupy our pages by copying in detail the lists, but refer the industrious student to the authorities themselves. In these we will see that Mackey names 25 Landmarks; Morris, 17; Simons, 15; Lockwood, 19; Oliver, 12. It is not so important to the Masonic student *how many* are the Landmarks, as *what is their nature*, what evidence we have for their antiquity and genuineness, and what evils grow out of removal and neglect.

THE PETITIONER

The expert operative Mason, when erecting his temporal structure, is careful to select none but proper materials—either of wood, stone, or metal—for the work. The durability of the structure, in fact, depends upon his selection of materials.

Upon the same principle acts the speculative or moral Mason, and the durability of *his work* depends mainly upon his success in the choice of "good men and true" for the mystic labor. He looks at the object presented before him for the moral structure with all the skill of a master, so that when the survey of the man is completed, he can, when the proper time arrives, express his final judgment by the silent but powerful machinery of the ballot, with the full conviction of right in the sight of God and of the Craft; for truly not every man who knocks at the door of our temple should gain admission!

The necessary qualification of candidates for initiation are conveniently divided into four classes: moral, mental, physical and social.

1. MORAL QUALIFICATION—Freemasonry recognizes no religious creed or dogma as a prerequisite to admission into the portals of her temple. All she requires under this head is that the candidate shall be of good moral character and shall believe in the existence of God as the Creator of all things, and in a future state of existence beyond the grave.

2. MENTAL QUALIFICATIONS—The mental qualifications refer to the security of the Craft. It is held that the stability of the Institution will be impaired by working into its mystic walls the ignorant and uneducated. The candidate, therefore, should at least be able to read and write, that he may the better appreciate the inculcations of Masonry. Mental imbecility, the result of idiocy, or too advanced age, or the excessive indulgence of passions, are absolute disqualifications.

3. THE PHYSICAL QUALIFICATIONS refer to sex, age, and bodily condition. They suggest the habit of industry taught in the Masonic emblem of the bee-hive, whereby we are taught to employ our time in the pursuit of some useful and honorable calling, both for self-support and that we may have a surplus out of which to relieve the distress of others.

As to *sex*, it has ever been maintained that Freemasonry, as an art, is limited *to men*. "No woman," is the emphatic expression of all ancient documents.

As to the requisite *age*, the custom of different countries varies. In Prussia, the candidate must be at least 25. In England and Ireland, the age of majority, 21, unless by dispensation from the Grand Master or Provincial Grand Master, nor then under 18. In Scotland, 18. In France, 21, but the son of a Mason who has rendered important service to the Craft may, by the consent of parent or guardian, be admitted at 18. Hanover, 25, but the son of a Mason at 18. In Hamburg, as in all the American States, the requisite age corresponds with the law of the country, which sets the legal majority at 21. [In recent years a few Grand Lodges have reduced the age for admittance to 18 or 19. Propositions to lower the age below 21 have been defeated in several Grand Lodges, while others have not considered changing.]

As to *bodily condition*, the legislation of Grand Lodges, both ancient and modern, is found to be nearly uniform. The ancient documents contain numerous injunctions under this head. "A candidate must be without blemish, and have the full and proper use of his limbs; for a maimed man can do the craft no good."—A.D. 926. "No person shall hereafter be accepted a Freemason but such as are of able body."—A.D. 1663. In one passage this explanatory clause is found: "No one who is maimed, or has a defect in his body which might render him incapable of learning the art, and of being made a brother."

This comment has justified Grand Lodges in making a freer construction of the law than when the Institution was more nearly operative. In England, which is the mother of the Craft as at present established, the law of bodily condition is entirely abrogated; the loss of limbs, of sight, of hearing, etc., being no bar to initiation. But in this country such change in a Grand Lodge constitution would be reckoned the removal of a Landmark. [Not any longer. Many jurisdictions permit men of varying handicaps to petition Lodges.]

Perfection in physical conformation is plainly impossible. There are few men who have not some defect of body outwardly or inwardly. The loss of a tooth, scantiness of hair, a scar upon the surface, might all be named *defects*. But these do not "render the candidate incapable of learning the art and of being made a brother."

4. SOCIAL AND GEOGRAPHICAL QUALIFICATIONS refer to the status of a candidate among men, the conditions of his birth, and residence. A candidate, in all the earlier records, was required to be "free born," as no person who was born in servitude should be made a Mason, for the

reason, so forcibly stated in the aforesaid records, "lest, when he is introduced into the Lodge, any of the brethren should be offended."—A.D. 926.

THE LAW OF RESIDENCE is one of the peculiarities of American Masonry most rigidly insisted upon. As no American Mason is allowed to be a member of more than one Lodge at the same time, the initiate is taught to apply to the Lodge *nearest his settled residence*, both because its members are best acquainted with his character, etc., and because the expenses of maintaining the interests of the Craft in that vicinity give them the right to the fees of initiation and after membership. Two or more Lodges, located in any town or city, hold concurrent jurisdiction over candidates within said town or city.

The only admissible exception to this rule is in the case of seafaring men in actual service, and officers in the military or naval service of government.

[Dual membership is now permitted in the majoriy of jurisdictions. Many allow Masons to be a member of as many Lodges as will accept them.]

JURISDICTION OF A LODGE

At the present time, in consequence of the increase of Lodges, it is difficult exactly to define the precise meaning that may be applied to this term. The jurisdiction of a Lodge is of two kinds—TERRITORIAL and PENAL.

The *Territorial* jurisdiction extends half way in every direction to the nearest Lodges within the territory of the Grand Lodge. In cities and towns where there are more than one Lodge, their jurisdiction is in all respects concurrent. This rule relates to the reception of candidates, therefore a Lodge cannot confer degrees upon a profane who has a fixed place of residence nearer another Lodge, without the consent of said nearest Lodge, by a vote of the majority of the members present, and at a stated meeting.

The *Penal* jurisdiction of a Lodge is the right of trial and enforcement of discipline over its own members (except the Master) without regard to their place of residence, and also of members of other Lodges living within its territorial jurisdiction, and unaffiliated Masons living or temporarily remaining therein. As a general rule, however, a Lodge should not proceed to try an offending brother until after due notice has been given to the Lodge to which he belongs, and in default of proper action on the part of the latter. Such notice, however, is rather a matter of courtesy than right, and may be given or not, as the Lodge in its discretion shall decide.

[Many jurisdictions now have state-wide concurrent jurisdiction which permits a man to petition any Lodge in the state. This change has usually been started on a trial basis, found advantageous in most cases, and made permanent.]

PROPOSING CANDIDATES

A candidate for initiation is proposed to the Lodge by two or more Master Masons. The petition sets forth the age, vocation, and residence of the candidate.

This petition, couched in respectful words, expresses a favorable opinion of the Institution, and pledges a cheerful obedience to all its established requirements.

The petition is signed by the autographs of the candidate himself, also of the members who recommend him. The latter are understood to vouch *from personal acquaintance*, for the facts stated in the petition, and to express their belief that he will prove worthy material for the mystic work.

The privilege of proposing candidates is one that inheres in every Master Mason of the Lodge who is in good standing. It is, however, one of the most responsible of all, and should be exercised with exceeding caution. No pressure upon the mind of a candidate is allowable to induce him to petition for initiation. All inducements, in fact, are improper, whether the promise of mercenary rewards, of social advantages or of important knowledge. The fact of the long existence of Freemasonry in the world, its strong and well-chosen membership, and the high aims set forth in its handbooks, and the public declamations of its officials, are sufficient to draw the good and true knowledge-seeker to the Lodge door. Personal friendship cannot be allowed to sway the mind in this; but the good of the Lodge and the benefit of the Fraternity must reign paramount.

A personal intimacy with the candidate, such as affords a knowledge of his antecedents, age, habits of life, etc., can alone justify a recommendation for initiation.

It should be held as good cause for discipline against an offending brother who has practiced a fraud upon the Craft previous to his initiation, by any misstatement as to age, residence, profession or other subject necessary to a fair acquaintance.

THE NUMBER OF INITIATES

The number who may be made at the same meeting of the Lodge is stated in the general regulations of 1720; "No Lodge shall make more than five new brethren at one time, unless by dispensation from the Grand Master." A strange confusion, however, exists among the authorities, some understanding the word *time* to imply "at one meeting;" others, "at one ceremony." The Constitution of the Grand Lodge of England itself defines the expression in the words, "No Lodge shall, under any pretence, make more than five new brothers in one day, unless by dispensation."

This rule is of such universal character as to preclude the necessity of enumerating more authorities; many of the Grand Lodge constitutions contain the fundamental law as above stated. The reason for such statutory provision is to check the Lodges in undue haste, and give the Master ample time to instruct the newly-made brethren.

LODGE ACTION

The candidate, having subscribed to the petition described in the last section, remains quiescent, awaiting the action of the Lodge having jurisdiction. The proposition is read by the Secretary to the Lodge, at a regular communication. The Master declares the petition received, and orders it referred to a committee for investigation. This committee, composed of three members appointed by the Master, take the petition in hand, and, each for himself, makes a series of inquiries into the age, profession, motive for wishing to become a member, residence, and standing of the candidate. The parties recommending the petitioner are first examined as being best able to affirm to his qualifications "to become an honorable member of the institution." The time given the committee, in this country, for these important investigations, is usually one month, or from one regular meeting to another. If further time is required the Lodge grants it. A majority of the committee must report to justify the Lodge in taking action on the report.

PETITION CANNOT BE WITHDRAWAN

The petition having been presented, received, and referred to the committee, is the property of the Lodge, and cannot be withdrawn. It must be acted upon by the committee, reported to the Lodge, and a ballot had in due order.

Some Grand Lodges permit a petition to be withdrawn by "unanimous consent." Other authorities permit this act in cases where it is discovered that the Lodge has no jurisdiction, or where the applicant is dead, or is not of age, or physically disqualified, or where the petition had not the consent of the petitioner, etc. In such rare cases the decision of the Grand Master may be sought.

ACTION UPON A PETITION

There is no law in Freemasonry in the United States more thoroughly universal than this—the fifth and sixth sections of the *Constitutions of 1721* requiring that all the brethren shall have timely notice, so that, by inquiry into the character and habits of the petitioner, they may be prepared to prevent a fractious member from being imposed upon the Lodge. [Therefore, every petition must be acted upon during a stated communication of the Lodge. Action at any other time is illegal.]

REPORT OF THE INVESTIGATING COMMITTEE

The report of the committee is usually couched in the words "worthy" or "unworthy" (or "favorable" or "unfavorable"), indorsed upon the back of the petition. This method seems defective. Some Grand Lodges say the Committee of Investigation shall not content themselves with saying that "they find nothing against the applicant," but must state what his standing and qualifications are. The report must be subscribed by at least a majority of the committee before the Lodge can receive it. Such a rule might well be made general.

The precise period when the report may be presented and the Lodge qualified to act being a local constitutional measure, the question must be controlled by the regulation of the Grand Lodge within whose jurisdiction the Lodge is at labor. This regulation is promulgated by the Grand Lodge of England, in the following words: "No person shall be made a Mason without a regular proposition at one Lodge and a ballot at the next regular stated Lodge." Such appears to have been almost universally adopted in similar language by the Grand Lodges of this country; and, if the exact words of the law are wanting in any of the Constitutions, the general usage of the Craft has furnished an equivalent authority for the regulation.

THE PROFICIENCY OF CANDIDATE

A candidate ought not to be advanced until he has made suitable proficiency in the preceding degrees, which is defined to be "the ability to

communicate the work and lectures to another in the established forms."
In many jurisdictions the secret ballot for each degree is rigidly enforced.

LODGE ACTION FOR ADVANCEMENT

The same requirements of qualifications, mental, moral, physical,
social, and geographical, that are essential to the initiation of a candidate, are equally essential to his advancement to the degree of Fellow
Craft, and subsequently to that of Master Mason.

Any permanent physical defect received after his initiation, whereby he
cannot perform the duties of Masonry, must therefore debar his progress
as much as any blemish in his *moral* character, or any serious removal
from *mental* soundness. Whatever tends to prevent a full compliance with
the necessity of receiving and communicating Masonic instruction is a
blemish. The partly-made Mason is thus treated with the same rigor as the
profane. This law of perfection is constructed so nicely that even though
the Lodge by accident, ignorance or inattention may have initiated a candidate wanting in some essential qualification, he must not be advanced.

A member of the Lodge has the right to object to the advancement of a
candidate, and no one has the right to demand his reasons therefor. But
should the brother objecting voluntarily give his reasons to the Lodge, for
its consideration, he must then submit to its determination, by the vote of
the members present. An objection to the advancement of a candidate
should not extend beyond the constitutional time applied to candidates.

In the large majority of jurisdictions a ballot is required for each
degree. A substantial theory upon this subject is that each degree is as
distinct from the next as each branch of Masonry is distinct from the
following one, so that no one can say he has *the right to* be advanced.

TRANSFER OF JURISDICTION

A well-defined law among American Lodges is that one Lodge shall not
interfere with the work of another in passing or raising its candidates. The
Ancient Charges declare that "None shall discover envy at the prosperity
of a brother, nor supplant him, or put him out of his work, if he be
capable to finish the same; for no man can finish another's work so much
to the lord's profit unless he be thoroughly acquainted with the designs of
him that began it." A Lodge cannot, therefore, confer a degree upon a
candidate who has received a degree in another Lodge without the consent of such Lodge, expressed in writing, and certified under seal.

When a Lodge confers the degrees at the *request* of another, it does not thereby acquire jurisdiction, and the fees belong to the latter, unless it sees proper to relinquish them.

An Entered Apprentice, whose Lodge has been declared extinct, and who applies to another Lodge to be advanced, must receive the unanimous ballot of the members present in the Lodge at the time his petition is voted upon otherwise, he must be declared rejected.

OBJECTION TO CANDIDATES

Objections by a member of the Lodge to the initiation of a candidate communicated even after election, is binding, and must be respected, nor can the reasons for such objections be demanded.

The objections, however, like the use of the black ball, are only binding and of force during the period recognized by the law of the Grand Lodge, in reference to rejections. If the candidate is again proposed, the objections must be renewed to prevent the applicant's admission.

The right of secrecy of ballot is destroyed only when the member chooses to make his objections known; then the secrecy is thrown off, and the reasons or objections become the subject of investigation by the Lodge, which may pass upon their validity, yet the member presenting his objections to the candidate cannot be deprived of his right to reject when he avows no vindictive hostility.

OBJECTION FROM VISITING BRETHREN

Our institution being world-wide, and every member thereof having a partnership interest in its welfare, should exercise vigilance in protecting it against the introduction of unworthy material. It is therefore admissible, that a brother visiting a Lodge may object to the initiation of a candidate if he knows of any good and sufficient reason why the candidate ought not to be made a Mason; but such objection is not sufficient in itself to stop the initiation. The brother should at once put the members (or more properly the Master) of the Lodge in possession of all the facts bearing upon the case, and upon which his objections are based, so that they, having "due and timely notice, may govern themselves accordingly." The Lodge may then judge of their sufficiency, and, if well-founded, they will, of course, refuse to initiate the candidate. Every Lodge is the judge of its own members; and to hold that a protest of objection against the initiation or advancement of a candidate made by a brother not a member of such Lodge, should have the same effect, and be respected the same as if made by one of its own members, would be equivalent to extending the ballot to all Masons the world over.

LODGE ACTION UPON PROPOSITIONS FOR AFFILIATION

The Ancient Charges declare, with emphasis, that "every brother ought to belong to some Lodge, and be subject to its by-laws and the general regulations of the Craft." The process of withdrawing from a Lodge is termed DIMITTING, and a brother thus withdrawn is styled a Dimitted Mason, or more tersely, Non-Affiliate. When he desires to be re-attached to a Lodge, he may make known his request by written petition to the Lodge having jurisdiction over him.

Such a petition must be accompanied with the certificate of his dimit from his last Lodge, together with the affiliating fee, if any, required by the by-laws. Should his petition be rejected, his certificate of dimit must be returned to him. No names of Masons recommending need be appended to this petition, but he must be a person known to the Lodge as a Mason.

The petition is received at a regular meeting of the Lodge, and referred to a committee composed of three Master Masons, who take charge of it, and subject it to the same course of inquiry as required upon propositions for initiation.

The petition for affiliation, when regularly accepted by the Lodge and referred cannot be withdrawn, but takes the same course as a petition for initiation. The action of the Lodge is by secret ballot.

If the Lodge rejects the petition for affiliation, it may be renewed at any and every regular meeting of the Lodge, at the pleasure of the non-affiliate.

THE LAW OF THE BALLOT

"The ballot is the Mason's great prerogative. It is a right which every member enjoys, and which he is bound to exercise faithfully, impartially and conscientiously. With him alone rests the responsibility of its use."

In the whole range of Masonic jurisprudence there is no subject of greater importance than this, and few themes branch into so many important particulars. The ballot in American Lodges is "the prudent way" referred to in the ancient law herewith quoted: "No man can be entered a brother in any particular Lodge, or admitted to be a member thereof, without the unanimous consent of all the members of that Lodge then

present when the candidate is proposed, and their consent is formally asked by the Master; and they are to signify their consent or dissent *in their
own prudent way*, either virtually or in form, but with unanimity; nor is
this inherent privilege subject to a dispensation, because the members of a
particular Lodge are the best judges of it; and if a fractious member
should be imposed on them, it might spoil their harmony or hinder their
freedom, or even break and disperse the Lodge, which ought to be avoided by all good and true brethren."

The system of voting by balls and in a covered box, has been found to
secure perfect freedom to every voter, and inviolable secrecy as to
observers. Various ingenious contrivances have been devised for this purpose, by whose aid expedition, convenience, secrecy and certainty are
pleasantly combined.

CANNOT DISPENSE WITH THE BALLOT

Under no circumstances is it within the scope or power of a Lodge to
dispense with the ballot on the admission of a candidate for the privileges
of Freemasonry or for membership. Should it occur that a person of more
than ordinary eligibility and honorable standing in the country desires to
be proposed, some of the members might, in the joy of their hearts, wish
to dispense with the formalities of the ballot on the ground that no objection could possibly exist or be raised against a gentleman of such exalted
position and irreproachable character, and, as a deserving compliment,
propose to elect him by acclamation. Such a proceeding would be unmasonic and wholly irregular, and would subject the Lodge to severe
discipline by the Grand Lodge. [The Grand Master, however, in most
jurisdictions, can dispense with the formality of the ballot box and "Make
a Mason-at-Sight." The new Mason then becomes an unaffiliated Mason
and must petition a Lodge of his choice for membership. He can be
elected only by a unanimous ballot.]

Nor is it proper to refuse to ballot on the application because the report
of the committee, or any portion thereof, should be unfavorable. The only legal answer to a petition for initiation or membership is *through the
ballot box*.

When the ballot is held on an application for affiliation, the same rules
apply as in the petition of candidates, but there is no delay required in
case of rejection in the presentation of a new application.

WHO ARE ENTITLED TO VOTE?

Under the head of MEMBERSHIP OF THE LODGE, the question, *Who are* entitled to vote? is more thoroughly considered. In American Lodges, with few exceptions, the ballot is confined to Master Masons. None but members of the Lodge, however, are allowed to participate in this act, visitors, of whatever official grade, having no privilege here, nor can any dispensing power be granted to remove this Landmark.

The division of the balls into white and black is the customary mode of distinguishing them, but lately the distinction between cubes and spheres is becoming popular as addressing itself more to the sense of *touch* and *sight*. The old mode of balloting was to pass the balls, by the aid of the Senior Deacon, to all entitled to use them. Each member took two balls, one of each color. The Senior Deacon passed the second time and collected them, each voter dropping the several balls into compartments of the box colored to correspond with the votes. If a black ball was dropped into the white compartment it expressed a rejection. The most popular mode of balloting now is for the Senior Deacon to pass the box to each voter, commencing with the Master, thus economizing time and securing absolute secrecy. [Or the ballot box is placed upon the Altar and the members approach it there and cast their ballot.]

THE RIGHT TO BALLOT

Every member of the Lodge present has the right to ballot for the admission or rejection of a candidate. This right can in no way be denied.

In the exercise of the right to vote upon the admission of candidates, no member who is permitted to be present can be deprived of his vote. A provision of the by-laws or a special act of the Lodge may disqualify a member from the exercise of his other franchises, or of holding office in his Lodge, in consequence of being in arrears beyond a certain amount, but the ancient law is imperative, and without equivocation, and requires that *every member present* SHALL VOTE. This right of the members to elect or reject their candidates is plainly called an "inherent privilege, not subject to a dispensation." The law being so positive in its character, it is not only *the right* but *the duty* of every member present, which he is compelled to perform, as without the unanimous consent of all present there can be no election.

EVERY MEMBER PRESENT MUST VOTE

The authorities are in accord upon this subject. From the responsibility of expressing the opinion whether the candidate should be admitted or rejected no member can shrink. No personal timidity forbids the deposit of a black ball if the applicant is unworthy; no prejudice should prevent the deposit of a white ball if he is worthy. Therefore all the members present *must vote*. No one can be exempt, except by the consent of the Lodge, which, if given, the Lodge assumes the responsibility, as it is no longer the act of a single individual.

VOTING SHALL BE SECRET

This admits of no controversy. The secrecy of the ballot is not governed by any law of a Grand Lodge, subordinate Lodge, or country. It is a Landmark. The impropriety of questioning a member as to his ballot is a matter of legislation, and a wilful violation of the secrecy of the ballot which should be met *with prompt discipline*. All remarks or discussions on the subject, in or out of the Lodge, upon the merits of a candidate are calculated to impair the secrecy, independence and usefulness of the ballot, and are therefore unlawful.

An unfavorable ballot does *not* stop further action. There is but one way of receiving a candidate, and but one way of rejecting one, and that is by the secret ballot. Every application for the degrees, or for membership, it matters not what the report of the committee may be, must be submitted to the ballot.

[Concerning the secrecy of the ballot: At the beginning of 1979 a Grand Master issued an edict ordering any Mason casting a black cube to report his reasoning to the W.M. If this wasn't done within 30 days, the W.M. had to declare the petitioner elected.]

ABSOLUTE UNANIMITY

This is demanded among American Lodges in the matter of the ballot. If the question is propounded by brethren who have come into our Order from other societies, Why so much reticence is necessary? We answer it is of the nature of Freemasonry that its work be elaborated in the secret recesses of the heart. There is no member of the Lodge works so much evil as the man with the loosened tongue. All the force of the Entered Apprentice's Degree lies in *secrecy;* the key to the Master Mason's Degree is in the legend of the man who died *rather than divulge.* Lycurgus, the great lawgiver, would have every man keep secret *whatsoever was done or said.* Pythagoras taught his scholars to remain absolutely silent for a certain number of years, by way of initiation. St. Ambrose in his Christian offices, places "the patient gift of silence" above all others.

The harmony and prosperity of the Lodge greatly depend upon this rule being enforced. Nor is it in the power of the Lodge to enact any form of by-law which shall prevent a member from voting on the petition of a candidate. There is no conflict of authorities under this head.

According to the Constitution of the Grand Lodge of England, no person can be made a Mason in, or admitted a member of a Lodge, if, on the ballot, three black balls appear against him; but the by-laws of the Lodge may enact that one or two black balls shall exclude a candidate. The rule in some American jurisdictions is to require at least two black balls to reject.

Having shown the right and duty of every member present to *cast his ballot,* it follows that this act, once performed according to the stringent rules of American Lodges,

THE BALLOT CANNOT BE RECONSIDERED

if it be unfavorable, except in such emergent cases as imperatively demand it. If it were found, on examination, that a non-member had voted, or that some of the votes had fallen out of the box, or into the wrong compartment of the box; if it were discovered that by oversight some member present had been neglected in the distribution of the ballots, in these similar cases the repetition of the balloting would be justified, not otherwise.

In the most of jurisdictions the custom has obtained, and with a sure foundation, that *one* black ball is sufficient to reject. But upon the *supposition* that the negative ballot might have been cast by mistake, it is considered correct and proper to pass the box the second time. This is only to make certain that there was no mistake made on the first ballot. If, upon the repassing of the ballot box, one or more negative ballots appear, the candidate must be declared rejected. If two or more black balls appear on the first ballot, the Master must declare the candidate rejected, even though a brother believes he voted by mistake.

Postponement of the ballot to an indefinite time, or the committee of investigation wilfully procrastinating their report, should not be allowed, except for good and sufficient cause, the facts being regularly reported to the Lodge, and the Lodge being satisfied with the statements made. Then, and under the circumstances as presented, a postponement would be justifiable.

REJECTED CANDIDATES

The analogy between the manner of selecting the materials—stone, wood, and metal—upon which operative Masons perform their work, and those manipulated by speculative Masons, fails when we come to consider the law concerning rejected candidates. The operative Mason having rejected a block of stone, or a stick of timber after critical examination, *it is rejected forever*. Not so with the speculative Mason. The materials passing under his hand may be rejected once and again, and yet be brought forward for another and another trial, so long as the Lodge or the individual maybe in existence. The question to be considered here is therefore the law of procedure concerning rejected applicants for Masonry.

The American rule limits the time within which the petition of a rejected applicant cannot be repeated. Some Grand Lodges set this period at twelve months, some at six months, and many are silent on this subject. In the absence of any Grand Lodge regulation, the subordinate Lodge may fix the time to suit its own convenience. If no time be stated, a new application may be made as often as the candidate may desire, and the Lodge be willing to accept.

CONTROL OVER A REJECTED CANDIDATE

The almost unanimous rule prevails among the Grand Lodges of the United States, and Masonic jurists are at accord in this matter, that "no Lodge can initiate a candidate previously rejected in another Lodge, without the consent of the rejecting Lodge."

ONE BALLOT FOR THE THREE DEGREES

With the view of facilitating the business of the Lodge, and as a rule of general practice when balloting on the petition of a candidate for the three degrees and membership. This rule may be changed at any time on the principle that a member of the Lodge has the right to demand a ballot for the second and third degrees, and such demand, when made, must be respected and complied with. But in the large majority of Grand Lodge jurisdictions three ballots are strictly adhered to, one for each degree. [Not any longer. As of 1979 only five Grand Lodges in the world required three ballots; the others required only one for election to all three degrees. However, the Master retains the authority to stop a candidate at any point. If he does, the candidate stands rejected as though a negative ballot had been cast.]

INDIVIDUAL MASONS

THERE are duties and privileges peculiar to each degree of Freemasonry. In general they are plain, simple, and easily understood. An examination of the "Ancient Records" affords the best knowledge of them.

In the labors of ancient architecture the ENTERED APPRENTICE was a bearer of burdens, the assistant and servant of the craftsman. His part was menial, having many *duties* but few *privileges*.

Advancing in honor as in knowledge, the craftsman or FELLOW CRAFT applied the tools and implements of operative Masonry to the materials of a building in the quarry, on the hill, at the forge, or whatever division of labor he was best fitted for. As his privileges were increased he was the more honored and respected among men. In theory he was reckoned a candidate for higher honors. He had a personal device or mark placed upon his work. Receiving wages for his labor, instead of the limited portion of food and clothing dispensed to the Apprentice, his companions were obligated to him, and he to them, not to wrong or defraud each other. Having distinguishing signs and signals peculiar to the grade of Fellow Craft, he was pledged to answer such and obey them, when they were within the scope of his duty and ability. Being liable to poverty, through sickness, want of employment, or unavoidable misfortune, he was under sacred engagements to aid and assist his companions, as they were to him.

Still advancing in learning, skill and honor, the MASTER MASON stood as the overseer of men. His place was equally in the *closet* among the rolls and records of architecture, and in the unfinished *edifice*, where men of all grades of skill were employed. All were subject to the commands of the Master of Masons. He was the medium between the "lord" (the wealthy and eminent person for whom the building was being erected) and the builders. The wages came from him, and so did the honors and rewards of fidelity, the punishments for idleness, vice and neglect. He was under solemn engagements to all Master Masons, and all Master Masons were, in like manner, to him, to be secret (discreet) and obedient to law, vigilant in answering a summons, charitable, honest. His obligations extended to the maner of selecting and advancing men into the degrees of Masonry. As his privileges were extended his responsibilities were equally enlarged.

The Entered Apprentice cannot demit from his Lodge as a Master Mason can, but when removing out of the jurisdiction, and with a view to becoming attached to another Lodge, he may have a certificate of his relation to Masonry and his moral standing and worthiness to be advanced. This is simply equivalent to a release from the law which gives every Lodge the right to finish up its own work. As he is not required to pay dues, he cannot be suspended for non-payment of dues, as a Master Mason.

THE ENTERED APPRENTICE

This term is applied to a person who has passed through the preliminaries of the petition for admission, the investigation as to qualifications, the ordeal of the ballot, and the initiation (or making) into the mysteries of the Institution in a legally organized body of Freemasons, and known as an ENTERED APPRENTICE MASON—a title at once recognized and respected by the whole fraternity.

At the revival of Masonry in England (1717), the private Lodges were allowed to confer on their members the first degree only, the Grand Lodge reserving to itself the power of passing and raising. On the appointment of Wardens they were passed in Grand Lodges, before their investiture, to the degree of a Fellow Craft, but no brother was admitted to the third degree until he had been chosen Master of his Lodge. Every Apprentice, at that period, had a vote on all questions in his Lodge, and even when any alteration was proposed to be made in the General Constitutions of the order, it was provided that a Fellow Craft, or even an Apprentice, might be allowed to address the chair on the subject under discussion, or to make any motion for the good of the Fraternity, "which shall be either immediately considered, or else referred to the Grand Lodge at their next communication." At the present time, however, the Entered Apprentice has no such priviledge. The vote and subscription to a Lodge commences when the candidate has attained his Master's degree, for an ancient law of Masonry provided that "initiation makes a man a Mason; but he must receive the Master's degree and sign the by-laws, before he becomes a member of the Lodge."

According to the present established rules of the Fraternity, initiation makes the man a Mason, but an Entered Apprentice only.

He has the right of visiting and sitting in all Lodges of the first degree, of receiving all the instructions which appertain to it, and of offering himself as a candidate for advancement, without the preparatory act of a formal, written petition.

RIGHT OF ADVANCEMENT

When an Entered Apprentice comes forward (equivalent to application) for advancement to the next higher degree, he is required to submit to an examination either in open Lodge or (in some jurisdictions) before a committee appointed for the purpose, that it may be known that he is prepared, by a knowledge of the degree already conferred, for advancement to another.

When the examination is satisfactory in the first or second degrees, it is usual for the Lodge to express its willingness to advance him by a secret ballot wherein one negative vote rejects him, without, however, affecting his standing as an Entered Apprentice or Fellow Craft; but if the objection is founded upon *moral* unfitness, specific charges should be preferred and a regular trial had. A ballot can be demanded and had only when the candidate applies for advancement.

A member of the Lodge has the right to object to the advancement of the candidate at any time before the obligation, and such objection is sufficient to prevent the progress of the candidate. But if the member voluntarily and openly divulges his reasons to the Lodge or elsewhere, they then become the property of the Lodge; and if they are wholly selfish, frivolous, revengeful, or vindictive, and are founded upon no moral or physical objections, he leaves open a fair inquiry *as to himself*, whether his action is correctly Masonic, and this his Lodge may investigate. An *abuse* of the right of ballot by a brother is a disciplinable offence, and hence, where a brother has waived his privilege of secrecy, and avowed an unworthy motive for balloting against a candidate, he is subject to charges.

In case of death the Entered Apprentice cannot be buried with the formalities of the Fraternity, nor can an Entered Apprentice take part in the procession of a deceased Master Mason.

Not being a member of the Lodge, the Apprentice is not required to pay dues; has no claims upon the funds of the Lodge; is not permitted to speak, vote, hold office, or serve on committees, and in case of death his family would not be entitled to pecuniary aid.

An Entered Apprentice has the right to be heard in his defence, if accused of any offence; but the trial must be before Master Masons, acting as a committee or commission, before whom he may be present, or he may be represented by counsel, who must also be a Master Mason. He is entitled to an appeal to the Grand Lodge, from the sentence of his Lodge, because it is the duty, imperatively, of the Grand Lodge to see that the rights of the humblest member of the Fraternity shall not be invaded, but that impartial fairness and justice shall be administered to all.

He may join in all public processions of the Craft (except funeral processions), such as laying corner-stones, dedicating public buildings and public works, and those connected with festive occasions. His place in such processions is in the van of the moving column, and on the right of line, when formed as such. [This is not permissible in most jurisdictions. The Entered Apprentice can only participate as can any of the general public.]

FELLOWCRAFT

After having satisfactorily complied with all the constitutional requirements in his examination as an Entered Apprentice, the candidate is entitled to claim his advancement to the second degree, wherein he finds that the responsiblities pertaining to the grade of a Fellowcraft are necessarily greater than those of an Entered Apprentice; and thus the aspirant learns that Freemasonry is truly a progressive Institution. He is now intrusted with those tokens which mark his advancement and prove his worth. He is taught that while the first degree inculcates a pure system of morality, founded on the Great Light which illuminates the Masonic altar, the second degree has a purely scientific reference. With this opportunity of acquiring knowledge he may improve his intellectual powers, qualify himself to become a useful member of the Society, and as an expert brother, strive to excel in that which is good and great and serviceable to his fellow man.

Fellowcrafts, like Apprentices, are required to make suitable proficiency before they can be advanced to the degree of Master Mason. Their privileges as to processions are the same as those of Entered Apprentices.

MASTER MASON

The candidate having been initiated as an ENTERED APPRENTICE, the symbolism of which is intended to represent the introduction of many into the arena of life's duties and struggles when he is to become a living and thinking actor; having passed through the degree of FELLOWCRAFT, when he is emblematically recognized as a companion and friend, and is a type of man advanced to a higher state, with faculties more fully developed, and longing, by the aid of science and philosophy, to explore and master the mighty secrets of the universe; having been raised to the sublime degree of MASTER MASON, the symbolism of which represents through the legend of the artist builder, the external war between good and evil, truth and error, right and wrong, the alternatives of victory and defeat, and the complete and final overthrow of error, the punishment of crime, and the reign of love and justice among the nations of the earth —and having subscribed to the by-laws of the Lodge and the Constitution of the Grand Lodge, is entitled to all the rights and privileges of the Institution. Every office in the Lodge is open to him, except that of Worshipful Master, which is not accessible until he has been elected and installed a Warden for the term of one year. Master Masons constitute the body, and are the active members of the Fraternity, as we have plainly shown above.

The privileges and obligations of a Master Mason, which form the essence of his duties, are of an extensive and important character. The following enumeration of his duties and prerogatives is given in evidence of their importance:

1. MEMBERSHIP, which gives the absolute right to sit in the Lodge; to vote on all questions that may come before the Lodge for discussion, and in the selection of officers, except when disqualified by the non-payment of dues, as may be prescribed by the by-laws of the Lodge, or in case of trial in which he is interested; to vote for all candidates for initiation, advancement or affiliation; to be tried by his peers; to serve on committees; to be relieved from the funds of the Lodge, when in sickness or distress; to be buried with the solemnities of the Order; to appeal to the Grand Master or Grand Lodge against the action of his Lodge or its Master; to avouch for a strange brother whom he knows to be a Mason; to visit a Lodge when at labor, if there be no objection from a member thereof; to hold any office in the Lodge; except that of Master, to which he cannot aspire, unless he has previously occupied the office of Warden for one year; to receive a demit or certificate of withdrawal; and to propose persons for the privileges and benefits of Masonry.

2. HONORARY MEMBERSHIP—This class of membership is of recent invention. It is of two kinds. The first includes such brethren as are distinguished as Masons. The title and position confer no other privileges than those of visiting the Lodge at pleasure, taking part in discussions, and of participating with the members of the Lodge on more equal terms than any other visitor; but in no case is an honorary member entitled to vote or hold office. [Honorary Membership in many jurisdictions elects the recipient to all rights and benefits of the Lodge. He can vote on all questions and can be elected to office.]

The second class includes those who are made honorary members of the Lodge to which they are already affiliated. This favor is usually bestowed upon such aged and faithful brethren as can appreciate the mark of distinction, and as a reward for long and useful services. In this case it exempts them from the payment of all dues or assessments, and from all *obligation* to unite in the labors of the Lodge, but deprives them of no privilege which they before enjoyed as a member. They are still eligible for office, and may serve on committees, and vote on all questions as heretofore. In either case honorary members are exempt from the payment of dues or assessments.

The same brother may be an honorary member of the first class of as many Lodges as choose to elect him, the mode of election, in every case, to be the same as in the election of active members.

3. AFFILIATING WITH THE LODGE—Membership acquired by affiliation gives to the brother all the rights and privileges that belong to any other member of the Lodge. Master Masons only are permitted to apply for affiliation, and the brother so applying must bring to the Lodge with which he wishes to affiliate a certificate of withdrawal or dimission from the Lodge of which he was formerly a member [but a dimit is not necessary in those jurisdictions permitting dual or plural membership.] The application must be presented by a member of the Lodge at a regular meeting, when the petition takes precisely the same course as in an original application by being referred to a committee of investigation, which committee will report on the character and qualifications of the candidate at the next regular meeting, and on this report the Lodge will proceed to ballot. If the ballot is unanimous in favor of the candidate he is admitted as a member on his complying with the requirements of the by-laws and signing that instrument. If, on the contrary, one or more black balls are cast at the ballot, he is declared rejected. However, such rejection does not affect the good standing of the brother as a Mason, and he may renew his application as often as he may desire. He may apply to any Lodge for affiliation, whether he resides within or out of its jurisdiction, except in those jurisdictions that have a different regulation.

4. THE RIGHT TO VISIT LODGES—A Master Mason in good standing has the right of visiting any Masonic Lodge, wherever he may go, provided the Lodge to which he applies will receive him. In general terms, the right of a Master Mason in good standing to visit a Lodge is subordinate to the paramount right of a Lodge to refuse him admission. The right of a member of any particular Lodge, while in his Lodge, is greater than the right of one who is a visitor and not a member; and when it is necessary to discriminate between the two, the superior right must prevail. There are other cases and circumstances in the affairs of a Lodge when it would be inexpedient to admit any but actual members thereof, as when the Lodge is engaged on business of a strictly private character, not designed or desired to go beyond the knowledge of its own members; or being about to transact such business as the trial of a member; or when the applicant cannot give satisfactory proof of his claims to the privileges of Masonry.

The brother making application to visit a Lodge has the right to examine the warrant of the Lodge; but the rule, generally conceded, requires the brother to produce his own papers before he has a right to call for those of the Lodge he proposes to visit.

EXAMINATION OF A VISITOR

To faciliate the examination of a visitor, it is well that he should be in possession of a Lodge certificate duly authenticated by the signatures of the Master, Wardens, and Secretary of the Lodge, with the seal thereof properly attached, testifying to the good and regular standing of the owner in his Lodge. Such a document, commonly called a diploma, will be of great value to a brother when he desires to visit Lodges in strange places, but it can be received only as diplomatic evidence of correctness. [Except for foreign countries, a current dues card is sufficient now.]

Too much diligence cannot be exercised in the examination of visitors, particularly when personally unknown to every member of the Lodge. In addition to the strict trial and due examination to be exercised by the committee, the visitor is required to pledge himself in what is sometimes styled the TYLER'S OBLIGATION [or Oath].

After the examination, if the visitor fails to exhibit a proper knowledge of the lectures and the esoteric part of Masonry to entitle him to a participation in its privileges, he is dismissed; but if, on the contrary, the committee is satisfied of the correctness of the brother's knowledge and good standing, he should be formally introduced by the Senior Deacon to the Master, who will welcome him to a seat in the Lodge and to the hospitality due to visitors.

To avouch for a brother is to bear witness for him and become responsible for his good standing as a Mason. The exercise of the right to avouch for a brother is an important and responsible privilege, and should never be resorted to until after a full compliance with that law which declares that you can only avouch for a man as a Mason after "strict trial, due examination, or lawful information."

The regulations by which avouchments should be governed are as follows: 1. A Mason may vouch for another, if he has sat in a Lodge with him. 2. When a brother whom you know to be a Mason vouches for another in person, the avoucher having sat in the Lodge with him. 3. A brother may vouch for another if he has subjected him to a skillful examination when authorized to do so by the Master of a Lodge, and finds him well qualified.

Every Master, at his installation, has agreed in the most solemn manner "that no visitors shall be received into his Lodge without due examination, and producing proper vouchers of their having been initiated in a regular Lodge." He should therefore be exceedingly vigilant in scrutinizing the qualifications of every strange visitor.

THE RIGHT OF DIMITTING

Actual membership in a Lodge being the *duty* of every Mason, it follows therefore as a reasonable deduction that such association or membership should not be dissolved or withdrawn without justifiable reasons. The right to withdraw from membership, or, as it is technically called to DIMIT, is an important right. It dissolves all immediate connection between the Lodge and the brother obtaining it. The separation does not, however, destroy the brother's obligations to the Order, or its control over him in the event of his violating the laws of the Fraternity or of the country. A Mason's obligations to the Order and its statutes are indefeasible.

There can be no doubt that a Mason in good standing, with no charges or arrearages against him, has the right to dimit, the approval of the Lodge first being had. The rule must always apply, that as the brother entered the Lodge with the consent, so should he depart with its approbation and fraternal recommendation. A Lodge, however, is bound to grant a dimit to a worthy brother (except the Master) against whom there are no charges pending or being prepared, or arrearages of any character standing against him on the books of the Lodge. In several jurisdictions, the law prevails that an elected and installed officer cannot dimit. This seems proper from a common-sense view of the subject.

If a member has been dropped from the rolls for non-payment of dues, he cannot lawfully become a member of another Lodge without first going back to the Lodge which dropped him and paying up all arrearages and getting a dimit from that Lodge in a regular way. A Mason dropped from the roll of membership of a particular Lodge does not thereby become an unaffiliated Mason in good standing. He occupies the position of one not in good standing, and cannot legally be affiliated in another Lodge while in that condition. But the system of "dropping from the rolls" is confined to a few States. In the most the failure to pay dues subjects the offender to suspension.

A dimit procured by fraud or to avoid investigation for unmasonic conduct, may, by subsequent action of the Lodge, be withheld, by a resolution of the Lodge, but unless it appears that one or the other of these charges is true, a Lodge cannot revoke a dimit once granted. By the action of a Lodge in granting a dimit, an application made in good faith, it loses jurisdiction over the member.

It is very improper for any Lodge to admit a visitor upon the authority of a dimit alone. Another and a much *severer test* should be applied to every one applying for admission into a Masonic Lodge. A visitor must *prove* himself, or be vouched for by a brother who knows him, to be entitled to the privileges of Masonry.

A dimit can only be granted by the Lodge. The document must be signed by the Master and Secretary, and have the seal of the Lodge attached.

When once a dimit has been granted and accepted, the brother dimitting can return to the Lodge in the same manner only as any other unaffiliated Mason would enter it.

The right to withdraw from a Lodge clearly conveys the right to refuse to pay dues or expenses of the Lodge; hence as the brother, by his own voluntary act of withdrawal from his Lodge, is deprived of the privileges of the fraternity, he should be exempt from taxation.

STATUS OF A DIMITTED MASON

When a Mason permanently withdraws his membership he dissevers all connection between himself and the *Lodge organization* of the Order. He divests himself of all the rights and privileges which belong to him as a member of that Organization. Among these rights are those of visitation, pecuniary aid, and Masonic burial. Whenever he approaches the door of a Lodge he is to be met in the light of a profane. But from the well-known maxim of "Once a Mason, always a Mason," it follows that a dimitted brother cannot by such dimission divest himself of all his Masonic responsibilities to his brethren, nor be deprived of their correlative responsiblity to him. He is still bound by certain obligations, of which he cannot, under any circumstances, divest himself, and by similar obligations is the Fraternity bound to him. Of these are such as secrecy, aid in the hour of pressing danger, and reverence and respect for a brother's family.

RIGHT OF TRIAL

The primary object of a Masonic trial is to demonstrate the innocence or guilt of a brother who is accused of unmasonic conduct, by a proper investigation into the facts of the case in the simplest yet most efficient manner, through the evidence of competent witnesses, before an impartial tribunal, who must conduct it in a regular and orderly manner, with a view of obtaining the truth, that impartial justice may be awarded. The rules and forms necessary for conducting Masonic trials are simple and easily understood. The great principle of law, which is the basis of all criminal jurisprudence, must be accorded to the accused—the benefit of every doubtful question and the presumption of innocence until proven guilty—and the accuser is entitled to the consideration of purity of motive and honesty of purpose, until facts to the contrary are established.

Every brother accused of an offence is entitled to an early, speedy, and impartial trial. His reputation and his rights as a Mason are sacred, whereby he is not only entitled to their enjoyment, but he has a claim to the assistance and protection of the whole Fraternity in maintaining and enforcing them, and he can, therefore, only be deprived of any of those guaranteed rights by the clearest and most indisputable proof, and after being afforded every fair opportunity of establishing his innocence. This subject is fully set forth under "Masonic Discipline."

The right to appeal to a higher tribunal or to a superior officer is sacred and undeniable.

An appeal may be taken from the decision of the Lodge or the Master to the Grand Lodge or to the Grand Master, and such decision may be set aside for irregularity.

DISPENSING RELIEF

Relief or assistance is an important tenet of a Freemason's profession and practice. The mutual dependence of man upon his fellow man for service and assistance in the execution of enterprises and designs for the general benefit of the community; for aid in adversity, comfort in sickness, and sympathy in misfortune, is so universally acknowledged that no society was ever known to prosper in the absence of some plan of benevolence which might embrace a prompt application of relief to all its worthy members who, by age, calamity, or suffering, should be reduced to indigence and want.

Accordingly, Freemasonry, as a beneficent association, has not been backward in making provision for its sick and impoverished members, distressed widows and helpless orphans. It is a beautiful element in the practically benevolent application of Masonry to be able to say, that "where it is best known it is most highly esteemed." If Masonry produces those blooming fruits of charity which all mankind commend, it is sure to be rewarded with universal approbation. The worthy and the good will eagerly embrace a system which produces so much practical benefit; and the Masonic Institution will be considered a public blessing to the community at large.

The right of a brother in good standing in his Lodge to apply for relief or assistance when in destitute circumstances, is one of the most ancient and well-established claims of the individual Mason upon the Fraternity wherever dispersed. It existed before the organization of permanent Lodges. In the old records, as early as the year 1600, we find:

§13. That every Mason must receive and cherish a strange brother, giving him employment, if he has any, and if not, he is directed to refresh him with money unto the next Lodge.

There is, therefore, no law or rule in Masonry more fully established than that of rendering relief to those justly entitled to it. Relief should not be donated to non-affiliates, or to Masons suspended or expelled. The moneys accummulated by the Fraternity are intended for the worthy, and for those only who contribute to the general stock of Masonry.

The claims of a widow of a Mason are destroyed by a subsequent marriage, but the claims of the children of a Master Mason are not impaired by the subsequent marriage of their mother.

THE RIGHT OF BURIAL

To give the last token of respect to the remains of one who has worked in the mystic labors of the Lodge, is one of the most sacred duties of Masons in Lodge assembled. The inherent craving *to be remembered after death* by those who professed friendship to us in life is as natural as it is powerful. Doubtless many persons are actuated to become Masons by observing the honors which Masons pay to their worthy dead.

Every Master Mason who dies in good standing has the right to be conducted to his last home, and to be committed to mother earth with the ceremonies of the Craft. The ceremonies are performed as a sacred duty, and as a mark of respect to the memory of a departed brother.

THE LODGE

A LODGE is understood to be the room or place in which a regularly constituted body of Freemasons assembles for work and the transaction of business connected with the Institution. The term is also used to designate the collection of Masons thus assembled, just as we use the word "church" to signify the building in which a congregation of worshippers meet, as well as the congregation itself.

A Lodge is defined to be an assembly of Masons, *just, perfect,* and *regular,* who together meet to share the beauties and mysteries of the Order, and to add new material to the sacred work. It is *just,* because it contains the Volume of the Sacred Law unfolded, together with the square and compasses; *perfect,* having the required number of members present to transact business in a regular and constitutional manner, and *regular,* from its warrant of constitution, which implies that it meets and works under the sanction of the legal Masonic authority of the jurisdiction in which the Lodge is held, subject to its by-laws and the general regulations. It is either particular or general, and will be best understood by attending it.—*Charges of* 1722.

No Lodge is recognized at the present day unless it has emanated from a Grand Lodge, and works in obedience to the regulations of its parent. Whatever may be the status of a Mason irregularly made, no countenance is given to an irregular (clandestine) Lodge.

Lodges, according to the American system, are recognized of two kinds, distinct in their character, and working under distinct and separate authority; the first, *Under Dispensation* from the Grand Master; the second, *Under Warrant* (charter) from the Grand Lodge.

In the formation of a new Lodge, which is technically termed a *Lodge under Dispensation*, a petition signed by not less than seven Master Masons in good standing is presented to the Grand Master, or other officer having authority to grant dispensations. There must be good reason for the orgainization of the Lodge at that time and place. The place of meeting must be designated, and the names of the first three officers stated. The petition must be recommended by the nearest chartered Lodge (in some States all the Lodges whose territory would be reduced), which must certify that the officers proposed are qualified to confer the degrees and give the lectures, etc.

The powers of a Lodge under dispensation are such as may be prescribed by the local regulations in force in the jurisdiction where it is located. The petitioners for the new Lodge must give notice to the old Lodge that they have signed such petition, and pay all dues to that time; but (in most of the States) they are not required to dimit from the Lodge until the charter is granted. This, however, like other rules, is subject to local regulations. Usually a Lodge U.D. has the same authority as a warranted Lodge except holding elections and installing officers.

CHARTERED LODGES

The powers, duties and privileges of a subordinate Lodge are such as are defined by its character, by the Constitutions and General Regulations of the Grand Lodge, and the Ancient Landmarks. They are divided into:

1. EXECUTIVE—In the direction and performance of its work under the control of its Master, and in all other matters in sustaining the Master, who has the primary executive power of the Lodge.

2. LEGISLATIVE—Embracing all matters relating to its internal concerns not in derogation of the Ancient Landmarks, the Constitutions and General Regulations of the Grand Lodge, or of its own particular by-laws.

3. JUDICIAL—Embracing the exercise of discipline and settlement of controversies between and over all its members (except the Master), and over all Masons and non-affiliated brethren within its jurisdiction, subject to an appeal to the Grand Lodge.

The powers of a chartered Lodge are divided into INHERENT and CORPORATE.

A Lodge by virtue of its *inherent* rights, as defined by Ancient Landmarks, established usages of Masonry, and when recognized by a Grand Lodge, has the power:

1. To retain its charter until lawfully surrendered, suspended, or revoked.
2. To fix its time and place (if not outside of the place named in the charter) of meetings.
3. To meet and do all the work of Craft Masonry.
4. To elect and initiate members, and reject any application for membership.
5. To elect and install its officers.
6. To make laws requiring its members to contribute to its funds.
7. To instruct its representatives, for their government, at all communications of the Grand Lodge.
8. To place on trial, for cause, its own members, sojourners, and unaffiliated Masons living within its jurisdiction.
9. To appeal to the Grand Master or Grand Lodge from the decision of the Master.
10. To make by-laws for its local government.

The *corporate* rights of a Lodge are conferred by its charter, and by the powers thereof they are entitled:

1. To representation in all communications of the Grand Lodge.
2. To protection while in the lawful exercise of its inherent rights.
3. To the enjoyment of all powers conferred by the Grand Lodge upon any constituent Lodge.

The acts for which a charter may be *forfeited* and the Lodge dissolved are:

1. Disobedience to the authority of the Grand Master or Grand Lodge.

2. Departure from the original plan of Masonry, and a violation of the Ancient Landmarks.
3. Disobedience of the Constitutions.
4. Ceasing to meet for one year or more.
5. Admitting clandestine Masons, or initiating known immoral candidates.

A Lodge may be *dissolved* by the voluntary surrender of its charter by its members, after special summons for that purpose, unless the minority opposed to such surrender consist of seven or more members, that number being the constitutional complement to *receive,* hence that number may *retain* the charter. The rule is now of almost universal practice in the United States.

The Grand Master may, for cause, arrest the charter of a Lodge, not to extend beyond the next annual communication of the Grand Lodge. Such suspension for the time arrests the work of the Lodge and prevents its meetings, but does not affect the Masonic standing of its members or destroy the legality of its charter.

DUTIES OF A LODGE

A Lodge by its acceptance of a charter, and its officers and members by their several Masonic obligations, are sacredly bound to obey the laws of Masonry. The duties of a Lodge:

1. To observe and preserve the ancient usages of Masonry.
2. To obey the Constitution and regulations of the Grand Lodge.
3. To render the Grand Master or his deputy all due respect and obedience.
4. Respectfully to hear all official communications from the Grand Lodge, the Grand Master, or any officer acting by their authority.
5. To be properly represented at the annual communications of the Grand Lodge.
6. To possess the proper jewels, clothing, etc., and a suitable seal.
7. To provide for its meetings a safe and suitable Lodge room.
8. To make, through its Secretary, the annual reports of its work and condition to Grand Lodge, and punctually to pay its annual dues.

For a persistent or inexcusable neglect by a Lodge, or of its officers, of any of the duties imposed; and for any deliberate violation of its obligations to Masonry or to the authority of the Grand Lodge or the edicts of the Grand Master, the charter thereof may be suspended or revoked.

GOVERNMENT OF THE LODGE

There is no plainer or more definite law in Masonry than that the Master must preside over his Lodge; but in case of his absence, from any cause, the Senior Warden, and in the absence of both, the Junior Warden shall summon the Lodge to order, and succeed to all the powers and privileges of the Master, as though the Master himself were present, provided the warrant shall be present. In the absence of the Master and the Wardens the Lodge cannot be opened. A Past Master can only preside when the Master or one of the Wardens is present and opens the Lodge, after which he may call such Past Master to the chair. Whoever occupies the chair legally controls the Lodge. Even the Grand Master, if present, can exercise no authority until he has taken the chair and assumed the gavel. [In most jurisdictions, however, a Past Master may open a Lodge to conduct a Masonic funeral or Memorial service.]

OFFICERS OF A LODGE

The prosperity, the success, and the usefulness of a Lodge, and its ability to discharge the duties and objects of Freemasonry, depend greatly upon the character and judgment of its officers.

The discipline of a Masonic Lodge, the order observed at its meetings, the obedience there exacted, and cheerfully rendered on the part of the brethren, make its government as nearly perfect as it is possible for human institutions to be. Intelligent and capable officers make good Lodges.

It is the imperative duty of the officers of a Lodge to be careful, prudent, and conciliating, positive in requiring obedience to the law; smoothing down all asperities of manner, spreading the cement of brotherly love and affection; rendering to everyone that due attention which should ever distinguish a band of brothers, and by their own example, exhibit the beauties of the Craft, admonish with kindness, and reprehend with justice.

Unity is the mainspring of Freemasonry. Destroy that, and the machinery will fall in pieces. It will be a difficult matter to preserve the links in the chain of unity unbroken, unless the Master pursues an accommodating policy, which may cause the brethren to be mutually pleased with each other's society, accompanied by an inflexible regard to discipline, which, while it allows freedom of action, will preserve inviolable the respectful submission that is due the Chair, as its undoubted and inalienable prerogative.

The duties, responsibilities and prerogatives of the officers of a Lodge are now well defined and consist of—1. A Master, who is styled Worshipful; 2. A Senior Warden; 3. A Junior Warden; 4. A Treasurer; 5. A Secretary; 6. A Senior Deacon; 7. A Junior Deacon; 8. Two Stewards, or two Masters of Ceremonies (sometimes both); 9. A Tyler. In addition to the above, many Lodges are provided with a Chaplain, Marshal, Organist (Musician), and Board of Trustees.

PAST MASTERS

By the term "Past Masters," it must be understood to allude to those who have been legally elected Masters of chartered Lodges, served their term of office, and are recognized as *Actual* Past Masters, and who are distinguished from those who have been seated in the *chair* in a Royal Arch Chapter. Their privileges are such as may be expressly given by the Constitution of the Grand Lodge, and, in addition, they are qualified to install any Master elect, when requested to do so, and to be present at the qualification of a Master elected to the chair.

A Past Master is always eligible to re-election, without further service, to any office in the Lodge of which he is a member.

He is eligible as a proxy or representative of the Grand Master to perform any duty when that officer cannot attend.

A Royal Arch *virtual* Past Master has no rights in a subordinate Lodge, and consequently cannot install a newly elected Master, or be present at the conferring of the Past Master's degree. This rule, however, is limited to a portion of the State jurisdictions.

Every Master Mason in good standing is the peer of a Past Master in matters of discipline, etc.

ELECTION AND INSTALLATION OF OFFICERS

The election and appointment of officers shall be held annually, at such time as is prescribed by the Constitution of the Grand Lodge, or the by-laws of the Lodge (usually the regular meeting preceding the festival of St. John the Evangelist, Dec. 27). Their installation must take place on the same evening, or within a reasonable period thereafter. Until such election and installation the incumbents in office shall hold over. No officer can be installed by proxy. [In most jurisdictions only the Worshipful Master cannot be installed by proxy.]

Previous to the annual election (if not already provided for in the by-laws), the Master should instruct the Secretary to call together the Lodge, notify every member of the amount of his indebtedness to the Lodge, and that in default of payment he will not be entitled to vote at such election.

Some opposition has been expressed against this doctrine on the constitutional provision that every member in good standing is entitled to one vote, but it is respectfully submitted that a member who fails to comply with the conditions of good standing, is not entitled to the immunities. [This latter view prevails today; any member in good standing is entitled to vote. This means a member, no matter how much he owes, who has not been suspended for non-payment of dues (SNP), is in good standing.]

A Lodge having failed to elect its officers at the constitutional time, the Grand Master may grant a dispensation to hold an election at another time to complete the work of the Lodge.

At the election two tellers are appointed, who shall receive and count the ballots, and announce the result, under the supervision of the Master. A ballot represents a brother's vote, which is the expression of whatever opinion he may entertain.

Nominations of candidates for office are in order, and the candidate must receive a majority of all the votes cast to be legally declared elected.

When the Constitution or the by-laws do not otherwise provide, the election of an officer may be taken by show of hands, or by a brother, selected for the purpose, casting one ballot, if there be no opposing candidate.

Every member of a Lodge in good standing is eligible to any office in his Lodge, except that of Master (who must have first been elected and installed a Warden for the term of one year).

The members of a Lodge cannot prevent the installation of the Master elect by objecting to it, but the acting Master, in his judgment, may postpone the installation until the case can be submitted to the Grand Master.

CHAPTER 12

FORMS AND BY-LAWS

[Most, if not all, Grand Lodges have their own forms for every purpose covered here. What follows is intended for any who may not have them, and also for historical purposes.

It is interesting to note how helpful this book was when it was first published in 1885. At the time few Grand Lodges had their own forms. Most had no fixed ceremonies. Many followed Macoy's suggestions almost totally.

Again, you are cautioned to follow the directives of your Grand Lodge. Use the forms prescribed by it. Where none are available, these will be found excellent substitutes.]

PETITION FOR A DISPENSATION FOR A NEW LODGE

To the W.M. Grand Master of Masons of the State of _____.

The undersigned petitioners, being Ancient Free and Accepted Master Masons, having the prosperity of the Fraternity at heart, and willing to exert their best endeavors to promote and diffuse the genuine principles of Masonry, respectfully represent—That they are desirous of forming a new Lodge in the _____ of _____, County of _____, and State of _____, to be named _____, No. ____. They therefore pray for letters of Dispensation, to empower them to assemble as a regular Lodge, to discharge the duties of Masonry in a regular and constitutional manner, according to the original forms of the Order, and the regulations of the Grand Lodge. They have nominated and do recommend Brother A B to be the first Master; Brother C D to be the first Senior Warden, and Brother E F to be the first Junior Warden, of said Lodge. If the prayer of this petition shall be granted, they promise a strict conformity to the edicts of the Grand Master, and the constitution, laws, and regulations of the Grand Lodge.

(This petition must be signed by not less than seven Master Masons, recommended by one or two Lodges. The constitutional fee must be forwarded to the Grand Master or Grand Secretary. On receipt of the Dispensation, the Master, Wardens, and brethren named therein will assemble, and open a Master's Lodge in due form. The three officers named must be present. But a Lodge is not constituted, or officers installed, until a charter is granted.)

* * * * * *

RECOMMENDATION FOR NEW LODGE

To the M.W. Grand Master of Masons of _____:

At a regular meeting of _____ Lodge, No. ____, holden at _____, on the ____ day of ____, 19____, the petition of several Master Masons, praying for a Dispensation to open a new Lodge at _____, in the County of _____, State of _____, was duly laid before the Lodge, when it was

Resolved, That this Lodge, being fully satisfied that the petitioners are Master Masons in good standing, and being willing to vouch for their Masonic abilities, does therefore recommend that the Dispensation prayed for be granted to them.

A true copy of the records.

_____ _____, *Secretary.*

(Seal.)

* * * * * *

FORM OF DISPENSATION FOR NEW LODGE

Grand Lodge of Free and Accepted Masons of the State of _____
To all to whom these presents may come, GREETING:

WHEREAS, a petition has been presented to me by Brothers _____, residing within this jurisdiction, praying, on account of the convenience of their respective dwellings, and for other good reasons, for a Dispensation to empower them to assemble as a legal Lodge, to discharge the duties of Masonry in the several degrees of Entered Apprentice, Fellowcraft, and Master Mason, in a regular and constitutional manner, according to the ancient forms of the Fraternity, and the Constitution and Regulations of this Grand Lodge;

And, WHEREAS, The said petitioners have been recommended to me as Master Masons in good standing by the Worshipful Master, Wardens and brethren of _____ Lodge, No. ____, under our jurisdiction; Therefore, I, _____ _____, Grand Master of the Grand Lodge of Free and Accepted Masons of the State of _____, by virtue of the authority in me vested, do hereby grant this my Dispensation, authorizing and empowering our trusty and well-beloved brethren aforesaid, to form and open a new Lodge in the _____ of _____, in the County of _____, and State of _____, to be called _____ Lodge, and therein to admit and make Entered Apprentices, Fellowcrafts, and Master Masons, in accordance with the ancient usages and customs of the Fraternity, obeying in all things the Constitution, Laws, and Edicts of this Grand Lodge, and not otherwise.

And I do hereby appoint our worthy brother, A B, to be the first Master; Brother C D to be the first Senior Warden, and Brother E F to be the first Junior Warden of said new Lodge.

And it shall be their duty, and they are hereby required to return this Dispensation with a correct transcript of all proceedings had under the authority of the same, together with an attested copy of their by-laws, to our Grand Lodge, at its next annual communication, for examination, and such further action as shall then be deemed wise and proper.

This Dispensation to continue in full force until the annual communication aforesaid, unless sooner revoked by me.

In testimony whereof, I have hereunto set my hand (Seal.) and seal, this _____ day of _____, A.D., 19____

_____ _____, *Grand Master*

* * * * * *

COMMISSION TO CONSTITUTE A LODGE AND INSTALL ITS OFFICERS

BY THE W.M. GRAND MASTER OF MASONS OF THE STATE OF _____.

To all to whom these presents may come, GREETING:

WHEREAS, the Most Worshipful Grand Lodge of _____, at its late annual communication, empowered, by warrant of constitution regularly issued, A B, Master, C D, Senior Warden, and E F, Junior Warden, and their successors, to assemble as a regular Lodge, at _____; and ancient Masonic usage requires that said Lodge shall be duly constituted;

Now, therefore, know ye, that I, _____ _____, Grand Master of Masons of the State of _____, reposing special trust and confidence in the skill, prudence and ability of Brother _____, Past Master (or W. Master) of _____ Lodge, No. ____, being unable to attend in person, have authorized and empowered our said Worshipful Brother to constitute, in form, the new Lodge at _____, to be known and designated as _____ Lodge, No. ____, and to install the officers of said new Lodge according to the ancient usages of the Craft; and for so doing this shall be his sufficient warrant.

Given under our hand and seal, at the City of _____, on the _____ day of _____, A.L. 59____, A.D. 19____.

_____ _____, *Grand Master.* (Seal.)

This form may be readily adapted to the appointing of a proxy for any other purpose. [Such documents as this approved by the Grand Master are usually attested to by the Grand Secretary, along with his signature and the seal of the Grand Lodge.]

* * * * * *

COMMISSION FOR REPRESENTATIVE (OTHER THAN MASTER AND WARDEN)

To all whom these presents may concern, GREETING:

KNOW YE, that we, the members of _____ Lodge, No. ____, reposing trust and confidence in the fidelity, skill, and Masonic abilities of our Worthy Brother _____, do hereby constitute and appoint him our representative in the Grand Lodge of _____, in case of the absence of the Worshipful Master and Wardens, at its next annual communication, to be held at _____ on the _____ day of _____, 19____, empowering him to act in our behalf, hereby ratifying and confirming whatsoever he may do in said capacity.

In testimony whereof, the Master of our said Lodge has set his hand, and caused the Secretary to affix the seal of the Lodge (Seal.)   thereto, this _____ day of _____, A.L. 59, A.D. 19____.

Attest: _____ _____, *Master.*

_____ _____, *Secretary.*

* * * * * *

COMMISSION FOR PROXY OF A MASTER, OR EITHER OF THE WARDENS OF A LODGE

To whom these presents may concern, GREETING:

KNOW YE, that I, _____ _____, Master of _____ Lodge, No. ____, held at _____ in the county of _____, do hereby constitute and appoint our worthy Brother _____ my proxy in the Grand Lodge of _____, empowering him to act in my behalf, and hereby confirming and ratifying whatsoever he may do in said capacity.

Given under my hand and the seal of said Lodge, (Seal.)   this _____ day of _____, A.L. 59____, A.D. 19____.

Attest: _____ _____, *Master.*

_____ _____, *Secretary.*

* * * * * *

PETITION FOR INITIATION AND MEMBERSHIP

To the W. Master, Wardens and Members of _____ *Lodge, No.* ____, *F. and A. Masons:*

The petition of the undersigned respectfully represents, that enteraining a favorable opinion of your ancient and honorable Institution, being unbiased by the improper solicitation of friends, and uninfluenced by mercenary or other improper motives, he is desirous of being admitted and becoming a member of your Lodge, if found worthy, promising a cheerful conformity to the usages and customs of the Order.

Place of residence is _____; age is _____ years; and his occupation is _____.   (Signed),   _____ _____.

    Recommended by _____ _____,

    _____ _____

* * * * * *

APPLICATION FOR AFFILLIATION

To the W.M., Wardens and Members of _____ *Lodge, No.* ____:

The undersigned, a Master Mason in good standing, and last a member of _____ Lodge, No. ____, located at _____, State of _____, respectfully prays to be admitted to membership in your Lodge.

    Dated, _____, 19____.

                Signed,   _____ _____.

    Recommended by _____ _____.

* * * * * *

REPORT OF COMMITTEE ON APPLICATION

The Committee upon the application of _____, report favorably (or unfavorably).

              Signed,   _____ _____

                          _____ _____ Committee

    Dated, _____, 19____.   _____ _____

* * * * * *

NOTICE FOR PAYMENT OF DUES

        HALL OF _____ LODGE, NO. ____. _____, 19____.

Brother _____:

Take notice, that your Lodge dues for the present year are now due, and payable on or before the _____.

The amount is $____, on payment of which I shall be pleased to hand you a receipt.   Fraternally,

    (Seal.)   _____ _____, *Secretary.*

[Note: Add the law of your Grand Lodge calling for the suspension, or possible suspension, of a member who is in arrears in his dues.]

* * * * * *

TO SHOW CAUSE WHY MEMBER SHOULD NOT PAY DUES, OR BE STRUCK FROM ROLL OF MEMBERS

HALL OF _____ LODGE, NO. ____.

_____, 19____.

To Brother _____:

You will take notice that you are required to pay the sum of $____, being the amount of dues owing by you to ____ Lodge, No. ____, or show cause at the next stated communication of the Lodge, to be held on the _____ day of _____, 19____, at ____o'clock, P.M., why your name should not be stricken from the roll of members, as provided by sec. ____ of the by-laws of this Lodge.

By order of the Lodge.

(Seal.)   _____ _____, *Secretary.*

* * * * * *

APPLICATION FOR DEGREES BY A PERSON WHO HAS BEEN ELECTED BY ANOTHER LODGE, OR HAS RECEIVED ONE OR MORE DEGREES THEREIN

To the W. Master, Wardens and Members of _____ *Lodge, No.* ____, *F. and A.M.:*

The undersigned respectfully shows that, on or about the ____ day of ____, 19____, he was duly elected as a candidate for the three degrees of Masonry by _____ Lodge, No. ____, located at _____, where he then resided, and thereafter duly received the first degree (or first and second degrees) of Masonry in said Lodge, that, for the sake of greater convenience (or other good cause), your petitioner prays that he may receive the remaining degrees in your Lodge.

The consent of _____ Lodge is hereto annexed (or show it to be impossible to obtain consent).

Dated, _____, 19____.

Signed,   _____ _____.

Recommender, _____ _____.

* * * * * *

APPLICATION FOR DISPENSATION TO AVOID DELAY

HALL OF _____ LODGE, NO. _____.

_____, 19_____.

To the M.W. _____ Grand Master of Masons of the State of _____:

M.W. SIR: Mr. A.B., having duly presented his application to be initiated, passed, and raised to the sublime degree of Master Mason in _____ Lodge, No._____, and imperative circumstances [state the nature thereof], making it necessary that he should proceed without delay, respectfully asks that a dispensation be granted, empowering said Lodge to confer degrees as soon as may be practicable.

Signed,   A_____ B_____.

I, the Master of _____ Lodge, No._____, certify that the application of A B presents a case for emergency, and recommend that the dispensation asked for be granted, and that he may receive the degrees accordingly, if found worthy.

Signed,   _____ _____, *Master.*

(Seal.)   _____ _____, *Secretary.*

DISPENSATION TO AVOID DELAY

OFFICE OF THE GRAND MASTER OF MASONS.

_____, 19_____.

To whom these presents shall come, GREETING:

Application having been made to permit _____ Lodge, No. _____, under this jurisdiction, to initiate, pass and raise A B to the sublime degree of Master Mason, who is unable, for certain reasons, to wait the time prescribed by our regulations, and the said Lodge consenting thereto:

Now, know ye, that I, _____ _____, Grand Master of Masons in and for said State, by virtue of the power and authority in me vested, do hereby authorize and empower said Lodge to proceed and confer the degrees without delay on said A B, in accordance with the ancient usages and customs of Freemasonry, and not otherwise; and for so doing these presents shall be their sufficient warrant.

Given under my hand, and the private seal of Grand

(Seal.)   Master, this _____ day of _____, 19_____.

_____ _____, *Grand Master.*

* * * * * *

NOTICE OF APPOINTMENT OF COMMITTEE

HALL OF _____ LODGE, NO. _____. _____, 19____.

Brother _____ _____:

Take notice, that at a stated communication of this Lodge, held this date, you were appointed on a committee to examine into and report upon _____. The committee appointed consists of Bros. _____.

Report to be called for at next stated communication.

Fraternally,

_____ _____, *Secretary.*

* * * * * *

DISPENSATION AUTHORIZING LODGE TO CONTINUE ITS LABORS AFTER LOSS OF ITS CHARTER

To all to whom these presents shall come, GREETING:

Know ye, that whereas it has been represented to us by W. Brother _____, Master of _____ Lodge, No. ____, that the charter of said Lodge has been lost (by fire or otherwise), and that the same cannot be found; and, whereas, the Master, Wardens and members are desirous of continuing the labors of said Lodge;

Now, therefore, by virtue of the power and authority in me vested, as Grand Master of Masons in the State of _____, do hereby authorize and empower the said Master, Wardens and members of _____ Lodge, No. ____, to continue their Masonic labors, and to perform all the functions of a regular Lodge in as full and complete a manner as if their charter was still in existence, until the next annual communication of the M.W. Grand Lodge, to which this dispensation shall be returned.

Witness my hand and seal, at the city of _____, the

(Seal.)   _____ day of _____, A.L. 59____, A.D. 19____.

_____, *Grand Master.*

* * * * * *

DISPENSATION TO ELECT A MASTER

THE MOST WORSHIPFUL GRAND LODGE OF ____ FREE
AND ACCEPTED MASONS

To whom these presents may come, GREETING:

Whereas, I have received official information that the office of Master of _____ Lodge, No. ____, has become vacant by the (death or permanent removal from the jurisdiction) of _____ _____, late Master thereof, and it is represented to me that it is important to the welfare of said Lodge that said office shall be filled, and a Master of said Lodge duly elected to supply said vacancy: Now, Know Ye, that I, _____ _____, Grand Master of Masons of the State of _____, do issue this, my special dispensation, authorizing and empowering said Lodge to proceed to fill said vacancy by the election of a brother to serve as Master until his successor is duly elected.

Given under my hand and private seal, at _____, this ____ day of _____, A.L. 59____, A.D. 19____.

_____ _____, *Grand Master.*   (Seal.)

A dispensation for the above purpose is seldom called for. The almost universal rule prevails, that in the absence of the Master, the Senior Warden assumes the responsiblities and duties of the Master.

* * * * * *

COMMISSION TO DEDICATE A MASONIC HALL

THE MOST WORSHIPFUL GRAND LODGE OF _____ FREE
AND ACCEPTED MASONS.

To all to whom these presents shall come, GREETING:

Whereas, _____ Lodge, No. ____, in the _____ of _____, has prepared and furnished a room, in which the members thereof desire to hold their meetings in future; and it is meet and proper that the same should be dedicated to Masonic uses with appropriate ceremonies: Now, Know Ye, that I, _____ _____, Grand Master of Masons of the State of _____, reposing special trust and confidence in the Masonic skill and ability of our Worshipful Brother _____, Master (or Past Master) of _____ Lodge, No. ____, have thought proper (being unable to attend in person), to nominate and appoint him to perform the ceremonies of dedication, according to the ancient usages of the Craft, and for so doing this shall be his sufficient warrant. And he is hereby required to report his acts and doings in the above service to this office.

Given under my hand and the private seal of the Grand Master, at ____, this ____ day of ____, A.L. 59____, A.D.19____. ' ____

_____ _____, *Grand Master.* (Seal.)

* * * * * *

COMMISSION TO LAY A CORNER-STONE

To whom these presents shall come, GREETING:

Whereas, _____ Lodge, No. ____, in the _____ of _____, has undertaken to erect a building in which the members thereof propose to hold their future meetings, and having requested that the corner-stone be laid with the appropriate ceremonies of the Order:

Now, Know Ye, that I, _____ _____, Grand Master of Masons in the State of _____, reposing especial trust and confidence in the Masonic skill and ability of our Worshipful Brother _____, A Past Master of _____ Lodge, No. ____, (R.W. Brother if a Grand Officer), have thought proper, being unable to attend in person, to nominate and appoint him to lay the corner-stone of the proposed building according to the ancient usages of the Craft, and for so doing this shall be his sufficient warrant. And he will report his acts and doings hereunto to this office.

Given under my hand and the private seal of Grand Master, at ____, this ____ day of ____, A.D. 19____, A.L. 59____.

_____ _____, *Grand Master.* (Seal.)

* * * * * *

PETITION FOR·CHANGING LOCATION OF LODGE

HALL OF _____ LODGE, NO. ____. _____, 19____.

To the M.W. Grand Master of the Grand Lodge of _____:

At the last regular meeting of this Lodge, the desire was expressed, and the sense of the Lodge taken in favor of removal from the present place of meeting to _____. Your permission for such removal is therefore respectfully solicited, and the same having been obtained, the further conditions in section ____ of the by-laws shall be carefully complied with.

(Seal.)   _____ _____, *Master.*

Attest: _____ _____, *Secretary.*

* * * * * *

APPOINTMENT OF DISTRICT DEPUTY GRAND MASTER

THE GRAND LODGE OF ____ FREE AND ACCEPTED MASONS

To all whom it may concern, GREETING:

Know Ye, That reposing special trust and confidence in the Masonic skill and ability of our Worthy Brother _____, a Past Master of _____ Lodge, No. ____, I do hereby appoint him to the office of District Deputy Grand Master of the _____ District of this Grand Jurisdiction, composed of the counties of _____, and embracing the several subordinate Lodges therein. He will be ob'eyed and respected accordingly.

This Commission is to continue in force (unless sooner revoked) until the next annual communication of the Grand Lodge.

Given under my hand and the private seal of the Grand Master, this ____ day of ____, A.L. 59____, A.D. 19____.

_____ _____, *Grand Master.* (Seal.)

* * * * * *

APPLICATION FOR A DIMIT

To the W. Master, Wardens and Brethren of _____ *Lodge, No.* ____, *Free and Accepted Masons:*

The undersigned, now a member of the Lodge, and having paid all known dues and assessments, requests that he may be dimitted from the Lodge.   Signed,

Dated, _____, 19____.   _____ _____.

* * * * * *

DIMIT

_____ LODGE, NO. ____, F. & A.M.

Acknowledging the jurisdiction of the Grand Lodge of the State of _____, to all whom it may concern, GREETING:

This certifies that Bro. _____, is a Master Mason, and was a member of this Lodge, in good standing, and having paid all dues, and otherwise complied with all legal requirements of the Lodge, we do cordially commend him to the fraternal regard of all true Free and Accepted Masons, wherever dispersed around the globe.

In testimony whereof, we have caused this dimit to be signed by the Master, and the seal of the Lodge this

(Seal.)   ____ day of ____, A.D. 19____, A.L. 59____.

_____ _____, *Master.*

_____ _____, *Secretary.*

BY-LAWS

No organization, including Masonic Lodges, can efficiently operate without some form or rules and regulations. In Freemasonry these regulations, and laws, come from the Grand Lodge. They were adopted over a period of years by trial and error.

The Constitutions of Freemasonry approved in 1723 were somewhat revised in 1738. These remain the foundation of all Freemasonry. They constitute, along with a few long-standing customs, the only Landmarks in Freemasonry. They cannot be changed.

Most Grand Lodges have the Constitutions as part of their book of law, by whatever name it is called. In addition, each has its own peculiar laws enumerated in the same book. It is to this, every officer and member must refer before taking any action in anything pertaining to Freemasonry. Never forget, the law is what your Grand Lodge says it is—not what this book, or anyone else, might claim it is.

Every Lodge must have By-laws. These are usually covered by your Grand Lodge. Nothing can be contained in them that is prohibited by the Grand Lodge. They must contain everything the Grand Lodge wants in them.

Most Grand Lodges prohibit the Lodge By-laws from referring to anything covered in its laws, rules, and regulations. Nothing can be included that will limit the authority of the Worshipful Master (in most jurisdictions). One Grand Lodge refused to approve Lodge By-laws containing these items:

1. Exempting ministers from paying dues.
2. Forbidding any Brother from holding officer in another Lodge.
3. Requiring attendance at Stated Communications.
4. Requiring newly Raised members to learn the Master Masons catechism.
5. Prohibiting smoking in the Lodge (this is left to the discretion of the Master in at least one jurisdiction).
6. Requiring a fixed percentage of dues, fees, and rentals to be turned over to the trustees for investment.
7. Exempting certain classes of members from paying dues.
8. Requiring dues to be paid in advance.

Any one of these may be allowed in your jurisdiction. This is the reason you must know your Grand Lodge law.

Some Grand Lodges exempt 50-year members from paying dues; others don't. Those that do usually won't permit this exemption to become a part of the By-laws because it's covered by a superior law. Those Grand Lodges refusing this exemption might let the Lodges do it, but still hold the Lodge accountable for the per capita tax.

Here is a set of suggested By-laws:

By-Laws
of ROBERT MACOY LODGE NO. 500, A.F. & A.M.
ARTICLE I
COMMUNICATIONS

The Stated Communications of Robert Macoy Lodge No. 500, Ancient, Free and Accepted Masons, shall be held in the Masonic Temple, 100 Freemason Street, New York, New York, on the Fourth Friday of each month at 7:30 p.m.; except December when it shall be held on the Second Friday at 7 p.m., which shall be the Annual Communication of the Lodge during which the officers will be elected.

ARTICLE II
DUES

Every member of this Lodge except the Treasurer, Secretary, Chaplain, Tiler, Honorary Members, and members with 50 or more years of membership in Freemasonry, shall be charged by the Secretary on the first day of January each year with the sum of Thirty Dollars ($30) per annum as dues. Any member six months in arrears in his dues shall be subject to suspension for non-payment of dues.

Note: The laws of your Grand Lodge must be followed for this section, as in all sections of your By-laws. Some jurisdictions will not permit certain officers to be exempt from paying dues; others will permit more than are listed here. Some will not permit 50-year members to be exempt. Then your Lodge may prefer to collect dues on a monthly basis, which was long the custom in thousands of Lodges.

ARTICLE III
FEES FOR THE DEGREES

The fees for the degrees in this Lodge shall be Two Hundred Dollars ($200), payable as follows:

Eighty Dollars ($80) for the degree of Entered Apprentice, of which Twenty Dollars ($20) must accompany the petition; Sixty Dollars ($60) for the Fellowcraft Degree; and Sixty Dollars ($60) for the Master Mason Degree.

ARTICLE IV
SALARIES

The Treasurer shall receive an annual compensation of Two Hundred Dollars ($200) payable in quarterly installments of Fifty Dollars ($50). The Secretary shall receive an annual compensation of Four Hundred Dollars ($400) payable in quarterly installments of One Hundred Dollars ($100).
The Tiler shall receive Ten Dollars ($10) for each communication he attends in this capacity.

ARTICLE V
ELECTIVE OFFICERS

The elective officers of this Lodge shall be: The Worshipful Master, Senior Warden, Junior Warden, Treasurer, Secretary, Senior Deacon, and Junior Deacon.

Note: Many jurisdictions will not permit these to be listed because they are covered by Grand Lodge law. In some Lodges, the Deacons are appointed; in some the Tiler is elected.

ARTICLE VI
APPOINTED OFFICERS

The appointed officers of this Lodge shall be: One Chaplain and no more than three Associate Chaplains, the Senior and Junior Stewards, the Marshal, and the Tiler.

ARTICLE VII
TRUSTEES

There shall be three trustees for this Lodge, the senior trustee to be dropped each year and a new one elected to serve a three year term; said trustees to be elected during the Annual Communication of the Lodge subject to appointment by the court having jurisdiction. The trustees shall make a report in writing of the funds invested by them for the Lodge. They shall have no authority whatsoever except that delegated to them for the investment of the funds at the direction of the Lodge.

> Note: Trustees are often a source of problems for the Lodge and its officers. Unless their specific duties are spelled out by the Grand Lodge and cannot be included in the By-laws, it would be well to include what your Lodge will and will not give them authority to do.

ARTICLE VIII
SPECIAL RELIEF FUND

Contributions made to the Special Relief Fund (or Charity Fund) of this Lodge will be handled by the Worshipful Master in the manner he deems appropriate. The balance in his possession will be turned over to his successor after the installation.

> Note: Not every Lodge has such a fund, but many do have large ones, and how they can be handled is part of the law of the Grand Lodge. In some Lodges this fund is kept separately by the Treasurer and paid out as the Master or Lodge may direct. If possible, this should be the Master's fund to use as needed. There are times when relief can't wait for the Lodge to meet or the Master to track down the Treasurer or some other officer who may have direct access to the fund.

ARTICLE IX
AFFILIATION

There shall be no fee charged for petitioners for membership in this Lodge who are members of other Lodges in this jurisdiction; those from other jurisdictions will pay the sum of Five Dollars ($5.00) which amount is to accompany the petition. As with all petitioners, there must be a unanimous favorable ballot to elect.

ARTICLE X
WITHDRAWAL OF PETITION

After a petition has been received and noted on the minutes, it shall not be withdrawn without the consent of three-fourths of the members present; after the report of the Committee on Investigations, it shall not be withdrawn. The Worshipful Master may respread the ballot once, and no more, if there is but one black ball appearing.

ARTICLE XI
EXAMINATION OF CANDIDATE

Before a candidate can be Passed or Raised he must stand examination in open Lodge in the degree previously taken; the ballot box shall be passed and the members will signify their approval of the examination by casting a white ball, or disapproval by casting a black ball, and there must be a majority approving the examination for him to be advanced. The Worshipful Master will examine the ballot and announce the result to the Lodge.

ARTICLE XII
MASONIC PUNISHMENT

There shall be no punishment inflicted upon a Brother whatsoever except for suspension for non-payment of dues. However, charges of un-Masonic conduct shall be preferred and presented in writing to the Lodge for any infractions of Masonic law. A copy of such charges shall be furnished the Brother and District Deputy Grand Master by the Secretary, who shall, if he deems it proper, and with the approval of the Grand Master, appoint a Trial Commission of Past Masters to try the case of the erring Brother. The Junior Warden of this Lodge, or his proxy, shall represent the Lodge during the trial.

ARTICLE XIII
ORDER OF BUSINESS

After the Lodge is opened, unless the Worshipful Master shall otherwise direct, the following order of business may be observed:

1. Calling Roll of Officers
2. Reading the minutes of the previous Communication.
3. Sickness and distress
4. Welcome visitors
5. Read the correspondence received.
6. Present new petitions and refer them to proper committees.
7. Receive reports of Committees
8. Ballot on petitions held over from previous Communication.
9. Present speaker or other program.
10. Confer degrees.

11. Receive and consider resolutions.
12. Consider unfinished business.
13. Dispose of any other business
14. Reading Minutes of present Communication
15. Closing.

ARTICLE XIV
MASONIC TEMPLE COMMITTEE

When Lodges in the same community join to raise funds for a new temple: Immediately after his installation, the Worshipful Master shall recommend two members to serve as the representatives of this Lodge for the Masonic Temple Committee. The Lodge may add to the recommendations. If there be more than two recommended, the Lodge shall, by secret ballot, elect two representatives by majority vote. These representatives shall keep the Lodge informed about any proposed changes considered by this committee. They shall present the views of the Lodge to this committee, and at no time oppose the wishes of this Lodge.

ARTICLE XV
REINSTATEMENT

All requests for reinstatement to membership in this Lodge shall be in writing and acted on as follows:

For suspension for non-payment of dues: Shall be held over for one month and if a majority are in favor he shall be restored to membership;

For suspension for un-Masonic conduct: Shall be held over for one month and will require a three-fourth majority vote in favor of restoration;

For expulsion for un-Masonic conduct: Shall be held over for one month and will require unanimous approval for restoration.

The ballot box shall be used in each case.

ARTICLE XVI
REQUESTS FOR DEMITS

A member requesting a demit shall have his request granted by the Worshipful Master, provided he is clear on the books of the Secretary and Treasurer, and has no charges pending or contemplated against him.

ARTICLE XVII
HONORARY MEMBERSHIP

A Past Master of any Lodge, or a member holding 50 years of continuous Masonic service, shall be eligible for election to Honorary Membership in this Lodge. His name may be prosposed at any Stated Communication, be held over for one month, then have a secret ballot taken. A unanimous favorable ballot shall be necessary to elect.

ARTICLE XVIII

These By-laws may be amended by submitting such proposal in writing to be read at a Stated Communication of this Lodge, and be held over until the next Stated Communication, during which time the membership shall be notified in writing of the present Article and the way it reads, along with the proposed amendment. It shall be brought up at the Stated Communication referred to, discussed, and require a three-fourths favorable vote for enactment. If approved by the Lodge, it shall be transmitted to the District Deputy Grand Master for his consideration, who will then submit it to the Grand Master for his approval or rejection. It will not be in effect until approved by the Grand Master.

More articles have been presented than 95% of the Lodges will ever require. There will also be special cases requiring items not covered here. For those whose Grand Lodges have no prescribed form, these should prove helpful.

These have been expanded in many cases to cover the law of many Grand Lodges. To add this to your By-laws would be unnecessary, and probably illegal. So, again you are reminded to study the law of your Grand Lodge before doing *anything.*

CHAPTER 13

COMMITTEES AND THEIR DUTIES
By Allen E. Roberts

"A Committee is a group of men who, individually, can do nothing, but who can, collectively, decide that nothing can be done."

This is an old and far, far too often true picture of committees. But it need not be true. You can prove it false.

Committees are composed of a chairman and a certain number of men. In Grand Lodges, and sometimes in Lodges, the number of men comprising a committee is determined by law. If you were to ask why the number was chosen, the chances are you'd receive no answer. Why? Because no one would know the reason why three, five, or six were written into the law.

As a rule, committees don't work. Everyone waits for the chairman to tell the members what to do. Too frequently the chairman doesn't know what's expected of him or his committee.

Over the years I've asked many Worshipful Masters why they appointed the committees they did. Almost without fail I receive the same answer: "Because my predecessors did." And, almost invariably, I'll be told the committees did nothing, but they were necessary.

A committee that does nothing is of no help to the Lodge. A committee that isn't necessary is also of no help to the Lodge. And because your predecessor may have done some particular thing could be an excellent reason for you not to do it.

A private looked out of his barracks window one morning. He saw a soldier watering the flowers around the flag pole. There was nothing unusual about that. It was done every morning. The private was distrubed, though. When the flower-waterer came in he asked him why he did it. "Because I was ordered to," said the soldier.

"I assumed that," said the private, "but in the pouring rain?"

This is the way too many of our Worshipful Masters operate. Because a thing has been done for years, it's continued. Our hundredth anniversary may have ended ten years ago, but we still have a Hundredth Anniversary Committee.

We have another failing with committees. We appoint them, then give them no direction. It's a good idea to have a Committee on Masonic Education. This is a subject we desperately need to cover in every Lodge in the world. But after the committee is appointed, what's it supposed to do? Take up a space for names in the bulletin? That's what often happens.

Who's in charge of the committees in your Lodge? The chairman? No. The Worshipful Master is. No committee can do anything without his approval. It's the Worshipful Master who must give it direction.

Having said that, let me add an important admonition—give your committees direction, but also give them plenty of leeway to use their creativity. Keep them under control, because that's your responsibility, but give them responsibility and as much authority as possible to do the job you want done.

It's a good idea to carefully select the chairman for each of the committees you want. Then let the chairman select the men with whom they wish to work. Their lists must be examined by you, the Worshipful Master, because you, and only you, can appoint them. Only under rare and reasonable circumstances should you veto a chairman's selection. Don't antagonize him before you even begin your year in the Oriental Chair.

How many men should you have on a committee? This will depend upon the committee, the circumstances, and what you want to accomplish. There can be no set rule. This year you might need five men on your Education Committee because you want to accomplish a certain purpose. Next year two may be enough. Nowhere in our list of committees will you find a certain number suggested. I cannot tell you what you need. I don't know your circumstances.

What committees should you appoint? Again, I have no way of knowing. A rural Lodge certainly needs different committees than one in a large city. Too often this is forgotten, not realized, or never considered by those in policy-making positions. We tend to think everyone thinks as we do.

There are some basic committees that will enhance any Lodge. A few of them will be listed. An idea of what one Master wanted these committees to accomplish will also be covered. These aren't fool-proof. They may not be what you need or want. But it will give you a reference point. You can determine what other committees you need and what you want them to accomplish.

Brother Macoy noted committees should be composed of like-thinking men. There isn't much I disagree with him on, but I do on this point. Committees should be well-rounded. In the "Building Committee" (which not many Lodges will need) you'll get an idea of what I mean.

Actually, you, the leader of your Lodge, should surround yourself with men who know more than you do! Too many disagree on this. But give it some thought. It's easy to find "yes men." They're plentiful. Will they help you? Will they fill in the blank spaces for the things you don't know? They certainly won't—unless you happen to be an individual who knows all the answers! Pick up a newspaper on any given day. You will find some official somewhere in a barrel of trouble. If you will take the time to find out why, you'll find he surrounded himself with "yes men." They didn't have the courage to let him know he was heading for disaster.

This is where *Teamwork* is invaluable. Teamwork is fun. *Teamwork is Constructive.* These two words—*"constructive"* and "fun" are the keys to a successful and progressive Lodge. Without fun (or happiness, if you prefer) your members are going elsewhere to find it.

The successful organization—profit or non-profit—is a happy place to work. A management consultant put it this way: "Business is fun. Companies that generate excitement about what they are doing are more successful than those that don't."

A Lodge isn't a business, you can argue. And you're correct. So that's all the more reason why it should be fun to be on committees. In the business world, as we all know, we're being paid to do a job. In the fraternal world we aren't. Here we're in a position to tell the Worshipful Master where he can go if we don't like what he wants us to do—outside the Lodge, of course.

How can you make it fun for your members to be on committees? By establishing the right committees, finding the right chairmen, letting them select their members, giving the committees direction, and then letting them set goals to make your Lodge successful.

We've got to make Freemasonry something to enjoy. I don't mean undignified tomfoolery found in some bodies. I mean we must share our philosophical values in such a way as to leave everyone with a sense of well-being. Conrad Hahn once put it this way: "Masons should radiate the joy of wisdom." This can come in many ways—knowledgeable Masonic speakers, song fests, quiz programs, social hours, excellent degree work.

And it can come from Teamwork. Rather than have our committees work (or loaf) as conventional ones often do, let them work as Teams. You and they will find Teamwork to be fun. Each member has an opportunity to share his knowledge with his fellows. There will be friendly give and take. The final consensus of the group will be a far better plan than anything one man alone could dream up.

Most important, by using Teamwork you will be helping to grow the Masonic leaders Freemasonry must have tomorrow. How proud the Worshipful Master can be to point to his successors and say they were better leaders of his Lodge than he was.

Committees are usually divided into two special classes: Standing and Special. In Grand Lodges, Standing Committees are established by law; Special Committees are selected by the Grand Master to accomplish certain objectives. Frequently, the Grand Master will appoint the same special committees as his predecessors did. Some are necessary, some aren't. "Custom" too often prevails even if it's useless.

In our Lodges, Standing Committees are often established informally. Sometimes they are part of the By-laws. This doesn't happen often, and in some jurisdictions they can't be named in the By-laws because this is prohibited by the Grand Lodge. In most jurisdictions, however, every Lodge must have certain committees because the Grand Lodge law makes it mandatory. If these aren't included in the list here, be sure to add them for your Lodge.

STANDING COMMITTEES

MASONIC EDUCATION

This is one of the most important committees any Lodge can have. On its ability will rest the success or failure of the Worshipful Master's year. Because of the amount of work expected of it, it should be divided into several sub-committees. The chairman should be among the most knowledgeable Masons in the Ldoge. He should select (and the W.M. appoint) Masons of varying interests. Among the directions the committee should receive are these:

1. *Provide a program for each Stated Communication.*

   These programs should be as varied as possible. They can include excellent *Masonic speakers* (stay away from speakers any civic club can have—you have one thing to offer your members they can't find better somewhere else, and that is Freemasonry); *Dedication programs,* which are often called Re-dedication nights, but until your members become dedicated they certainly can't be re-dedicated.

   And here are a series of other suggestions: *Anniversaries, Birthdays, Past Masters' Night, Patriotic Night, St. John's Night, Spelling Bee (Masonic), Debate, Quiz, Panel Discussion* (with questions from the floor), *Masonic Motion Pictures,* (available from The Masonic Service Association), *Masonic Song Fest, Masonic Sojourners' Night, Masonic Musicale,* and on and on.

2. *Provide a five minute talk on some phase of Freemasonry for each Stated Communication.*

3. *Answer questions placed in a question box a month earlier.*
A question box, along with index cards and pens, can be placed in the reception room before each Communication. Encourage the members to write out any question about Freemasonry they want to know more about. At the end of the meeting a member of the committee will take them and research the answers. These will be recited at the following Communication.

4. *Enlarge (or start) the Lodge library.*
Someone who likes to read and is familiar with Masonic books, should be appointed Librarian and work with this committee.

5. *Write and distribute a monthly newsletter.*
Whoever is selected as the Editor should work closely with the Committee on Public and Internal Relations. This publication can be the backbone of your Lodge. It will keep your members informed of what has happened and what's about to happen. You can have the best program in the world, but if no one knows about it, it will go nowhere. It takes good communication to make anything a success.

6. *Plan occasional activities.*
Your Lodge shouldn't stay in a shell. It should share its activities with the families of its members and even the community. Programs should be provided to include them, such as *Family Nights, Father and Son Dinners, Picnics, Musical Programs, Banquets, Talent Nights, Song Fests, Widows' Dinners, Church Services, Blood Banks, Trips,* and so on.

7. *Provide special Masonic festivities.*
Freemasonry once widely celebrated the Festivals of St. John the Baptist (June 24) and St. John the Evangelist (December 27). These should be revived. They can be by holding *Table Lodges,* or by having *Dedication Breakfasts* followed by attending a church in a body. Other special occasions can readily be found and celebrated.

It will be readily seen that this is an important committee, and sub-committees will be needed. If this outline is followed, the Lodge will have a successful year, and credit will go to the Worshipful Master as well as the committees. Visitors, a barometer of how good a Lodge is, will be plentiful. More important, the attendance of members of the Lodge will increase.

ATTENDANCE

1. The Line Officers will be the key men. Each will telephone the members on his list before every function of the Lodge. This will result in every member receiving one or more personal calls each month.
2. The member called will be informed about what the Lodge is doing. In turn, the member should inform the caller of sickness or any other distress in his family, or that of another.
3. Transportation will be furnished by members of this committee, or volunteers, for those who need it.
4. Calls to the members immediately upon news of a Masonic funeral or Memorial Service are most important. Many members don't read the notices in the newspapers.
5. The Worshipful Master will inform the chairman of the Public and Internal Relations Committee about what he wants the membership to know. This chairman will then contact the Line Officers. The Worshipful Master will contact all appointed officers, especially the Tiler.

PLANNING

1. Although a chairman and specific number of men will be appointed to this committee, every member of the Lodge should be considered an ex-officio member. Each member should present his ideas on improvements the Lodge should make to a regularly appointed member of the committee.
2. The duties, in general, will consist of the following:
    a. To make long and short range plans for the future and present benefit of the Lodge.
    b. To improve the appearance of the Temple inside and out.
    c. To bring the ideas of the committee and members-at-large, after they have been thought through, to the attention of the Worshipful Master, who will determine if they should be brought before the Lodge for action.

Several years ago a Senior Warden was disturbed because no one knew where his Lodge was heading. It had never had a Planning Committee, or anything resembling one. He was determined to change the slipshod way things were being done. He found an old-time Mason who knew Masonry and something about goal setting and planning. Together they found a cross section of the membership who agreed to serve on a new committee.

A Planning Committee was born. As a result the Temple property was rebuilt. This brought new members into the Lodge. It also brought in two appendant bodies and two youth organizations. It added zest to the work of the other committees. Consequently the programs and outside activities improved (they had to—there were none before).

The committee was continued over the years, and ten years after the birth of the Planning Committee, a new Temple was built. The immediate and long range plans paid off with a tremendous increase in attendance, better facilities, and community spirit.

Perhaps you will find the type of members on this committee interesting. There was a management consultant, a carpet-layer, a cloth mill foreman, a construction superintendent, a baker, a lawyer, a banker, an electrician, and a retired musician. There wasn't a "yes man" among them. Everything brought up was discussed thoroughly. A majority vote was never taken on any proposition—they reached a consensus of opinion. Everything this committee brought before the Lodge was adopted without any trouble. The members recognized the "gold mine" it had.

VISITATION

1. The primary duty of the members is to visit the sick and shut-ins; to pay the respects of the Lodge to the families of deceased members; to visit the widows; to send cards, and flowers when deemed important, to the sick; to report needy cases to the Worshipful Master who will in turn report to the Committee on Relief.

RELIEF

1. Will investigate every case reported of members, their families, or widows who might require assistance; report the results of the investigation to the Worshipful Master. He will determine what immediate or long term assistance is required and have the committee provide it.

There may be jurisidictions where the Worshipful Master cannot provide financial assistance immediately if required, but I know of none. I do know of one case, though, where the Worshipful Master didn't know what he could or couldn't do. This actually happened not too long ago.

About ten o'clock one February evening the Senior Warden of a country Lodge received a phone call. The daughter of the widow of the long-term Tiler said her mother was without food or heating oil. The Senior Warden went to the home, and found what she said to be true. He went home, called the Worshipful Master and told him what he had found.

"There's nothing I can do about it," said the Master. The Lodge doesn't meet again for two weeks."

"My Brother," said the Senior Warden, not too gently, "there's plenty you can do. You can see that she gets oil and food right now."

"But I can't spend the Lodge's money without its consent, and even if I could, it's ten forty-five. Nothing's open."

"Give me the word and I'll see that she has food and oil," said the Senior Warden.

"If I do someone in the Lodge can prefer charges against me," cried the Master.

"Should that happen I'll not be Master next year, because I'll be the first one to ask the Grand Lodge to yank our charter," said the Senior Warden.

"All right, then. Go ahead. But you remember you talked me into it," the Master told him.

The oil dealer was a member of the Lodge. He was called and immediately said he would deliver the oil. The leading grocer in the town didn't belong to the Lodge, but he was a Mason. He readily agreed to open his store. He did and loaded the trunk of the Senior Warden's car with groceries.

It was about 11:30 before he carried the groceries into the widow's home. She and her daughter had tears streaming down their faces. The house had already started to warm up. He stayed with them to have a cup of coffee while the daughter fixed her mother a hearty meal. It was one in the morning before he returned home. But he was happy.

What happened in the Lodge two weeks later? The Worshipful Master hesitatingly told the brethren what he had done with its money. The applause was deafening!

EMPLOYMENT

1. Will assist any member in need of employment, or seeking a change in his position.

RITUAL

1. Teach candidates the catechism (lectures) of the various degrees.
2. Provide competent teams for the conferral of the degrees when requested to do so by the Worshipful Master.
3. Teach the lectures and floor work by conducting weekly classes.
4. Teach the funeral and other ceremonies to those interested, especially the Line Officers.
5. Be ready to comply with every ritualistic need of the Lodge when requested by the Worshipful Master.

INDOCTRINATION

1. Visit every petitioner of the Lodge at a time convenient to him and his family.
2. Explain the background of Freemasonry to the petitioner and his wife; be prepared to answer the many and varied questions they will ask.
3. Learn the man's background, his likes and dislikes; shortly after leaving the man's home, make a written list of this background, including his work and hobbies, to become an "inventory" of the man for future appointments to committees and help in the various phases of Lodge work.
4. A member of this committee will become the petitioner's Mentor or Big Brother; to work with him throughout his early days in Masonry; take him to his Lodge meetings and to visit neighboring Lodges; and answer the questions that will arise as he learns his ritualistic work from a member of the Ritual Committee.

INVESTIGATING

1. To be appointed by the Worshipful Master as petitions are received. Robert Macoy had this to say:

   > *Those who are charged with the duty of investigating the character and other qualifications of applicants for the privileges of Masonry, hold positions of distinction and trust. They are, of necessity, the inspectors to examine the material wherewith to add wisdom, strength and beauty to the universal Masonic temple. Carelessness, indifference or negli-*

gence in the discharge of this responsible duty are of the nature of misdemeanors.

The applicant should be given to understand that his character is subjected to the closest scrutiny, and that friendship, personal consideration, or favoritism, must not control or bias Masonic action. He is informed that he must pass the scrutiny of investigation and the ordeal of the ballot, as all have done who went that way before him. If there be a doubt in regard to his fitness to become a Mason, let the Lodge have the benefit of the doubt. Remember that the dignity, honor, and reputation of the Institution are in your hands.

A fearless discharge of this duty may, for a time, subject the committee to the frowns, and possibly the abuse of the rejected and his friends, but faithfulness and courage will, in the end, command the plaudits of every lover of the Institution.

2. Reports on the petitioner should be obtained from courts, the police department, credit bureaus, and other places necessary.

3. As the Indoctrination Committee does, members of this Committee should meet with the petitioner, but not necessarily his family. What Macoy notes above should be covered with the petitioner.

4. A complete report of the investigation should be presented to the Worshipful Master prior to action on the petition. He should be kept honestly and fully informed.

SOJOURNING MASONS

1. To be appointed by the Worshipful Master at the beginning of his year.

2. The committee should make every effort to learn who are the Masons from other jurisdictions and other sections of the state. When satisfied about their Masonic standing, they should be urged to participate in the activities of the Lodge. Many of them will become members.

3. Keep in mind that Freemasonry is universal, yet every Mason should have a local Masonic home.

STEWARDS

1. Appointed by the Worshipful Master at the beginning of the year.

2. The Senior and Junior Stewards are officers of the Lodge and will be in charge of this committee. As officers they are expected to be present for every communication of the Lodge, and properly dressed. They will prepare all candidates for the degrees.

3. The committee will be responsible for furnishing refreshments for each Stated Communication. It will prepare, or supervise, all dinners for the Lodge, including those for special occasions.

4. The committee will work closely with the Committees on Masonic Education and Public and Internal Relations.

5. It will assist the Secretary in mailing notices and collecting Lodge dues.

FINANCE

1. It will serve as the "watch dog" of the treasury, keeping the Worshipful Master informed of the financial condition of the Lodge.

2. For projects costing substantial sums of money, it will report on the best method of financing them, if feasible; if not, why not.

3. It will audit the books and records of the Secretary and Treasurer before the Annual Communication, reporting in writing its findings to the Lodge.

RECEPTION

1. Composed of all officers, Past Masters, and others selected by the Master.

2. That the Lodge may be known as a "friendly Lodge," all visitors, new Masons, and members who haven't been present for some time will receive a hearty welcome, along with a sincere invitation to return often.

3. It will make certain all visitors sign the registration book, or attendance slips. These names will be given to the Master as soon as possible so he can greet them at the proper time during the communication.

4. Anything worthy of note should be passed along to the Master for whatever action he may want to take.

YOUTH

1. Will work with and for the Masonic-related youth groups in the area, particularly those sponsored by the Lodge.
2. Will also support youth groups in the community, such as Little League ball clubs, Girl and Boy Scouts.
3. Establish and present awards, with the permission of the Lodge, for outstanding Scholarship or other ability to selected youth.

PROPERTY AND BUILDING

1. Will supervise the work of the janitor and others charged with keeping the Lodge properly clean.
2. Will make frequent inspections of the Lodge property to make certain it is kept in good repair.
3. Will handle all repairs required to keep the rental property in satisfactory condition.
4. Will supervise the cleaning and maintenance of the groups meeting in the Temple.
5. May authorize necessary work up to the amount of [$200] without the necessity of consulting the Master of the Lodge, but will make a report to the Master and the Lodge during the following communication.

MASONIC HOME

1. Will visit the Masonic home periodically and meet with its guests.
2. Will work closely with the Superintendent of the Home and assist him in any manner possible.
3. Will provide bimonthly programs (talks, Bible lessons, motion pictures) for the guests of the Home.
4. Assist in fund raising drives for the benefit of the Home.

ANNIVERSARY

1. Plan for special celebrations during the anniversary year of the Lodge.
2. Work with the Finance Committee on plans for financing the proposed events. Work with the Public and Internal

Relations and Masonic Education Committees on plans for the celebrations.

Note: This can be a continuing committee. Every year there are occasions for celebrating some special event in the history of the Lodge. Special emphasis should be placed on some particular event periodically. For instance: 100th, 50th, 25th, 10th anniversaries of the chartering of the Lodge. A little thought will bring out dozens of other occasions for celebrating.

PUBLIC AND INTERNAL RELATIONS

1. This committee will be composed of a cross section of the membership. Its chairman will be a member familiar with working with people and the media.
2. It will assist the Masonic Education Committee with the monthly newsletter.
3. It will work with every other committee to improve the public relations of the Lodge and Freemasonry. It will also work with them to improve internal (membership) relations.
4. It will prepare all newsworthy items to be issued to the local news media (radio, TV, magazines, newspapers, Grand Lodge publication, national publications).
5. It will strengthen the weakest link in every Lodge—the lack of communication—by keeping the officers and members informed.

Note: Frequently Public Relations Committees are appointed on the Grand Lodge level. These are excellent choices. Freemasonry is in "the people business" and it does have a public image, sometimes good, sometimes bad. A good Public Relations Committee can improve the image.

Too often, however, we forget (if we thought about it) Freemasonry can't have a good public image if it doesn't have a good internal image. Its members reflect the Organization. The image-making must start with the membership. The members can't reflect the beauty of Freemasonry if they know nothing about it. That's why Masonic Education is absolutely necessary.

The day of the anti-Mason is not past. Freemasonry is still being attacked in the media, by dictators, and even the news media. It is most important to see the media receiving the proper information. Only specialists, particularly those who know what Freemasonry stands for, should be passing out information for general consumption.

A good Public and Internal Relations Committee should be a "must" in every Lodge and Grand Lodge.

This list of committees is by no means complete. Every Lodge will need others not covered here. Every committee listed here can be used in every Lodge. Even if your jurisdiction doesn't have a Masonic Home, the same committee can function in the community. Substitute "Masonic Home" with "Community Homes." Many Masons or their widows will be found in them.

But the Lodge shouldn't keep itself isolated from the community. Its work shouldn't be confined to only Masons and their families. It should reach out to all who can use its assistance. Freemasons should be in the forefront with assistance in times of crisis or distress.

Freemasonry is the greatest force for good the world has ever known. But it is only where it is put to work properly. Where it is working for mankind, it is a vital force in the community.

May your Lodge, Worshipful Sir, be at the top of the list of those bringing goodwill to the Craft.

Index